Introduction to
Public Services for
Library Technicians

LIBRARY SCIENCE TEXT SERIES

Introduction to Public Services for Library Technicians

MARTY BLOOMBERG

1972

LIBRARIES UNLIMITED, INC., LITTLETON, COLO.

Copyright © 1972 Marty Bloomberg
All Rights Reserved
Printed in the United States of America

Library of Congress Card Number 72-89629
International Standard Book Number 0-87287-055-3

LIBRARIES UNLIMITED, INC.
P.O. Box 263
Littleton, Colorado 80120

TABLE OF CONTENTS

Chapter 5
Reference Services

Chapter 6
Reference Sources: The Library Catalog

Chapter 7
Reference Tools: Library Classification

Chapter 8
Reference Work: Bibliographic Citations

Chapter 9
Reference Materials

Chapter 10
Reference Materials: Almanacs and Yearbooks

Chapter 11
Reference Materials: Dictionaries and Their Supplements

Chapter 12
Reference Materials: Encyclopedias

Chapter 13
Reference Materials: Biographical Information

Chapter 14
Reference Materials: Bibliographies

Chapter 15
Reference Materials: Atlases and Gazetteers

Chapter 16
Reference Materials: Directories and Handbooks

Chapter 17
Reference Materials: Indexes

Chapter 18
Reference Materials: Humanities

Chapter 19
Reference Materials: Social Sciences

Chapter 20
Reference Materials: Science

Chapter 21
Reference Materials: Specialized Non-Book Materials

Chapter 22
Reference Materials: Government Documents

Chapter 23
Library Cooperation and Interlibrary Loan

Chapter 24
Reference Services: Special Materials and Services

PREFACE

This text is meant to serve as a general introduction to public services and reference materials for library technicians and other non-professionals. The materials presented will give the reader a foundation on which to develop library skills through practical work experience.

The materials presented in the text are primarily for the library technician and other non-professionals working in a small or medium-sized public library or academic library. By small and medium-sized library, the author means a library with a collection of between 50,000 and 500,000 items and a staff of 15 to 75 employees. This range is large, and because each library combines a number of different objectives, functions, and services, it becomes impossible to describe a typical library.

This text is not a guide for establishing or maintaining a library. Reading the text will not provide an adequate background for assuming major responsibilities in a public services department without work experience. However, reading the text should make practical work experience or on-the-job training more meaningful and thereby allow for earlier acceptance of responsibility.

The author wishes to thank the many librarians who so willingly gave their time to answer questions and discuss their libraries' public service operations. Thanks go also to those librarians and library technicians who read parts of the manuscript and offered many valuable suggestions. My appreciation goes especially to Mrs. Linda Evans, who read, typed, and criticized the entire manuscript. Last, but certainly not least, my thanks to my wife, Leila Bloomberg, who edited, proof-read, and generously criticized the first drafts of this text.

M. B.

CHAPTER 1

GENERAL INTRODUCTION TO THE LIBRARY

INTRODUCTION

The purpose of this text is to introduce the library technician and non-professional to the various aspects of a public services operation.[1] The material covered in the text should help the reader accomplish two goals: 1) to develop a foundation of knowledge leading to an understanding of the purpose of public services, and 2) to introduce a basic core of reference materials upon which skills can be developed.

This text alone will not provide sufficient background to allow the library technician to assume major responsibilities in a public services operation. Mastery of the skills for successful work experience at the library technician level requires several years of experience under the guidance of a librarian or experienced library technician. The need for experience is particularly important for reference work, which is mostly non-repetitive and constantly presents new challenges. Hopefully, this text will help the library technician understand some of the major functions of public services operations and principles.

ROLE OF THE LIBRARY TECHNICIAN

In recent years the library profession has devoted much research toward defining the various levels of library personnel and their education requirements. Librarians, as a result of these studies, are making new efforts both to define professional duties and to free the librarian to perform them. The most important way to free librarians is to give the clerical and preprofessional tasks to well-trained non-professionals.

A tentative and unofficial list of library personnel classes with training requirements has been developed in a working paper by Lester Asheim and the Office for Library Education of the American Library Association. The table below is from a paper by Lester Asheim in which these five classes of library personnel are discussed:[2]

Table 1
Levels of Library Personnel

	Definition	Education
Professional Specialist, e.g.,	subject specialist language specialist information scientist administrator	Education beyond the Master's degree: 6th-year post-Master's; Ph.D.; Master's in other subject field; continuing education in many forms
Librarian	general practitioner	Master's degree

Library Assistant	preprofessional responsibilities at a high level	Bachelor's degree (with or without minor in library science); Bachelor's degree plus library course work at graduate level short of Master's degree
Technical Assistant	simple, routine tasks; special skills tasks	2 to 4 years college; a degree (with or without library technical-assistant courses); post-secondary training in special skills
Library Clerk	typing, filing, operation of business machines	Business school or commercial course

The levels, definitions of tasks, and educational requirements have not yet been generally adopted by libraries. Any attempt to compare the four job levels in the above table with actual library positions will reveal the difficulties involved in making generalized statements.

A more concise definition of a Technical Assistant was offered by another committee of the American Library Association:[3]

> Performance of such work (at the Technical Assistant level) primarily requires skills peculiar to library work, such as knowledge of circulation systems, ability to perform simple cataloging and classification, to use book lists, dictionaries, encyclopedias and other elementary reference aids, to apply clearly established methods, skills, and procedures to the service needs of a library under the supervision of a librarian.

The materials in this text are suited for training personnel at the Library Assistant and Technical Assistant levels. The term Library Technician, as used in this text, refers to a person with at least two years of college and some courses in library science.

THE LIBRARY TECHNICIAN IN PUBLIC SERVICES

The table on pages 18 and 19 provides an overview of public service tasks and the levels of personnel likely to be responsible for performing the work. The table is a guide only and should not be considered as a "how it should be" table. The types and functions of libraries are too varied to allow any hard and fast rules of who should do what without close study by the supervisory personnel.

The role of the library technician in public services is basically one of supervisory responsibility and the answering of directional and simple reference questions. As stated above, these duties will vary from library to library. In a small public or school library the library technician, who may be the only person on duty a good part of the time, will handle all phases of public service work. In large public or academic libraries the circulation activities may be run

16

by library technicians while their role in reference may be relatively restricted.

The function of the library technician, regardless of the library, is to assume the clerical and semi-professional duties which have heretofore been performed by librarians. As the role of the library technician develops, the librarians may now be free to devote their full time to the duties for which they were trained.

PUBLIC SERVICES OPERATIONS—AN OVERVIEW

Public services usually consists of two operations—circulation and reference. Both have direct contact with the library's public and are responsible for satisfying patron needs as far as possible. In fact, the only reason for the existence of most libraries is to serve a specific group of people. In the final analysis a library is judged by most patrons on the performance of its public services operations. This fact should never be forgotten.

The circulation operation has four primary tasks: 1) charging out material to library patrons, 2) checking in returned materials, 3) returning materials to their proper places on the shelves, and 4) performing housekeeping tasks necessary to keep the collection usable and in good order.

The reference service is primarily concerned with answering the questions of the library's users. The questions will range in scope (depending on the library) from the directional "Where are the restrooms?" to research questions requiring several hours or even days of a librarian's time. Other responsibilities of reference service may include interlibrary loans, instruction in using library resources, classroom instruction, compiling bibliographies, establishing special vertical files, and creating appealing displays, bulletin boards, and exhibits.

Although books are still the mainstay of most libraries, the modern library collection is made up of many different materials. Public services operations must be prepared to handle microfilm, films and filmstrips, newspapers, art prints, records, tapes, periodicals, and government documents.

RESPONSIBILITIES AND ETHICS OF LIBRARY WORK

All library personnel should be aware of the library's unique place in our society. The library, considered one of the basic institutions of our democratic society, is the one place where people can find material containing different viewpoints on all subjects. The best statement of a library's responsibilities is the "Library Bill of Rights":*

1. As a responsibility of library service, books and other library materials selected should be chosen for values of interest, information and enlightenment of all the people of the community. In no case should library materials be excluded because of the race or nationality or the social, political, or religious views of the authors.

2. Libraries should provide books and other materials presenting all points of view concerning the problems and issues of our times; no library

*Reprinted by permission of the American Library Association.

Table 2

Public Service Activities	Librarian	Library Technician	Library Clerk	Part-time or Student Help
General				
1. Establishing operating policy	X			
2. Assigning personnel	X or	X		
3. Public relations	X or	X	X	X
4. Book selection	X			
5. General supervision	X or	X		
Circulation				
6. Selection of circulation system	X			
7. Patron registration			X	X
8. Non-routine registration	X or	X		
9. Typing and other clerical work			X	X
10. Charging out materials			X	X
11. Discharging materials			X	X
12. Maintaining files		X	X	X
13. Identifying overdues and carrying out overdue procedure			X	X
14. Collecting fines			X	X
15. Dealing with disputed fines	X or	X		
Collection Maintenance				
16. Supervise collection maintenance		X		
17. Reshelving			X	X
18. Shelf reading			X	X
19. Shifting material on shelves			X	X
20. Inventory			X	X
Reserve Book Collections				
21. Working with faculty	X or	X		
22. Circulation functions			X	X
Interlibrary Loan				
23. Accepting requests	X or	X		
24. Interpreting loan code	X or	X		
25. Bibliographic and location search		X		
26. Receiving and returning material			X	X

	Librarian	Library Technician	Library Clerk	Part-time or Student Help
Reference				
27. Initial patron contact at reference desk	X	X		
28. Answering general information and directional questions		X	X	
29. Answering simple reference questions within limits established by the library		X		
30. Interviewing patrons and answering reference questions	X			
31. Compiling bibliographies	X			
32. Explaining use of library catalog and periodical indexes	X	X		
33. Bibliographic work under librarian's direction		X		
34. Recommending material for purchase	X	or X		
35. Typing and other clerical work			X	X
Miscellaneous Activities				
36. Establishing subject headings for vertical files	X			
37. Upkeep of files and assignment of subject headings under librarian's direction		X		
38. Working on displays, bulletin boards, exhibits	X	X		
39. Demonstrating use of audiovisual equipment		X		

materials should be proscribed or removed from libraries because of partisan or doctrinal disapproval.

3. Censorship should be challenged by libraries in the maintenance of their responsibility to provide public information and enlightenment.

4. Libraries should cooperate with all persons and groups concerned with resisting abridgment of free expression and free access to ideas.

5. The rights of an individual to the use of a library should not be denied or abridged because of his age, race, religion, national origins or social or political views.

6. As an institution of education for democratic living, the library should welcome the use of its meeting rooms for socially useful and cultural activities and discussion of current public questions. Such meeting places should be available on equal terms to all groups in the community regardless of the beliefs and affiliations of their members, provided that the meetings be open to the public.

While it is the librarian's responsibility to carry out the policies stated in the "Library Bill of Rights," he must depend on all library personnel for assistance. This is particularly true of high ranking non-professionals who may have as much contact with the public as the librarian has.

The professional ethics demanded of librarians in performing their duties are similar to those of other professions.[4] While they may apply directly only to librarians, they will nonetheless have an effect on the conduct of all library personnel.

The library's patron puts trust in the library to perform its duties competently, and the librarian makes a claim to be able to do this best because of his special training. Some people feel that the patron must depend on the library to offer truly good service, since he often might be in no position to judge the quality of that service.

In reference or information work every inquiry is equally important and every patron is entitled to expect reasonable efficiency. The setting of priorities is a librarian's decision. Every reasonable effort should be made to help the patron as soon as possible. Any time a non-professional is asked a question which he cannot answer, he has an obligation to refer it to a librarian. There is no place here for ego-building or wounded pride since the patron has every right to expect that the information he receives will be correct and that he has received it from an authoritative source. Library personnel, including librarians, who feel obligated to answer every question personally and who are reluctant to seek help will probably not be suited for a position of responsibility in a library.

All library personnel have an obligation to keep library matters confidential. A patron has the right to assume that any questions he may ask and any material he charges out will not be a subject of conversation outside of the library. Just as the physician has a duty to keep patient matters confidential, so does his nurse or any other employee in his office who may see the records. The librarian has this obligation, but so do the non-professionals working in the library. The best example of this obligation might occur in the special library of a company. It is likely that library personnel will be familiar with the research being done on new products under development. Loose talk outside the library might reveal information to the competition, thus placing them in a better position. As you can see,

Figure 1
Organization Charts[5] of Public Services

(a) Small Libraries

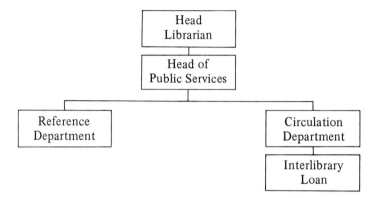

(b) Larger Libraries

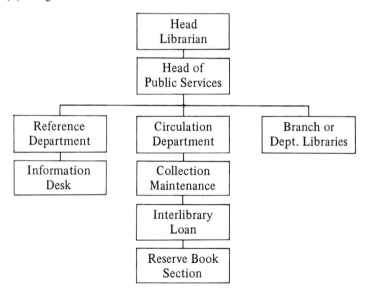

this type of information could involve millions of dollars for the companies involved.

All library personnel have a right and an obligation to offer constructive criticism about library matters. Such criticism, however, must be offered to the proper library administrator. To express any criticism to a patron is improper and might subject the offender to disciplinary action.

Lastly, the library is not the private domain of the library personnel. The patron must be served first. Library personnel must be cautious about checking out material and depriving the patrons of its use. For example, if one library employee after another checks out a book that happens to be on the bestseller list, together they can deprive library patrons of its use for weeks or months. Common sense and good judgment are essential.

FOOTNOTES

1. Also called "reader's services." We will use the term "public services" in this text.

2. Lester Asheim, "Education and Manpower for Librarianship," *ALA Bulletin* 62:1099 (October 1968).

3. ALA Report of Joint Ad Hoc Committee of Library Administration Division and Library Education Division on Sub-Professional or Technician Class of Library Employees. Chicago, 1967. p. 4. Also see Appendix A for a description of library technician duties as given in U.S. Civil Service classifications.

4. See Appendix B for the "Code of Ethics for Librarians."

5. To study the organization of some of our largest universities, see Louis Round Wilson and Maurice F. Tauber, *The University Library: The Organization, Administration and Functions of Academic Libraries*, 2nd ed. New York, Columbia University Press, 1956. Also see Rutherford D. Rogers and David C. Weber, *University Library Administration.* New York, H. W. Wilson, 1971.

BIBLIOGRAPHY

American Library Association. *A.L.A. Glossary of Library Terms.* Chicago, 1943.

American Library Association. Library Education Division. "Criteria for Programs to Prepare Library Technical Assistants," *ALA Bulletin* 63:787-94 (June 1969).

American Library Association. Library Education Division. "Library Education and Manpower: ALA Policy Proposal," *American Libraries* 1:341-44 (April 1970).

Asheim, Lester, editor. *The Core of Education for Librarianship.* Chicago, American Library Association, 1954.

Asheim, Lester. "Education and Manpower for Librarianship," *ALA Bulletin* 62:1096-1118 (October 1968).

Bowler, Roberta. *Local Public Library Administration*. Chicago, International City Managers' Association, 1964.

Brewer, Margaret L., and Sharon O. Willis. *The Elementary School Library*. Hamden, Conn., Shoe String Press, 1970.

Bryan, Alice I. *The Public Librarian*. New York, Columbia University Press, 1952.

Butler, Pierce. "Librarianship as a Profession," *Library Quarterly* 21:235-47 (October 1951).

Canadian Library Association. *The Library Technician at Work: Theory and Practice*. Ottawa, 1970.

"Code of Ethics for Librarians," *ALA Bulletin* 33:128-30 (February 1939).

Corbett, Edmund V. *The Public Library and Its Control*. 2nd rev. ed. London, Library Association, Association of Assistant Librarians, 1966.

Davies, Ruth Ann. *The School Library: A Force for Educational Excellence*. New York, R. R. Bowker, 1969.

Delaney, Jack J. *The New School Librarian*. Hamden, Conn., Shoe String Press, 1968.

Ellsworth, Ralph E. *The School Library*. New York, Center for Applied Research in Education, 1965.

Evans, Luther H., and others. *Federal Departmental Libraries: A Summary Report of a Survey and Conference*. Washington, Brookings Institution, 1963.

Gaines, Ervin J. "The Personnel Needs for Tomorrow's Main Libraries," *Library Trends* 20:742-56 (April 1972).

Johns, Ada Winifred. *Special Libraries: Development of the Concept, Their Organizations, and Their Services*. Metuchen, N.J., Scarecrow Press, 1968.

Leger, J. L. "Library Technicians," *California School Libraries* 39:116-23 (March 1968).

Leigh, Robert D., and Kathryn W. Sewny. "The Popular Image of the Library and the Librarian," *Library Journal* 85:2089-91 (June 1, 1960).

Library Association. *Professional and Non-Professional Duties in Libraries*. London, Library Association, 1962.

Lyle, Guy R. *The Administration of the College Library*. 3rd ed. New York, H. W. Wilson, 1961.

Mahar, Mary Helen. *School Library Supervision in Large Cities*. Washington, U.S. Department of Health, Education and Welfare, Office of Education, 1966.

Monypenny, Phillip, and Guy Garrison. *The Library Functions of the States*. Chicago, American Library Association, 1966.

Palovic, Lora, and Elizabeth B. Goodman. *The Elementary School Library in Action*. West Nyack, N.Y., Parker Publishing, 1968.

Petru, William C., editor. *The Library: An Introduction for Library Assistants.* New York, Special Libraries Association, 1967.

Reynolds, Michael M., compiler. *Reader in the Academic Library.* Washington, NCR Microcard Editions, 1970.

Robinson, Charles W. "Promise and Fulfillment (More or Less)," *Library Journal* 93:3756-59 (October 1968).

Rogers, Rutherford D., and David C. Weber. *University Library Administration.* New York, H. W. Wilson, 1971.

Rudnik, Mary Chrysantha. "What Every Librarian Should Know About Library Technical Assistants," *Wilson Library Bulletin* 46:67-72 (September 1971).

Sass, Samuel. "Library Technicians—Instant Librarians," *Library Journal* 92: 2122-26 (June 1, 1967).

Saunders, Helen E. *The Modern School Library: Its Administration as a Materials Center.* Metuchen, N.J., Scarecrow Press, 1968.

Shaffer, Dale Eugene. *The Maturity of Librarianship as a Profession.* Metuchen, N.J., Scarecrow Press, 1968.

Sharp, Harold S. *Readings in Special Librarianship.* New York, Scarecrow Press, 1963.

Shores, Louis. "Library-Technician: A Professional Opportunity," *Special Libraries* 59:240-45 (April 1968).

Sinclair, Dorothy. *Administration of the Small Public Library.* Chicago, American Library Association, 1965.

Smith, D. L., and E. G. Baxter. *College Library Administration, In Colleges of Technology, Art, Commerce and Further Education.* London, Oxford University Press, 1965.

Steele, Carl L. "Library Technicians—The Big Controversy," *Special Libraries* 60:45-49 (January 1969).

Steinke, Eleanor G. "Orientation and Training for the Non-Professional Library Staff," *Medical Library Association Bulletin* 50:36-41 (January 1962).

Strauss, Lucille J., and others. *Scientific and Technical Libraries: Their Organization and Administration.* New York, Interscience, 1964.

"The Subprofessional or Technical Assistant: A Statement of Definition," *ALA Bulletin* 62:387-97 (April 1968).

Swartout, Charlene R. *The School Library as Part of the Instructional System.* Metuchen, N.J., Scarecrow Press, 1967.

Thompson, James. *An Introduction to University Library Administration.* Hamden, Conn., Archon Books and Clive Bingley, 1970.

Wasserman, Paul, and Mary Lee Bundy, compilers. *Reader in Library Administration.* Washington, NCR Microcard Editions, 1968.

Wheeler, Joseph L., and Herbert Goldhor. *Practical Administration of Public Libraries.* New York, Harper & Row, 1962.

Wilson, Louis Round. *Education and Libraries.* Hamden, Conn., Shoe String Press, 1966.

Wilson, Louis Round, and Maurice F. Tauber. *The University Library: The Organization, Administration, and Functions of Academic Libraries.* 2nd ed. New York, Columbia University Press, 1956.

CHAPTER 2

CIRCULATION SERVICES: PATRON REGISTRATION

INTRODUCTION

Registration for a library card is often the patron's first contact with a library. (This is most likely the case in a public library, but it is less true in an academic or special library.) In any library, however, registration should be a trouble-free and simple procedure for both the patron and the library personnel.

Personnel at the registration point must be completely familiar with registration procedures and prepared to answer a variety of directional and informational questions about the library's resources and services. The importance of good service at this contact point cannot be overstated. Library personnel who cannot answer simple directional or informational questions or who seem annoyed with patron requests can create a negative impression of the whole library which may take a long time to overcome.

There are several general reasons for patron registration. The more important ones are: 1) to identify those people who have the right to withdraw materials from a library, and in some cases the right to use a library; 2) to give a patron some special form of identification to enable him to charge out material—a borrower's card; 3) to get statistical data on the ages, occupations, and geographic characteristics of the library's patrons in order to plan for the best service.

The final reason for registration has particular importance for public libraries. In this era of rapid social change, it is important for a library to know who it is serving and, perhaps more important, who it is not serving. Thus, the seemingly simple act of registration can produce statistics which are of great importance to a library.

The routines of registration are easily mastered and can be handled by clerks or part-time help under the library technician's supervision. The routine procedures of registration and the personnel responsible for them vary depending on the size and function of a library. The remainder of this chapter contains a general discussion of registration in different kinds of libraries. Because daily work details vary greatly among libraries, they are not discussed here but are left to the arena where they are best learned—working in a library.

PUBLIC LIBRARIES

Registration work is probably more important in a public library than in other types of libraries. As the probable first point of contact, registration presents an excellent opportunity for creating good public relations. The library technician should be aware of this opportunity and should make certain that other library personnel also realize this. An irritable, uninterested clerk can give the patron a negative picture of an entire library.

The first step in registration is usually to have the patron fill out a registration form (Figure 1). Information often requested includes the patron's name, phone number, current address, and possibly occupation and/or employer.

Figure 1
Registration Form

(a) Front

```
┌─────────────────────────────────────────────────────────────┐
│                    Registration Card                         │
│                                                              │
│  Date_____  No._____           │
│                                                              │
│  Print Name:    First    Initial   Last    Phone No.         │
│  Mr.                                                         │
│  Mrs._____        │
│  Miss                                                        │
│                                                              │
│  No., Street, Box, Route            Post Office              │
│                                                              │
│  _____        │
│                                                              │
│                         School_____         │
│                         Grade 1 - 2 - 3 - 4 - 5 - 6          │
│                               7 - 8 - 9 - 10 - 11 - 12       │
└─────────────────────────────────────────────────────────────┘
```

(b) Verso

```
┌─────────────────────────────────────────────────────────────┐
│              Instructions for Completing Cards               │
│                                                              │
│  Print name, telephone number and home address legibly.      │
│                                                              │
│  Students: Print name. Name after "School" and circle        │
│  grade. Print first name of father above your name.          │
│                                                              │
│  Sign the card. A parent must sign for a child in 1st through │
│  8th grade.                                                   │
│                                                              │
│  Hand in both cards and show proof of local residence, such  │
│  as a driver's license.                                      │
│                                                              │
│                  PROTECT YOUR CARD                           │
└─────────────────────────────────────────────────────────────┘
```

Registration for juveniles may involve a separate form and request different information. The parent usually signs the form and accepts the responsibility of helping the library enforce its rules. Several forms are used for this category of users; one is reproduced as Figure 2.

In recent years many libraries have formed library systems or entered into other kinds of cooperative agreements which allow patrons to use all libraries in an area by registering at any one library. In at least one state a person registered in a public library can take material from any other public library by presenting his borrower's card. In some library systems registration in one library gives the patron privileges in any library in the system. Figure 3 presents an example of a borrower's card.

Figure 2

```
┌─────────────────────────────────────────────────────────────────┐
│                                                                   │
│                    JUVENILE APPLICATION FORM                      │
│                                                                   │
│  RIVERSIDE PUBLIC LIBRARY      RIVERSIDE COUNTY FREE LIBRARY       │
│                                                                   │
│  Dear Parents:                                                    │
│                                                                   │
│  Your child has requested a free library card from the Riverside  │
│  Public Library–Riverside County Free Library. With this card he  │
│  may borrow books for two weeks, if you give permission.          │
│  To borrow these books your child must promise to take good care  │
│  of them and to pay for any damage or loss. A fine is charged for │
│  each juvenile book which he does not return on time.             │
│  If you wish your child to have his own library card, please write │
│  your name and address and sign your name on this paper.          │
│  We should like to help your child become acquainted with these   │
│  books which will give him pleasure, knowledge, and a better life. │
│                                                                   │
│  ──────────────────────────────────────────────────────────────  │
│  Child's full name                                                │
│  ──────────────────────────────────────────────────────────────  │
│  Home Address                               Street               │
│  ──────────────────────────────────────────────────────────────  │
│  City                                       Telephone            │
│  ──────────────────────────────────────────────────────────────  │
│  Child's school                                                   │
│  ──────────────────────────────────────────────────────────────  │
│  Grade                                      Age                  │
│  ──────────────────────────────────────────────────────────────  │
│  Name of parent or guardian                                       │
│                                                                   │
└─────────────────────────────────────────────────────────────────┘
```

Another innovation in libraries has been to eliminate registration and special library identification cards. Instead, the patron uses standard forms of identification such as a driver's license, credit card, or social security card. In a smaller library it might be possible for the library staff to rely on personal recognition of patrons. Elimination of registration procedures, when possible, can free much clerical staff time for other activities.

Another group of borrowers to be provided for are non-residents. This may include students in local colleges and universities or people temporarily working in the area. Most public libraries make provisions for these patrons. The same registration procedures can be used, the difference being that the borrower's card is dated to expire sooner than residents' cards; the card may be a different color or have other special characteristics for immediate identification. Some-

28

Figure 3

```
┌─────────────────────────────────────────────────────────────┐
│                    Borrower's Card                            │
│                                                               │
│   Expires                        No.                          │
│   Print Name:     First    Initial    Last        Phone No.   │
│      Mr.                                                       │
│      Mrs.                                                      │
│      Miss                                                     │
│   ─────────────────────────────────────────────────────────  │
│   No., Street, Box, Route              Post Office            │
│   ─────────────────────────────────────────────────────────  │
│   I Agree to Observe all Library Rules:                       │
│                                                               │
│   ─────────────────────────────────────────────────────────  │
│   Signature (Parent must sign for child grades 1-8)          │
│   Married Women−Please use example: Jane Jones (Mrs. Fred R.) │
│   ─────────────────────────────────────────────────────────  │
│   Riverside Public Library         School_____    │
│   Riverside County Free Library    Grade 1 - 2 - 3 - 4 - 5 - 6│
│   Member of Inland Library System      7 - 8 - 9 - 10 - 11 - 12│
└─────────────────────────────────────────────────────────────┘
```

(a) Front

(b) Verso

```
┌─────────────────────────────────────────────────────────────┐
│              GENERAL LIBRARY RULES                            │
│                                                               │
│   Everyone using the library must have a card.               │
│                                                               │
│   This card must be presented when borrowing.                │
│                                                               │
│   Immediately notify library of change of address.           │
│                                                               │
│   Cards are not transferable.                                │
│                                                               │
│   The person whose signature appears on the face of this     │
│   card is responsible for loss or damage to any item         │
│   borrowed with the card and for payment of overdue fines.   │
│                                                               │
│   Loan period: 14 days, except when "7 days" appears in or   │
│   on the item borrowed. Renewals are permitted.              │
│                                                               │
│   Fines are charged in accordance with current policy and    │
│   are computed for each day the library is open.             │
│                                                               │
│   Your card expires on date shown on reverse side. Please    │
│   renew on or before that date.                              │
└─────────────────────────────────────────────────────────────┘
```

times non-residents must pay a special fee for the borrower's card, which may be partially or wholly refundable.

A public library may keep its own file of registered patrons or there may be a centralized file of registered patrons for an entire system or geographic area. An important clerical duty is to keep these files current, eliminating inactive names. Most borrower's cards expire at regular intervals, which forces people to reregister. Files are kept updated when cards are removed for those people who do not reregister. Some libraries have eliminated this task by using lists of registered voters in lieu of registration, and the latest list of voters is the current list of registered library users.

ACADEMIC LIBRARIES

The main responsibility of the academic library is service to its students, faculty and staff. Usually the library has no separate registration for these three groups. Faculty and staff are given identification cards entitling them to library privileges because they work for the institution (Figures 4, 5). Students are normally granted library privileges when they register for the current academic term. Registration in the institution automatically includes registration in the library. Students are usually required to have one of two forms of identification: 1) an identification card issued when the student registers for the current academic term, or 2) a receipt for fees paid for the current academic term. In some cases the library has a list of currently registered students issued by the registrar's office and may only require that the student verbally identify himself and check this against the list. This list is also helpful if a student should forget to bring his identification card or receipt.

Figure 4
Staff Identification Card

California State College, San Bernardino

is a member of the staff of the
California State College, San Bernardino

Staff Member's Signature

President

This Identification Card Expires 9-1-72

Academic libraries have several other kinds of users who require some form of registration to be handled in the library. These special users include local residents, students at other institutions, local school teachers and school administrators, and alumni (Figure 6). Each of these groups is handled in a different way depending on local circumstances. When the librarian develops a policy for these groups he always keeps in mind the institution's primary responsibility—service to the institution's own students, faculty and staff. The services offered to special users, therefore, are related to two factors: 1) the resources of the institution and their ability to support use by all groups, and 2) the number of special borrowers desiring to use the library.

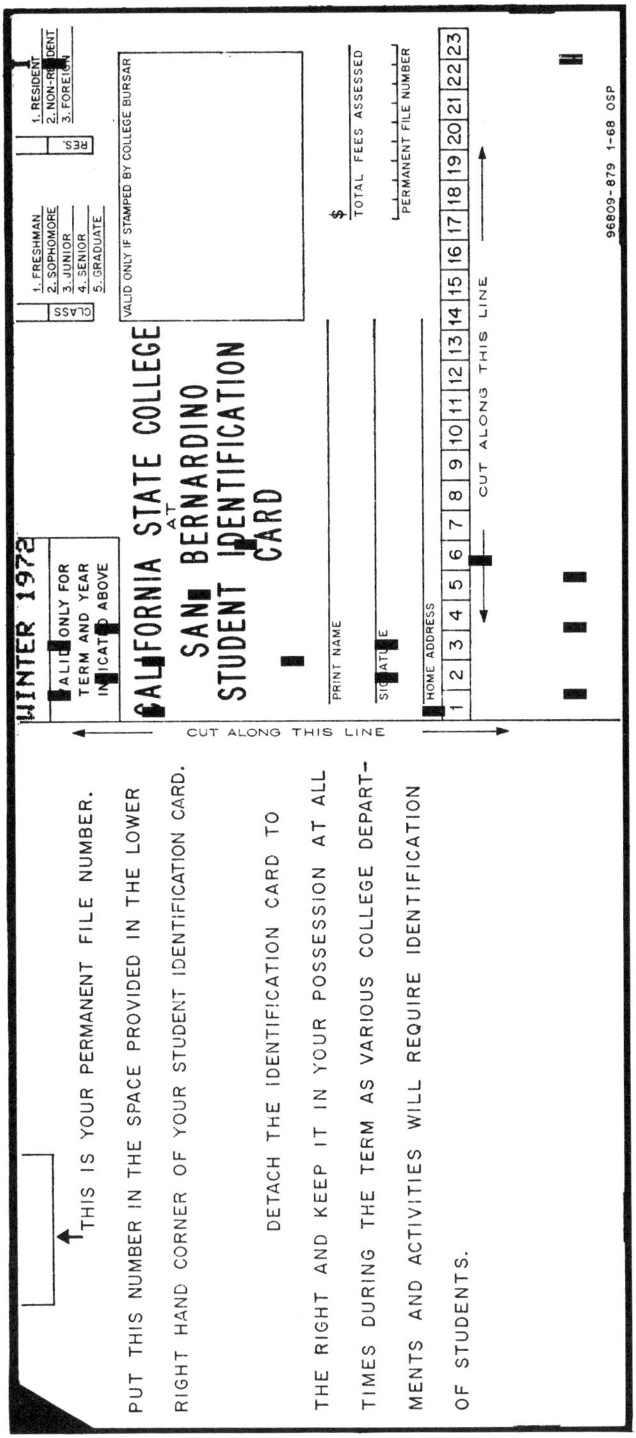
WINTER 1972

VALID ONLY FOR TERM AND YEAR INDICATED ABOVE

CLASS

1. FRESHMAN
2. SOPHOMORE
3. JUNIOR
4. SENIOR
5. GRADUATE

RES.

1. RESIDENT
2. NON-RESIDENT
3. FOREIGN

CALIFORNIA STATE COLLEGE AT SAN BERNARDINO STUDENT IDENTIFICATION CARD

VALID ONLY IF STAMPED BY COLLEGE BURSAR

PRINT NAME

SIGNATURE

HOME ADDRESS

$ TOTAL FEES ASSESSED

PERMANENT FILE NUMBER

1 2 3 4 5 6 7 8 9 10 11 12 13 14 15 16 17 18 19 20 21 22 23

CUT ALONG THIS LINE

96809-879 1-68 OSP

CUT ALONG THIS LINE

THIS IS YOUR PERMANENT FILE NUMBER.

PUT THIS NUMBER IN THE SPACE PROVIDED IN THE LOWER RIGHT HAND CORNER OF YOUR STUDENT IDENTIFICATION CARD.

DETACH THE IDENTIFICATION CARD TO THE RIGHT AND KEEP IT IN YOUR POSSESSION AT ALL TIMES DURING THE TERM AS VARIOUS COLLEGE DEPARTMENTS AND ACTIVITIES WILL REQUIRE IDENTIFICATION OF STUDENTS.

Figure 5
Student ID Card

Figure 6
Special Borrower's Card

UNIVERSITY OF CALIFORNIA • LIBRARY CARD
Riverside, California

Expires: _____ | GEN.
Lib. Status

Name ....

Business address .... City .... Zip Code

Home address .... *[signature]* .... City .... Zip Code
Librarian

Date of issue ....

Signature of Borrower

Most academic libraries allow special users to use materials in the library but do not allow them to charge out materials. There are many variations to this policy, and some types of special users—such as local public school teachers—are often given full library privileges. Many academic libraries charge a fee to some special borrowers. The fee may be refundable when the borrower turns in his special card. The library technician should be aware that policies for special users are not arbitrary but are based on many factors. Because the library technician will have to answer questions about special users' privileges, he must be completely familiar with the library's policy and the reasons for the policy.

There are two other developments in academic libraries which make their collections more easily available to special borrowers. One is to give all students in a system common identification cards that allow them to use any library in the system. The California State College System is currently working on a common identification card which would allow a student registered on any campus to have library privileges on all 19 campuses. The second development consists of cooperative agreements among local colleges which allow a student at any college to use any other cooperating college. No special registration is necessary, since students use the individual college's identification cards.

Figure 7
Cooperative System Library Card

| INTER-LIBRARY COURTESY CARD |
| (Inland Empire of Southern California) |
| Faculty ☐ |
| Name _____ Graduate ☐ |
| Area of Interest _____ |
| FROM _____ TO _____ |
| Card Expires   Librarian |

32

SPECIAL LIBRARIES

Special libraries have specialized subject collections and generally serve a limited clientele. A special library can be either a separate independent library or part of a larger library. A special library of a company or government agency is a type of independent library. A rare book collection or music collection can be part of a larger library yet be restricted in its services.

Registration of patrons for special libraries can take a variety of forms. First, employment with a company or government agency will give a person library privileges. Second, registration as a general library user may also include special library privileges. Third, a temporary borrower's card may be issued for a limited time to people needing to use a special library. Often in the latter case the user must be a researcher or specialist before a special library will give library privileges. There are thousands of special libraries and, of course, infinite variations in the manner of borrower registration.

BIBLIOGRAPHY

"First State Library Card Adopted in New Hampshire," *Library Journal* 95:3726 (November 1, 1970).

"Fully Automated Registration System Instituted at Los Angeles Library," *Library Journal* 91:3134 (June 15, 1966).

Holmes, J. L. "Nonresident Borrowing Agreement with Resident Businesses," *ALA Bulletin* 56:171 (February 1962).

Josey, E. J. "Community Use of Academic Libraries," *Library Trends* 18:66-74 (July 1969).

"Metropolitan Denver OK's Single Card," *Library Journal* 94:491 (February 1, 1969).

Petru, William C., editor. *The Library: An Introduction for Library Assistants.* New York, Special Libraries Association, 1967.

"Registered Voters Are Registered Library Users," *ALA Bulletin* 63:1500-1501 (December 1969).

"Statewide Library Cards Issued to Marylanders," *Library Journal* 93:2786 (August 1968).

Tauber, Maurice F. *Technical Services in Libraries: Acquisitions, Cataloging, Classification, Binding, Photographic Reproduction, and Circulation Operations.* New York, Columbia University Press, 1953.

CHAPTER 3

CIRCULATION SERVICES:
CIRCULATION CONTROL SYSTEMS

INTRODUCTION

Charging out materials from the library is one of the most important functions of a public services operation. The contact at the circulation desk is the only one for many patrons. It is essential, therefore, that library personnel at this service point be aware of the value of good public relations. The library's circulation control system must be easy to use for both the patron and the library staff, since a cumbersome or complex system may appear as an obstacle to the patron rather than as a help. In order to provide the best service, all personnel in circulation work should understand the circulation control system.

The reason for circulating materials out of the library is to allow the borrower the convenience of using them whenever and wherever he desires. Most libraries, however, have certain materials which are not allowed to circulate, or which have only limited circulation. This may be because of the rarity, the value, or the format of the materials; for example, non-circulating items might include rare books, reference materials, or reels of microfilm.

Figure 1
Label for Non-Circulating Reference Book

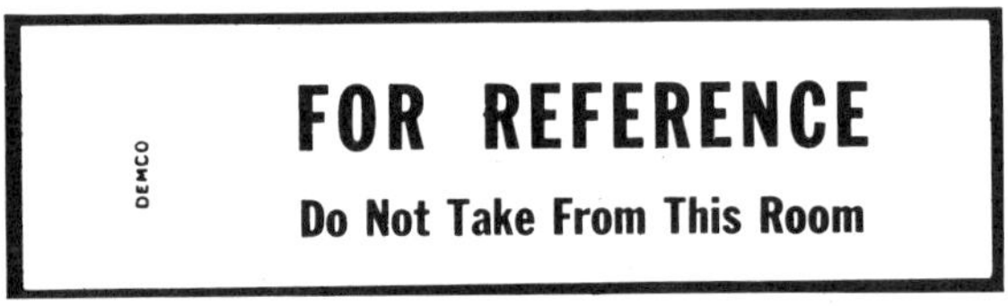

FOR REFERENCE

DEMCO

Do Not Take From This Room

Charging out materials, while very important, is only "the tip of the iceberg" of all the work performed by a circulation department. Other duties may include discharging (checking in) materials, overdue and fine work, reserve book control, shelving, general shelf maintenance, shelf reading, shifting materials, inventory control, and interlibrary loan.

The material in this chapter will cover the purposes and characteristics of circulation control systems. Several of the most popular systems will be described. Although some general duties will be discussed, not many details of the daily routine work will be included, since there is no set pattern for these daily routines and great variations exist among libraries. Even libraries using the same system can have very different ways of handling materials. The best way to learn the actual operation of a system in a library is by working in the circulation department. The operating routines can be mastered in a short time.

SELECTION OF A CIRCULATION CONTROL SYSTEM

Selecting a circulation control system is often one of the first decisions made in a library. The system selected must be coordinated with the processing of materials for use. Before material can be made ready for use, it must be known if the circulation control system will require a book pocket and book card, only a date due slip, or a punched card. The method of circulating books may affect how other library operations are set up. Care and study are necessary when a system is chosen because once it is operating any change or major modification will be costly and time-consuming. Many factors will be involved in the selection of a circulation control system. Four of the most common ones are discussed below.

The first factor is the size of the library collection and the expected amount of circulation. Some systems, well suited to a smaller volume of circulation, would be inadequate in a larger library. And, of course, the opposite is also true: an automated system may be needed in a library circulating 500,000 items a year, but it would be far more than is necessary in a library circulating 50,000 items a year.

A second factor is the cost of the system. Three elements are involved here: 1) the initial cost of processing and equipment; 2) the cost of ongoing processing, equipment maintenance and supplies; and 3) the cost of personnel needed to operate the system. Although this kind of analysis is complex and requires detailed research, it is essential. Over a period of time a carefully selected circulation system may save many thousands of dollars.

A third factor is the type of patron the library will serve. The basic decision here is the kind and amount of borrower participation built into the system. Some systems require that the borrower merely hand the material to library personnel, who then do everything necessary to charge it out. Other systems require that the borrower fill out cards with the author and title of the item, the borrower's name, and his identification number. In a public library, where patrons range from the semi-literate to the university graduate, the circulation control system must accommodate as many as possible. To avoid the errors possible in borrower participation, a public library might use a system in which the patron hands over the material and the library personnel do the actual charging-out. At the other end of the spectrum is the academic or special library. Since it serves a select clientele from whom relatively error-free participation can be expected, this type of library may save personnel time by letting the patron do as much as possible.

A final factor in the selection of a circulation control system is the service given to the patron. To some degree all of the preceding factors must be balanced with the library's standards of what constitutes good service. *The circulation control system must be compatible with the needs of the library's users and the overall purpose of the library.* The least costly system, for example, might not be selected if it would not be suitable in a particular library.

CHARACTERISTICS OF CIRCULATION CONTROL SYSTEMS

Each circulation control system has certain characteristics which determine its value to a library. The characteristics discussed below are found in all systems, but in varying degrees. When selecting a system it is necessary to consider the importance of each characteristic for a library's operation.

First, the system must be easy for the patrons to use and for library personnel to operate. An unnecessarily complex or cumbersome system may result in poor service and poor public relations if the patron views it as an obstacle to his needs rather than a help. Simplicity and ease of use might be the most important quality of any circulation control system.

Second, the system should allow the library to identify who has borrowed material, the material borrowed, and the date it is due to be returned. All systems can provide this information, but they vary greatly in the efficiency with which it can be retrieved. In some libraries this information may not be needed instantly. In academic libraries, however, one requirement might be that the borrower's name and due date be available only a short time after the material is charged out.

Third, the system must provide some record of overdue materials. The library must have this information to send overdue notices, to provide a record for fines, and to add to a list of materials for possible replacement. All systems provide this information, but again it is a matter of how rapidly the information can be retrieved. In some libraries identification of overdue material is done weekly, while in others daily identification is necessary.

Fourth, it is important that the system provide easy retrieval of reserved materials. Patrons often request materials already out on loan. The patron should be able to leave a request to be notified when the material is returned and available for his use. At some point the system must allow for returned materials to be checked against reserve requests and held for the next borrower. Reserve work is an important service and when well run can be a good public relations tool.

Last, the system should allow easy retrieval of statistics required by the library. For some libraries a manual or semi-automated system provides sufficient statistics with minimal effort. Other libraries, which may need complex statistics on reading patterns or collection-use, will require a computerized or semi-computerized system.

SELECTED CIRCULATION CONTROL SYSTEMS

There are currently about 30 different circulation control systems being used in American libraries. Most of them, however, are not widely used. In a survey of libraries it was shown that five systems were in general use far more than the other systems.[1] They were: 1) Newark system, 2) Gaylord system, 3) Photographic systems, 4) Marginal punched card systems, and 5) IBM card systems. Our discussion will be limited to general descriptions of those systems.

The reader should remember that each library has special needs and may alter a circulation system to meet those needs. Even libraries which use the same system may have great variations in operating details.[2] For this reason the following descriptions of the major systems are general and do not cover specific operating details. As with so many library functions, the best way to learn is through practical work experience under the guidance of an experienced library technician or librarian. The reader would benefit greatly by visiting libraries to see various systems in operation.

Newark System

This circulation control system is the most widely used of all systems. It is simple for patrons and library staff and is suitable for most libraries. There are two basic variations of the system: 1) a "self-charge" method which requires borrower participation, and 2) a "staff-charge" method with no borrower participation.

Using the "self-charge" method the borrower will remove the book card (Figure 2) from the book pocket (Figure 3) and write his name, identification number, or other required information on the first available blank line.

Figure 2
Book Card

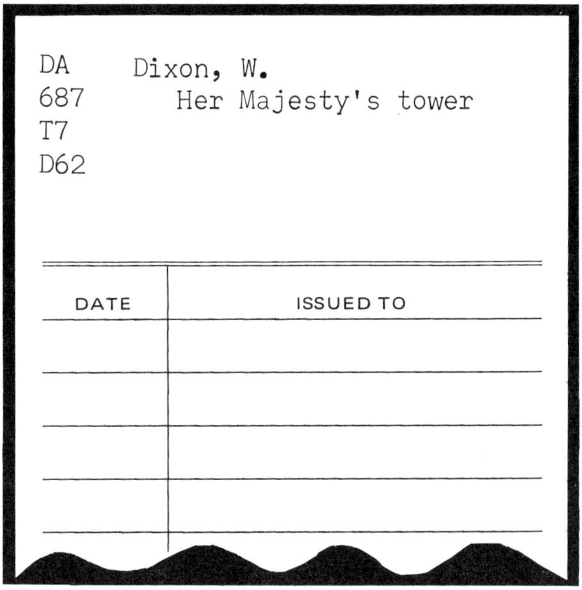

```
DA    Dixon, W.
687      Her Majesty's tower
T7
D62
```

DATE	ISSUED TO

The borrower then gives the book and completed book card to the library clerk, who stamps the due date in the book and on the book card. At this time the borrower may be asked to show his library registration card or some other form of identification. The book card is then ready to file by due date and in order by call number. One possible variation is to file book cards by author instead of call number. In this system it is necessary to have the call number, author's name, and title on the book card and book pocket.

The "staff-charge" methods differ in that a library staff member and not the borrower fills out the information on the book card. The borrower will give the material to be charged out and his library card to the clerk. In this method

Figure 3
Book Pocket with Date Due Printed on the Pocket

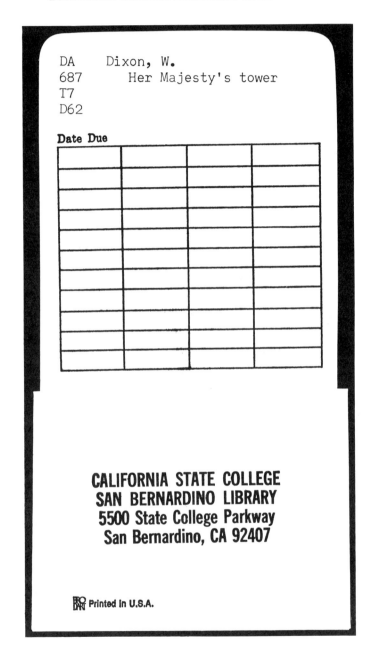

DA   Dixon, W.
687   Her Majesty's tower
T7
D62

Date Due

CALIFORNIA STATE COLLEGE
SAN BERNARDINO LIBRARY
5500 State College Parkway
San Bernardino, CA 92407

Printed In U.S.A.

Figure 4
Paste-In Date Due Slip Used to Cover Filled-Up
Date Slip on Printed Cards

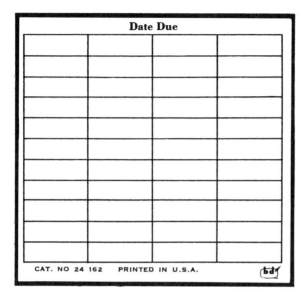

each borrower will have an identification number on his library card and this number will be placed on the book card instead of the borrower's name. The remaining steps are the same as in the "self-charge" method. "Staff-charge" is more expensive to operate because of the extra staff time involved. It should, however, reduce the number of errors, which take time to trace down and correct.

When material is returned, pulling the book card from the file discharges it. This ends the borrower's responsibility. The book card is placed back into the book pocket, and the material is ready for circulation again.

A library using the "self-charge" variation will need to maintain a file of registered borrowers by name. However, for the "staff-charge" variation it will be necessary to maintain two registration files—one filed by identification number and one filed by borrower's name. Since only the borrower's identification number is on the card, the second file must be used to identify the borrower if material is overdue or if other problems arise.

Gaylord System

This circulation control system is named for the manufacturer of the electric book charger used in charging out materials. It is similar to the Newark system except that a machine is used to fill in the information on the book card, which frees both the borrower and the library personnel from this time-consuming task. This system requires no borrower participation. When the borrower registers with the library, he will be given a library identification card with certain information (usually an identification number) embossed on a metal plate (Figure 5).

39

Figure 5
Library Identification Card with Embossed Metal Plate

In the newer variation of the charging machine, it is possible to use an all-plastic identification card which can print a maximum of four lines on the book card.

If the identification card with the embossed plate is used, a registration file of borrowers by both name and identification number will be needed, since only the identification number will appear on the book card (Figures 6 and 7). With the plastic identification card, the borrower's name can be printed on the book card, thus eliminating the need for a registration file by identification number.

Figure 6
Registration File Card with Identification Number

No. 37187
PLEASE PRINT
Last Name   First   Middle
Address
City   Phone No.
Do Not Fill Out Below
Librarian   School or Organization

Figure 7
Book Card Showing Only Borrower's Identification Number

Note that the left top of the card is notched. This is done by the machine each time the card is used so the dates will be printed below the previous one. With re-use the card will be notched all the way to the center.

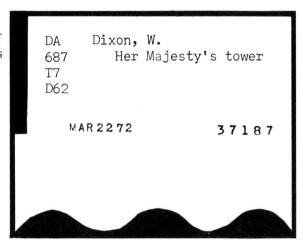

```
DA      Dixon, W.
687          Her Majesty's tower
T7
D62


    MAR 22 72                    3 7 1 8 7
```

To charge out material the borrower presents the material and his identification card to the attendant. The book card is removed from the book pocket and inserted into a slot in the charging machine. The identification card is inserted into another slot and the machine automatically prints the information—borrower's name or identification number and a due date—on the book card. Then a pre-dated date due card is placed in the book pocket (Figure 8). The book card is now ready to be filed by due date and in order by call number or author.

Material is discharged by removing the book card from the file and placing it back into the book pocket. When the date due card is removed from the pocket, the material is ready for circulation.

Photographic Charging

This type of circulation control system is characterized by the use of equipment to photograph each transaction on microfilm and the use of a transaction number to identify it. Many different companies manufacture equipment for this type of circulation control system and each piece of equipment may have a unique quality suitable to a particular library. Below is a general description of photographic charging. The reader must realize that the details of operating the systems will vary with the equipment used and with the requirements of a library.

The borrower presents the material to be charged out, along with his identification card, to the attendant. In this circulation control system the identification must have the borrower's name but it will not necessarily be a library card. The identification could be a driver's license, credit card, or some kind of membership card. The book is placed on the machine with the book pocket in position

Figure 8
Date Due Card

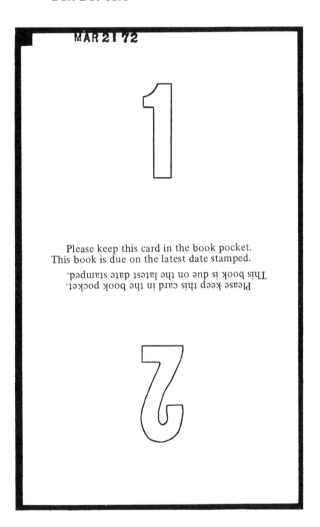

Note the notch on
the top left of the
card. The machine
automatically
notches the card
with each use so
the due dates will
be printed below
the previous one.

to be photographed. Then the borrower's identification and the dated and
numbered date due card—the transaction slip with the transaction number—
are placed on the machine in position to be photographed (Figures 9 and 10).

The photograph will include all the information needed to identify the
material, the borrower, and the due date; that is, the author, title and call
number of the material, the borrower's name, and the due date. If the author,
title, and call number are not on the book pocket, a book card with this information will be necessary.

Figure 9
Transaction Slip
with Date Due and
Transaction Number

Figure 10
Information Photographed on Microfilm: Borrower's Identification,
Book Pocket with Call Number, Author, and Title, and
Transaction Slip with Due Date and Transaction Number

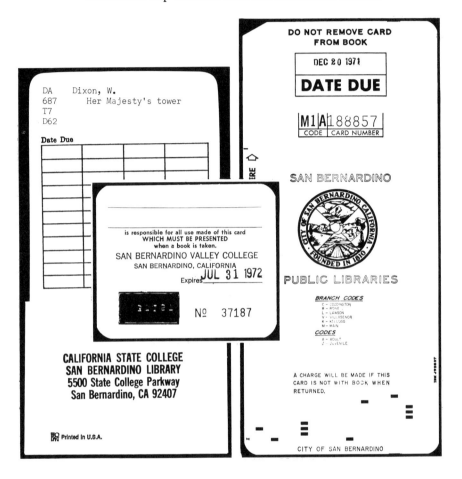

The numbered transaction slips are kept in sequence and will be in numerical order on the microfilm. The microfilm is not referred to again unless the material becomes overdue and it is necessary to locate the charge information.

To complete charging out the material the attendant inserts the dated transaction slip into the book pocket and the transaction is completed.

Material is discharged when the material is returned and the transaction slip is removed from the book pocket. There are several methods of checking which material has been returned and which is overdue. One way is to use a serial-number sheet (Figure 11). The attendant checks the due date on the transaction slip and matches it with the corresponding due date on the serial-number sheet. As material is discharged the transaction slip number is crossed off the serial-number sheet. After a time the numbers not crossed off will be

Figure 11
Serial-Number Sheet

Note that this is only a partial section.

1	51	101	151	201	251	301	351
2	52	102	152	202	252	302	352
3	53	103	153	203	253	303	353
4	54	104	154	204	254	304	354
5	55	105	155	205	255	305	355
6	56	106	156	206	256	306	356
7	57	107	157	207	257	307	357
8	58	108	158	208	258	308	358
9	59	109	159	209	259	309	359
10	60	110	160	210	260	310	360
11	61	111	161	211	261	311	361
12	62	112	162	212	262	312	362
13	63	113	163	213	263	313	363
14	64	114	164	214	264	314	364
15	65	115	165	215	265	315	365
16	66	116	166	216	266	316	366
17	67	117	167	217	267	317	367
18	68	118	168	218	268	318	368
19	69	119	169	219	269	319	369
20	70	120	170	220	270	320	370

considered overdue. The microfilm record—in sequence by transaction number—can be checked for the borrower's name so that overdue procedures can be started.

In a larger circulation operation it may not be feasible to use a serial-number sheet because of the high volume. In this situation it is possible to have the transaction number key-punched into the transaction slip. When the material is returned the key-punched transaction slips are sent to a computer center. The computer can be programmed to print out lists of transaction numbers returned and those not returned.

Marginal Punched Cards

This circulation control system is named for the special cards used to charge out material (Figure 12). No special equipment is needed except for a needle to sort out overdues. The system is more often used in college and university libraries than in public or special libraries. Borrower participation is required often to a greater degree than in other circulation control systems.

Figure 12
Marginal Punched Card

Note: Some cards are the same as IBM cards except that they are punched marginally rather than internally.

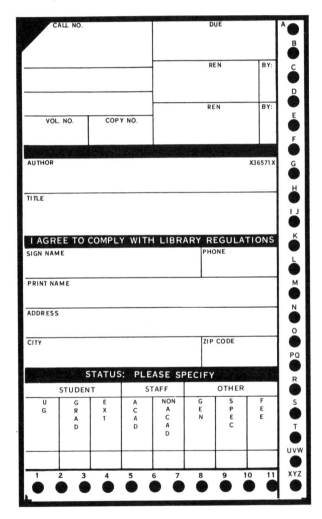

To charge out material, the borrower goes to the circulation area and fills out one card (Figure 12) for the item to be charged out. As Figure 12 illustrates, the borrower must fill out quite a bit of information. When the card is filled out, it is presented to the desk attendant, along with the material. The attendant will check the information on the card with the material, and the borrower will be asked to present his library identification card. The material will have a date due slip (Figure 13) but probably no book pocket. The due date is stamped on the date due slip in the material and on the marginal punched card. The charge-out procedure is then completed.

Figure 13
Date Due Slip

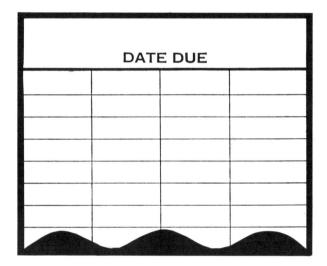

The marginal punched card is filed by due date and by call number within the date file. When material is returned it is discharged by pulling the marginal punched card from the files. If only a date due slip is in the material, nothing else needs to be done; it is ready for circulation.

The holes on the sides and bottom of the marginal punched card (Figure 12) are notched by the hole representing the due date. A needle inserted into a file sorts the overdues; all cards which are notched on the margin for a particular date will be separated from all cards not notched on that date (Figure 14).

IBM Card Systems

The IBM card system is not one system, but rather a number of systems that all use an internally punched 80-column card (Figure 15). Unlike the marginally punched card, the internally punched card must be used with data processing equipment. In a high-volume circulation control system the use of data processing equipment to semi-automate the system saves a considerable

47

Figure 14
Marginal Punched Card with Notch for Due Date

CALL NO.		DUE		A
VOL. NO.	COPY NO.	REN	BY:	B C D E F
		REN	BY:	
AUTHOR			X36571X	G H I J
TITLE				K

I AGREE TO COMPLY WITH LIBRARY REGULATIONS

SIGN NAME	PHONE	L M N O
PRINT NAME		
ADDRESS		
CITY	ZIP CODE	PQ

STATUS: PLEASE SPECIFY

	STUDENT			STAFF		OTHER			R S T UVW XYZ
U G	G R A D	E X T	A C A D	NON A C A D	G E N	S P E C	F E E	
1	2	3	4	5	6	7	8	9	10	11	

amount of personnel time. Also, if the library has access to the computer itself, the system can be programmed to yield sophisticated circulation statistics.

The IBM system is a borrower-participation system, but the required information is usually limited to the borrower's identification number and name (Figure 16). The IBM book card, which is already in the book pocket, has the call number, author, title, and accession number of the material punched into the card. The borrower removes the book card and fills in the required information. This method requires a borrower identification card, but not one which will be needed for use in any equipment. The attendant stamps the due date on the book pocket and the material is then charged out.

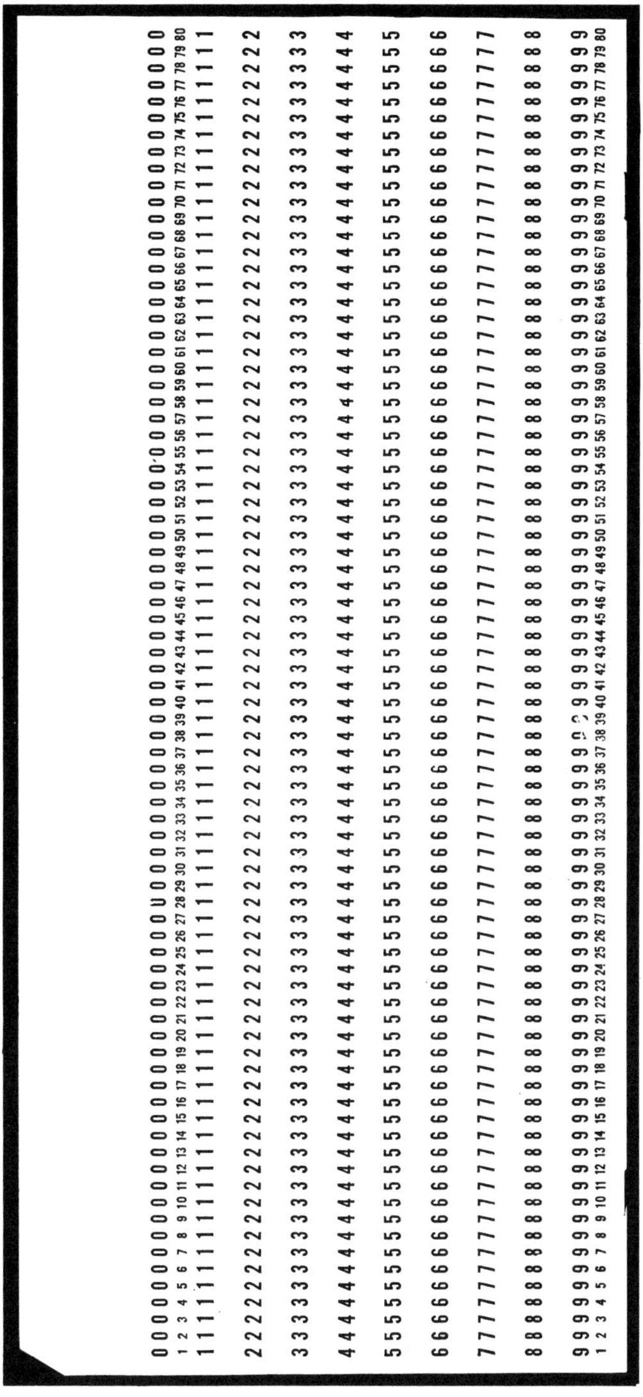

Figure 15
80-Column
Internally
Punched Card

49

Figure 16
IBM Book Card
with
Information
Punched In

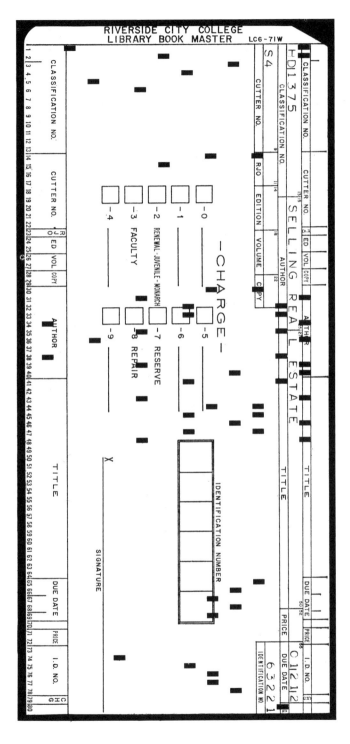

Another popular method requires the use of special embossed plastic library identification cards and an added piece of equipment. When the material is charged out, the special plastic identification card is inserted into a machine along with the book card (Figure 16). The machine automatically prints the borrower's name or identification number and punches the information on the book card and date due card. At the same time, all of the internal punches on the book card are made on the date due card (Figure 17). The due date is also printed on the date due card, which is then inserted in the book pocket, completing the charging-out process.

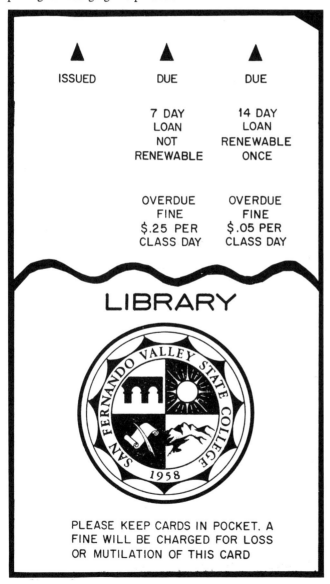

Figure 17
Date Due Card
with
Loan and Fine
Information

In both systems the book cards are processed and a duplicate book card is keypunched. Both cards—the one signed by the borrower or with his name printed on it and the duplicate card—are filed by due date in order by accession number or by call number. When the book is returned the file of book cards is checked and the old book card is withdrawn. The new duplicate card is inserted into the book pocket. If a date card is used, it is pulled and the book card is placed back into the pocket. The book is now discharged and ready for circulation.

The use of internally punched cards and a computer make it possible to produce special lists and statistics that are all but impossible when manual systems are used. A library using internally punched cards can produce lists of materials charged out by either call number, accession number, or author. Thus, by consulting a printed list, a borrower could immediately tell what materials are charged out and when they are due. The flexibility of this system is great, and it is especially useful in high-volume operations.

CIRCULATION OF NON-BOOK MATERIALS

Although the circulation control systems we have described are capable of handling all kinds of library materials, many libraries choose to handle certain non-book materials separately, with special forms. Borrower participation is usually required. Also, the loan periods for these materials may be different from those for books. Nearly every library develops its own special forms for charging out non-book material. To charge out such materials the borrower will fill out a special charge card for whatever kind of material is involved (Figures 18 through 24). As the examples below illustrate, libraries handle non-book circulation in a variety of ways.

Figure 18
Special Charge Card for Periodicals

```
┌────────────────────────────────────────────────────────────────┐
│              *ONLY ONE ITEM PER CARD*                            │
│                    PERIODICAL                                    │
│  Call Number                                          Date Due   │
│         Title: _____                 │
│                                                                  │
│         _____  _____  _____                │
│         Date of Periodical    Volume     Number                 │
│                                                                  │
│         _____  _____              │
│               Signature              I.D. Number                │
│                                                                  │
│         MUST BE RETURNED TO CIRCULATION BOOK DROPS              │
└────────────────────────────────────────────────────────────────┘
```

Figure 19
Special Charge Card for Periodicals and Pamphlets

PERIODICALS AND PAMPHLETS
CHARGE CARDS

Please fill our charge card for each title you wish
to check our and present at Loan Desk.

Title _____

_____

Date of Periodical

_____

_____

Borrower's Name

_____

ID Number _____

Do not write below this line
=====================================

Date Due _____

Figure 20
Special Charge Card for Periodicals and Reference Books

PERIODICAL AND REFERENCE
CARD

Charge Out Date _____

Title _____

_____

Date of Periodical _____

_____

Signature _____

Due _____

Total No. of Periodicals
Charged Out _____

Figure 21
Special Loan Card

Figure 22
Special Charge Card for
Occupational Guide

SPECIAL LOAN	OCCUPATIONAL GUIDE
Call No.	Number
Author	
Title	Borrower's Name
Borrower's Name	ID Number
ID No.	
Date Due	Date Due
Authorized by:	

Figure 23
Special Charge Card for Government Documents

ONLY ONE ITEM PER CARD

GOVERNMENT DOCUMENT

Call Number   Date Due

Title: _____

_____   _____
Signature   I.D. Number

MUST BE RETURNED TO CIRCULATION BOOK DROPS

Figure 24
Special Charge Card for Non-Accessioned Material and Pamphlets

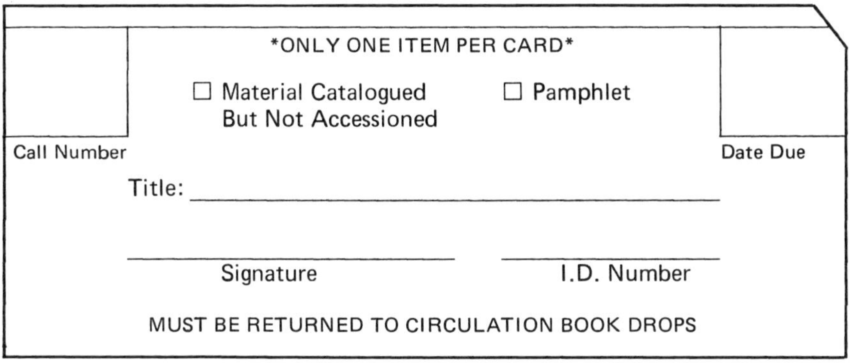

```
┌──────────────────────────────────────────────────────────────────┐
│              *ONLY ONE ITEM PER CARD*                              │
│                                                                    │
│   ☐ Material Catalogued      ☐ Pamphlet                           │
│     But Not Accessioned                                            │
│ Call Number                                        Date Due        │
│     Title: _____              │
│                                                                    │
│     _____      _____            │
│        Signature                   I.D. Number                     │
│                                                                    │
│     MUST BE RETURNED TO CIRCULATION BOOK DROPS                     │
└──────────────────────────────────────────────────────────────────┘
```

While it may be possible to use the same circulation control system for both special materials and books, most libraries choose not to do so. The cost of controlling these special materials is often lower if a separate system is used. Also, many of the special materials do not have a large enough circulation to justify anything but the simplest and least costly system.

LOAN PERIODS

Libraries usually set limits on the length of time a borrower can keep library materials. These limits are established so that the materials will be returned and made available to other library users. The length of the loan period may depend on the size of the collection, amount of use, purpose of lending materials, and the clientele served. Loan periods for most materials are for one to four weeks. Special materials (such as periodicals, pamphlets, phonorecords, or films) are usually lent for shorter periods of one to seven days. These periods, of course, vary depending on the library.

Libraries with smaller collections and high circulation would tend to have shorter loan periods in order to make material available to as many borrowers as possible. Libraries with larger collections could allow longer loan periods. The librarian must take all of the aforementioned factors into consideration when establishing loan periods.

Some libraries also limit the total number of items a patron may borrow at one time or the number of items he may borrow in any one subject area. This is often done in smaller libraries where one patron could deplete an entire subject unless limits were set. The larger the collection, the less need there is for limiting borrowing.

Figure 25 provides a summary of major operations in circulation and check-in procedures.

Figure 25
Circulation and Discharging Procedure

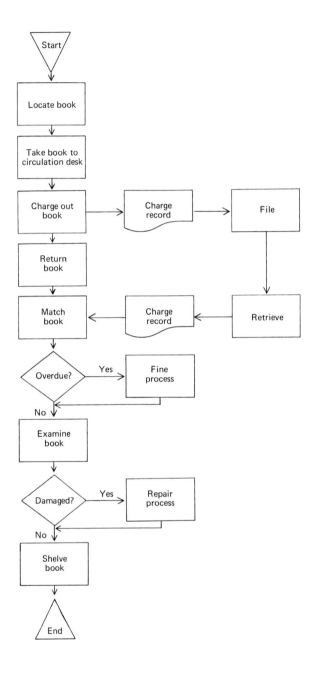

FOOTNOTES

1. George Fry and Associates, Inc. *Study of Circulation Control Systems: Public Libraries, College and University Libraries, Special Libraries.* Chicago, Library Technology Project, 1961. pp. 36-38. For complete descriptions of all circulation control systems, read this volume and Helen Geer, *Charging Systems.* Chicago, American Library Association, 1955. There are also, of course, many articles in professional literature on this subject; a small number of them are included in the bibliography at the end of this chapter.

2. The author visited four libraries using the Newark system, two libraries using marginal punched cards, and three using IBM cards. Listening to descriptions of their daily operations made it apparent that differences existed between the libraries using the same system. Knowing how to work with a system in one library was no guarantee that one could step into another library using the same basic system without learning a whole new series of procedures.

BIBLIOGRAPHY

Bauer, Harry C. "Circulation Service and Public Relations," *Library Trends* 6:52-65 (July 1957).

Boyer, Calvin J. "On Line Circulation Control–Midwestern University Library's System Using an IBM 1401 Computer in a 'Time Sharing' Mode," in *Proceedings of the Clinic on Library Applications of Data Processing, 1969.* Urbana, University of Illinois, School of Library Science, 1970. pp. 135-43.

Birnbaum, Henry. *General Information Manual–IBM Circulation Control at Brooklyn College Library.* New York, International Business Machines, 1960.

Bloss, Meredith. "Transaction Charging," *Library Journal* 78:1285-88 (August 1953).

Booser, Ronald J. "The Use of Data Processing Equipment for the Control and Circulation of Magazines," *Special Libraries* 51:297-300 (July-August 1960).

Bousfield, Humphrey G. "Circulation Systems," *Library Trends* 3:164-76 (October 1954).

Geer, Helen. *Charging Systems.* Chicago, American Library Association, 1955.

George Fry and Associates, Inc. *Study of Circulation Control Systems: Public Libraries, College and University Libraries, Special Libraries.* Chicago, Library Technology Project, 1961.

Hagerty, M. M. "Reserve Book System; a Positive View," *Wilson Library Bulletin* 26:387-88 (January 1952).

Hamilton, Robert E. "The Illinois State Library 'On-Line' Circulation Control System," in *Proceedings of the Clinic on Library Applications of Data Processing, 1968.* Urbana, University of Illinois, School of Library Science, 1969. pp. 11-28.

Harris, Michael H. "The 357 Data System for Circulation Control," *College and Research Libraries* 26:119-120+ (March 1965).

Harvey, John, editor. *Data Processing in Public and University Libraries.* Washington, Spartan Books, 1966.

Hayes, Robert M., and Joseph Becker. *Handbook of Data Processing for Libraries.* New York, Becker and Hayes, 1970.

Hocker, Margaret L. "Punched-Card Charging System for a Small College Library," *College and Research Libraries* 18:119-22 (March 1957).

Hood, Marjorie. "Circulation Work," in Guy R. Lyle, *The Administration of the College Library.* 3rd ed. New York, H. W. Wilson, 1961. pp. 96-127.

International Business Machines. *General Information Manual: Mechanized Library Procedures.* New York, (n.d.).

Jordan, Robert T. *Tomorrow's Library: Direct Access and Delivery.* New York, R. R. Bowker, 1970.

Kimber, Richard T. *Automation in Libraries.* New York, Pergamon Press, 1968.

Kirkwood, Leila H. *Charging Systems.* New Brunswick, N.J., Graduate School of Library Science, Rutgers, The State University, 1961.

Lansberg, William R. "Current Trends in the College Reserve Room," *College and Research Libraries* 11:120-24 (April 1950).

McCoy, Ralph E. "Computerized Circulation Work: A Case Study of the 357 Data Collection System," *Library Resources and Technical Services* 9:59-65 (Winter 1965).

McGaw, Howard F. *Marginal Punched Cards in College and Research Libraries.* Washington, Scarecrow Press, 1952.

Parker, Ralph H. "Adaptation of Machines to Book Charging," *Library Trends* 6:35-41 (July 1957).

Pizer, Irwin H. "A Mechanized Circulation System," *College and Research Libraries* 27:5-12 (January 1966).

Rift, Leo R. "An Inexpensive Transaction Number Charging System with Book Record," *College and Research Libraries* 18:112-18 (March 1957).

Surace, Cecily J. "Library Circulation Systems: An Overview," *Special Libraries* 63:177-88 (April 1972).

Tauber, Maurice F. *Technical Services in Libraries.* New York, Columbia University Press, 1954.

Yenawine, Wayne S., editor. "Current Trends in Circulation Services," *Library Trends* 6:1-100 (July 1957).

CHAPTER 4

CIRCULATION: COLLECTION CONTROL

INTRODUCTION

As stated in the preceding chapter the circulation of library materials is only a small part of circulation work. Most library users, familiar only with the act of charging out materials, have little or no conception of the less visible but equally important work performed to make sure materials are readily available. The time and personnel involved in charging out material may represent only a fraction of the effort needed for all the circulation activities related to collection control.

In this chapter we will discuss the other activities involved in circulation control. They include discharging materials, overdue procedures, reserve books, reserve book collections, reshelving, shelf-reading, shifting materials, inventory, and general maintenance.

Our concern in this chapter will be the importance of and reasons for each activity. The specific details of how each activity is performed in a library will not be dwelt upon. The diversity of methods used in collection control work among libraries makes it difficult to describe daily routines. Again, the best way to learn work routines is by doing the work in a library circulation department.

DISCHARGING MATERIALS

The various ways to discharge borrowed materials were discussed in the section on circulation control systems. Regardless of the circulation control system being used, the result of discharging is the same—the record of a loan is removed or cancelled and the borrower's responsibility ends.

Once material has been discharged, it is inspected for wear or damage. If it is badly damaged, the borrower may be charged a fee. In general it is at this point in the circulation that needed repairs can most easily be spotted. Torn pages, loose bindings, missing labels must be repaired before the material circulates again since, if it is not repaired, the material may be damaged beyond repair and require replacement. When repairs are needed, materials may be placed on a special repair shelf and a mending slip inserted in the item (Figure 1).

The importance of good public relations must not be forgotten when evaluating the discharging process. Few things are more irritating to a borrower than mistakes in the discharging process. For example, the borrower will resent receiving overdue notices for materials already returned. The fact that there may be a shortage of personnel or a heavy workload will be of little concern to the patron; his impression will be that the library is inefficient. The library technician or clerk who supervises a circulation department must be aware of the total possible effect of each step in the operation. Such awareness is particularly important if the operation has direct dealings with library patrons.

Figure 1
Mending Slip

```
MENDING SLIP

☐ Needs new label on spine
☐ Torn page(s) _____
☐ Loose page(s) _____
☐ Repair weak or loose hinge
☐ Torn or loose cover
☐ Needs rebinding
☐ Miscellaneous: _____
  _____
  _____
  _____
```

RESERVE BOOKS

Patrons often request that materials be held for them when returned by another borrower. One of the characteristics of a good circulation control system is its ability to identify holds—reserve requests—when material is returned. Patrons are usually requested to fill out a hold or reserve request (Figures 2, 3), and when the material is returned it is set aside and held until it can be picked up by the patron who reserved it. The hold/reserve card is usually attached to the charge record so that the material can be identified in the discharging process. When material is returned, the hold/reserve request card is mailed (or in some cases the patron may be phoned). In all cases the material is reserved for only a limited time—usually a few days.

Figure 2
Hold Request

```
HOLD REQUEST

NAME_____
ADDRESS_____
PHONE _____ DATE _____
AUTHOR_____
TITLE_____
CALL NUMBER_____
```

Figure 3
Hold Request Which Can Be Mailed to the Patron

```
┌─────────────────────────────────────────────────────────┐
│              FORM FOR RESERVE NOTICE                       │
│                                                            │
│  Call No._____Date of Request_____19_____  │
│                                                            │
│  Title_____  │
│                                                            │
│  Author_____  │
│                                                            │
│  Not wanted after_____  │
│  ========================================================  │
│  A copy of this book has been reserved for you today,      │
│                                                            │
│  _____, and will be held until_____.      │
│                                                            │
│  Please bring this notice with you when you call for the book. │
│                                                            │
│                  Per_____          │
│                                                            │
└─────────────────────────────────────────────────────────┘
```

OVERDUE MATERIAL AND FINE PROCEDURES

Libraries handle their overdues and fine procedures in a variety of ways. In recent years there has been a general trend to lower or eliminate fines in many libraries. During this same time, however, some libraries have reinstated or even increased fines because a fineless system failed to work for them.

Libraries which use fines should be sure that information about them is easily available to the borrower. The fine rates can be printed on the borrower's card, on the transaction card inserted in the book pocket, or in the library handbook. They may also be posted on a sign at the circulation desk.

The fine rate is not always established by the library; it may be set by the library's governing body. In a public library the librarian sometimes makes recommendations on a fine policy, but the library board of trustees may be the only body with legal authority to establish the policy. In a college or university library the librarian will often make recommendations to the president or other governing body with authority over the library. The library technician should be aware that fine policy is not arrived at haphazardly, but is based on many factors. Few libraries have complete freedom to set policy, but must conform to the desires of various governing bodies.

Fine rates will often vary for different types of loans. For example, fines for short-term loans are often higher than for longer term loans. There may be a different fine rate for children or juvenile borrowers. Usually these rates will be lower than those used for adults. Some libraries have a policy of rescinding fines for borrowers who say they are unable to pay. Some libraries have tried temporary moratoriums to encourage the return of overdue material. If the overdue

61

material is returned within a specified period of time the fine will be cancelled.

Remember that the purpose of fines is not to punish borrowers, but to protect the rights of all library patrons. Fines are used to encourage the timely return of material so that other patrons will be able to use them.

When overdue material is identified, a notice is mailed to the borrower (Figure 4). The way overdue material is identified , of course, depends on the circulation control system being used. If the borrower does not respond to the first notice, second and third notices may be sent as new deadlines come due.

Figure 4
Overdue Notice

DID YOU FORGET?

Please return the following overdue book(s) drawn on your library card No._____

AUTHOR   TITLE   DUE

                                    DAPHNE WALKER, Librarian
EL PASO COUNTY LIBRARY
FABENS, TX 79838   By _____

The number of notices sent is a matter of library policy. Records are maintained on notices sent and the eventual resolution of the loan (Figure 5). A bill is made out (Figure 6) when a fine is charged, and a receipt is issued when it is paid. If the fine remains unpaid, legal action may be taken. In all cases, the decision as to whether or not to take legal action rests with the librarian. Public libraries may work with the city or county legal department to take action against borrowers who fail to respond to overdue notices. Libraries sometimes take action against borrowers guilty of flagrant violations in hopes of deterring other patrons from committing similar violations. In academic institutions the library may work with the registrar or business office to withhold transcripts or degrees from students with unpaid library fines.

COLLECTION OF FINES AND FEES

Collecting fines is an important responsibility because it involves handling

Figure 5
Fine Slip for Record Keeping

```
┌─────────────────────────────────────┐
│                                      │
│            FINE SLIP                 │
│                                      │
│   Card No...............................│
│   Name .................................│
│   Address ..............................│
│   Call No. .............................│
│   Author ...............................│
│   Title ................................│
│   Date Loaned ..........................│
│   Date Due .............................│
│   Date Returned ........................│
│   1st Notice Sent.......................│
│   2nd Notice Sent ......................│
│   3rd Notice Sent ......................│
│   Messenger Sent .......................│
│   Reported Lost ........................│
│   Fines Due...................$...........│
│   Messenger Fee ..............$...........│
│   Price of Book ..............$...........│
│   Total ......................$...........│
│   Rec'd Payment.........................│
│                                      │
└─────────────────────────────────────┘
```

Figure 6
Bill for Overdue Materials

BILL FOR LIBRARY MATERIALS

Cost of material: $ _____

Processing fee: $ __3.35__

Fine: (15¢ per day excluding Sundays and days the $ _____
      library is closed. From date due until returned
      or paid for.)

Damage to material: $ _____
      TOTAL DUE IF MATERIAL IS NOT RETURNED $ _____ plus fine

California State College, Fullerton   COLLEGE LIBRARIAN
Pay all fees in the Circulation Department   Mr. E.W. Toy, Jr.

63

money. Fines must be calculated carefully; since a fine is a poor public relations device to begin with, miscalculation of the amount of the fine will only exacerbate the situation. In some libraries, usually academic, the fine money is not collected by the library. Instead, a bill stating the amount of the fine is issued by the library and the fee is paid at the business office or other appropriate agency on campus. Although the policy varies, fines for overdues often do not revert to the library but go to a general fund of the governing body of the library.

Another situation in which the library must collect money involves lost books. Generally the borrower is charged the original cost or the replacement cost of the material, and often a set fee will be added to cover the expenses of replacement (Figure 6). A lost book which costs $4.95 to replace might be billed at $5.95—the cost of the book plus a replacement fee of $1.00. The replacement fee is often suspended for inexpensive materials, and sometimes the patron is not charged at all for low-cost items.

Many libraries have special fees for rental collections. Some academic libraries have rental reserve collections and some public libraries have rental collections of currently popular materials. If multiple copies of particular works are needed but their purchase is not justified, the library might purchase multiple copies for rental and thereby recover, or partially recover, their costs. Again, as with fines, rental fees must be calculated correctly and must be collected. When libraries have rental collections the fees are usually collected in the library and not by any outside agency.

The library technician may not do the actual collecting of fines and fees. Nevertheless, since he will probably supervise the operation, the technician must be aware of library policy and be able to solve most problems that may arise. Just as important, the library technician must know when to consult the librarian on special problems.

SHELVING MATERIALS

Shelving materials is one of the most important aspects of collection control. Unless a library has an accurate and efficient shelving operation, good overall library service will be difficult and in come cases impossible to offer. Backlogs of unshelved materials may cause delayed service and require valuable staff and patron time to locate them. Misshelved materials are as good as lost and are of use to no one until they can be found. In larger collections it may take many hours of searching to locate such materials.

Materials for shelving usually come from one of three sources: 1) materials newly processed sent to the circulation department for first shelving, 2) circulated materials which have been returned and discharged, and 3) materials used in the library and not reshelved by the patron. (NOTE: Most libraries actively discourage patrons from reshelving materials. The chance of mistakes from patron reshelving is great primarily for two reasons: 1) patrons may not understand the importance of accurate shelving and therefore may approach it haphazardly, and 2) they may not understand the system used to shelve material.)

The details of how materials are handled in a shelving operation vary from library to library. All materials may be brought to a central location where they are sorted and placed in order. In some larger libraries there may be shelving and sorting areas on each floor with special procedures to send books to other floors when necessary. Books are usually placed in rough order on shelves and then placed in exact order on book trucks just prior to shelving.

Most library materials are shelved in classification number order. The format of some material (such as microfilm, slides or films) may require a different method of shelving, but generally these materials will have some classification or accession number to allow for orderly shelving. Some books require special handling even if format is no problem (such as rare books, special collection materials, and oversize books). The library technicians must be familiar with all of the special shelving problems. Although the library technician will do little or no shelving, it will be necessary to train and supervise clerks and student assistants to handle all phases of the shelving operation.

The two most common classification systems found in libraries are the Dewey Decimal Classification and the Library of Congress Classification. The Dewey Decimal Classification may present more problems in shelving because of the numbers to the right of the decimal point. It is important to remember that, since those numbers are decimal-fractions, .16 is smaller than .9 and will therefore file before the latter. Below, some classification numbers are given in the order in which they will appear on the shelves:

581.21	581.3	581.31	581.4	581.498	581.5
D4	E73	A4	A47	R3	J6

Notice that .498 files before .5 because in a decimal system it is the lesser number. The second line is a cutter number for the author's name. This number serves to keep items with the same classification number in alphabetical order. For example:

512	512	512
A3	A47	D6

The Library of Congress Classification is arranged first by the letters and then by the numbers. The third line is the author number which, like the cutter number used with the Dewey Decimal Classification, serves to keep material in alphabetical order. Notice that the author number in the examples below is treated like a decimal—D47 is shelved before D5:

L	L	LA	LB	LD	LD
7	7	96	3063	4701	4701
D47	D5	G5	R71	R19	R2

In some Library of Congress classification numbers there are two sets of letter/number combinations. When this occurs, continue to file line-by-line, treating the numbers as decimals:

DC	DC	DC	DC	DC
801	801	801	801	801
A96	A96	A96	V57	V57
G3	G68	H7	G5	H9

It is important for the library technician to see that the staff members responsible for shelving understand the classification system and its relation to shelving materials. Also, those shelving must understand the importance of correct shelving and how it relates to good library service. Shelving is a tiring and dull job if performed for lengthy periods; the supervisor must establish schedules so that one person does not shelve too long and thereby become careless.

RESERVE BOOK COLLECTIONS

Reserve book collections are usually associated with academic libraries. These collections are composed of materials reserved by the faculty for their classes. Because a course must be completed within a limited period of time—a semester or quarter—the materials cannot be lent for the regular loan period, or few people in a class could use them. If everyone in a class of 40 people must read a chapter from a particular book, the loan period of the book must be greatly restricted.

To place materials in a reserve collection, the faculty member fills out a special form listing what he will require. These lists must usually be sent to the library well in advance of the starting date of the class so that the material can be gathered together. Items are removed from the shelf; if they are in circulation, they are recalled (Figure 7). When material is placed in a reserve collection, this is noted in the library catalog. If the library uses a card catalog, a special clear plastic cover will be placed over the cards for a particular item. At the top of the plastic cover the word "Reserve" will be printed informing the patron that the material will not be found on the shelves, but in the special reserve collection (Figure 8).

Figure 7
Reserve Material Recall Notice

California State College, Fullerton

The following material charged out to you is needed by the library. Please return it to us by _____.

If you fail to return the material by that time, you will be charged a fine of 15¢ per day on each item from that date. Please place this card in the pocket of the book and return it to the Circulation Counter of the library. Thank you.

Date: _____

Figure 8
Clear Plastic Reserve Book Card Jacket

RESERVE BOOK

NE   Museum of Graphic Art.
505   American printmaking, the first 150 years.
M8   Pref. by A. Hyatt Mayor. Foreword by Donald
H. Karshan. Introd. by J. William Middendorf
II. Text by Wendy J. Shadwell. [New York,
1969]

180 p. illus. (part col.) ports. 26 cm.
Bibliography: p.175-178.

1.Prints, American-Catalogs. I.Title.

A special circulation control system is used for reserve book collections. Depending on the projected demand for the materials, the loan period may vary from seven days to one hour. The faculty member who places the material on reserve will also set the loan period; different items on the same list may be assigned different loan periods.

Reserve materials are set apart from the regular collection. They are usually kept in a special reserve book room or on special shelves in the circulation area, depending on the size of the reserve collection. Some reserve material collections are kept on closed shelves, which means the borrower does not have direct access to them. In this case the patron gives the desk attendant the author, title, and call number of the desired material, which is pulled and given to the borrower. In some libraries reserve collections are kept on open shelves but materials cannot be removed from the reserve room.

One of the more popular ways to shelve reserve materials is to group them together under the name of the person reserving them. As stated above, reserve materials are most often charged out under their own special circulation control system, using special reserve charge cards. To charge out material the borrower gets the material from the shelves or, if closed stacks are used, requests material from the library attendant. The patron signs his name or identification number on a special charge card (Figure 9), although in some systems he must also fill in the author and title of the material. The date due is stamped or written in on a date due slip. The charge card is then filed by call number, by author, or by the loan period. Because of the relatively short loan periods, these files are searched frequently for overdues. If books are lent for two-hour periods, it is necessary to check the file for overdues every two hours.

Figure 9
Reserve Material Charge Card

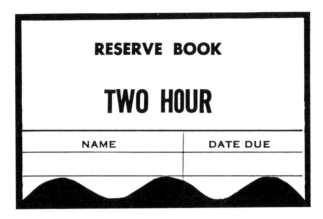

In academic libraries the reserve materials operation can be quite large; however, once a reserve policy is established, a librarian has little to do with the daily routines. Thus, the library technician may play an important supervisory role.

SHELF READING

To keep the library collection in good order it is necessary to read the shelves systematically from time to time. This is accomplished by reading the classification numbers on book spines (or on any other types of materials) to see that the materials are in proper order. A collection in which much of the material is out of order is difficult to use and can waste a lot of patron and staff time locating particular items.

As the clerk or student assistant reads the shelves, misshelved items should be placed in correct order. The shelf reader should also look for damaged material and loose or defaced labels and should remove this material so that it can be repaired.

Although the library technician will probably do little shelf reading, except perhaps to revise work of new personnel, he will assume major responsibility for supervising the shelf-reading operation. He will establish schedules to insure that the entire collection is shelf-read at regular intervals. Some of the more heavily used parts of the collection might require frequent shelf reading, while other parts of the collection may need to be checked only occasionally. The library technician, therefore, must be thoroughly familiar with circulation statistics and in-library reading patterns in order to identify the more heavily used parts of the collection.

Needless to say, shelf reading is tedious work. Most shelf readers can maintain accuracy, and perhaps some enthusiasm, for 30 to 45 minutes. When scheduling personnel to do this work, the library technician must consider these limitations.

SHIFTING MATERIALS

As a library's collection grows the shelves become full and eventually some shifting of materials is required. Shelves are not arranged randomly, but require planning by the librarian. In formulating these plans the librarian attempts to: 1) place more frequently used materials in easily accessible places near circulation areas, 2) keep closely related materials together, 3) place seldom used materials so they do not take up the most valuable space, and 4) place periodical indexes near the periodical collection.

Although it is the librarian who makes shelving decisions, the library technician must be aware of the rationale behind the decisions. The library technician should be alert for the shelving problems, or possible shelving problems, throughout the library. These problem areas should be reported to the librarian along with any recommendations for their solution.

INVENTORY AND SEARCH ROUTINES

A complete inventory of a library collection is costly and time-consuming. While only a few years ago many libraries carried out an inventory every two or three years, this is no longer the case. The relatively low book losses in most libraries require regular inventories less frequently. In fact, some libraries do not inventory at all, but only check requests for material which cannot be found on the shelves.

While complete inventories are often avoided, many libraries take a continuous partial inventory. At regular intervals the shelf list for a particular subject area is compared with the material on the shelves. Usually the subject areas inventoried are the most heavily used, where lost material should be replaced as soon as possible. The lesser used parts of the collection will be inventoried less often or not at all.

Regardless of the frequency or scope of inventories the methods used by libraries are similar. The shelf list is compared to the materials actually on the shelves. Missing items are noted and then checked with the circulation files listing the materials out on loan. If the material is neither on the shelves nor on loan, it may be considered as probably missing. It could, of course, be in use in the library, in the shelving area, at the bindery, or misshelved. The missing items will be listed on special forms (Figures 10, 11), and noted in the shelf list, and searched for again—a procedure which may be repeated several times. Then if the item has still not been located, it is declared missing, and the cards are removed from the card catalog. The librarian is given a list of items declared missing, and he will decide if replacement is necessary.

When a patron requests material which he is unable to find on the shelves and which is not on loan, a special search procedure is undertaken. The same search procedures may be used if the borrower claims he returned an item which library records show as still on loan. The call number, author, and title are written on a special search form and a search is carried out by a clerk or student assistant (Figures 10, 11). The patron's name and address will usually be written on the search form so that he can be notified if the material is found. The number of search locations listed on Figure 10 shows how time-consuming a search can be. However, it is an important service, and libraries make every effort to locate missing material when requested.

Figure 10
Missing Material Search Form

SEARCH FORM

Call no. _____

Author _____

Title _____

_____

_____

Search taken ___

Card Catalog ___			
Shelves ___			
Carts ___			
Circ. files ___			
Bk. repair areas ___			
Missing bk. list ___			

Figure 11
Patron Request Form to Locate Returned Material

Name _____ **INQUIRY CARD** Date _____

Local Phone _____ Clerk _____

Accession No. _____

Call No. _____

Date Due _____ REMARKS:

Returned ___ Autopage ___ Overdue

___ Library ___ On Time

Searches:

Date _____ By _____

Date _____ By _____

Date _____ By _____

Date _____ By _____

Figure 12
Inventory Procedure

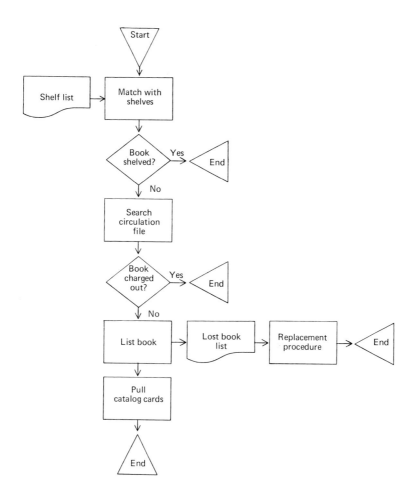

Start

Shelf list → Match with shelves

Book shelved? — Yes → End

No ↓

Search circulation file

Book charged out? — Yes → End

No ↓

List book → Lost book list → Replacement procedure → End

Pull catalog cards

End

STATISTICS

All libraries keep circulation statistics of one kind or another. Some may keep statistics of the number of items loaned; other libraries break down the circulation statistics according to classification, type of borrower, format of material, or a combination of these (Figure 13).

Figure 13
Monthly Circulation Statistics Sheet With Daily Totals

Month: Day:	1	2	3	4	5		Totals
No. of Student Loans							
No. of Faculty Loans							
Reserve Book Loans							
Curriculum Material Loans							
Phono-Record Loans							
Periodical Loans							
Totals							

Figure 14
Circulation Statistics by Decimal Classification

Month: Day:	1	2	3	4	5	Totals
000						
100						
200						
300						
400						
500						
600						
700						
800						
900						
Totals						

Figure 15
Daily Record of Statistics

DAILY RECORD

Date _____

BOOK CIRCULATION		ADULT	JUVENILE
Generalities	000		
Philosophy	100		
Religion	200		
Social Sciences	300		
Language	400		
Pure Sciences	500		
Technology	600		
The Arts	700		
Literature	800		
History	900-909 930-999		
Geography, Travel	910-919		
Biography	920		
Total Non-Fiction			
Fiction			
Total Book Circulation			
Periodicals			
Pamphlets			
Paperbacks			
Rental			
Total Circulation			

Signature _____

Those libraries using internally punched cards and computer equipment can easily produce statistics of the type shown in the forms above. Daily, weekly, or monthly print-outs of circulation statistics can be produced almost on demand, and no manual record-keeping is required. Complex reader profile analysis (who reads what, their educational level, grade point average, residential district, etc.), which can be performed quickly by machines, would require an almost prohibitive number of hours if performed manually. In any case, statistics of one kind or another are kept in all libraries.

SCHEDULING

A library technician will normally have administrative duties in circulation work. One of the more important of these will be establishing work schedules to see that all of the functions in the department are performed on a regular basis. In addition, library staff must be assigned to circulation desks during all hours the library is open. This scheduling, which can be a complex job, is usually done in ccoperation with the supervising librarian. The typical library schedule below shows the great number of hours a library is open and the special periods which present scheduling problems (Figure 16).

Figure 16
Schedule of Library Hours

UNIVERSITY OF CALIFORNIA, RIVERSIDE
LIBRARY CALENDAR

REGULAR SCHEDULE

Monday through Thursday	8:00 a.m. to MIDNIGHT
Friday	8:00 a.m. to 5:00 p.m.
Saturday	10:00a.m. to 5:00 p.m.
Sunday	2:00 p.m. to MIDNIGHT

WINTER QUARTER 1972

January 1, Saturday (New Year's Day)	CLOSED
January 2, Sunday	CLOSED
January 3, Monday (Quarter begins)	8:00 a.m. to 5:00 p.m.
January 4, Tuesday—Feb. 20, Sunday	REGULAR SCHEDULE
February 21, Monday (Washington's Birthday) . .	2:00 p.m. to MIDNIGHT
February 22, Tuesday—March 9, Thursday . . .	REGULAR SCHEDULE

Extended Hours for Final Exam Period

March 10, Friday	8:00 a.m. to MIDNIGHT
March 11, Saturday	10:00 a.m. to MIDNIGHT
March 12, Sunday	2:00 p.m. to MIDNIGHT
March 13, Monday—March 17, Friday .	8:00 a.m. to MIDNIGHT
March 18, Saturday (quarter ends) . .	8:00 a.m. to NOON

March 19, Sunday	CLOSED
March 20, Monday—March 23, Thursday	8:00 a.m. to 5:00 p.m.
March 24, Friday (Spring Holiday)	CLOSED
March 25, Saturday	REGULAR SCHEDULE
March 26, Sunday	CLOSED

One other area which requires scheduling is shelf reading. The library technician sets up a schedule of the classification numbers to be read and assigns clerks or student assistants to read them on a regular basis. By means of such careful scheduling, the library technician can be sure that heavily-used areas of the collection are checked regularly.

BIBLIOGRAPHY

NOTE: Only a few of the citations listed here deal with fines. Because most of the articles on fines are only one or two pages in length and very limited in scope, it did not seem to serve any purpose to list many of them. The reader should look under the subject entry "Fines, fees, etc." in Library Literature.

"ALA Statement on Overdues," *Library Journal* 86:1114 (March 15, 1961).

American Library Association. Statistics Coordinating Project. *Library Statistics: A Handbook of Concepts, Definitions, and Terminology.* Chicago, American Library Association, 1966.

Beck, R. E., and J. R. McKinnon. "Development of Methods and Time Standards for a Large Scale Library Inventory." In B. R. Burkhalter, editor, *Case Studies in Systems Analysis in a University Library.* Metuchen, N.J., Scarecrow Press, 1968. pp. 48-75.

Benford, H. L., and others. "Analysis of Book Reshelving." In B. R. Burkhalter, editor, *Case Studies in Systems Analysis in a University Library.* Metuchen, N.J., Scarecrow Press, 1968. pp. 76-89.

Bluh, P. "A Study of an Inventory," *Library Resources and Technical Services* 13:367-71 (Summer 1969).

Braden, I. A. "Pilot Inventory of Library Holdings," *ALA Bulletin* 62:1129-31 (October 1968).

Bristol, R. P. "Simple Reserve System," *Special Libraries* 60:659-60 (December 1969).

"California Library's Experiment Supports Abolition of Fines," *Library Journal* 88:4339-40 (November 15, 1963).

"Chicago P.L. Amnesty: Landslide of Books," *Library Journal* 93:502 (February 1, 1968).

"Cops' Midnight Raids Net Library Scofflaws, Rite Town," *Publisher's Weekly* 179:41-42 (February 20, 1961).

Dennis, Donald D. *Simplifying Work in Small Public Libraries.* Philadelphia, Drexel Institute of Technology, 1965.

George Fry and Associates, Inc. *Study of Circulation Control Systems: Public Libraries, College and University Libraries, Special Libraries.* Chicago, Library Technology Project, 1961.

Hagerty, M. M. "Reserve Book System: A Positive View," *Wilson Library Bulletin* 26:387-88 (January 1952).

Jahoda, G., and others. "Academic Library Procedures for Providing Students with Required Reading Materials," *College and Research Libraries* 31: 103-106 (March 1970).

Jesse, William H. *Shelf Work in Libraries.* Chicago, American Library Association, 1952.

"LJ's Survey of Accession and Inventory Practices," *Library Journal* 84:1048-52 (April 1, 1959).

Rogers, Rutherford D., and David C. Weber. *University Library Administration.* New York, H. W. Wilson, 1971.

"Special Shelfreading Project During the Summer of 1968," *Library of Congress Information Bulletin* 27:649 (October 24, 1968).

Weyhrauch, E. E. "Automation in the Reserved Book Room," *Library Journal* 89:2294-96 (June 1, 1964).

Wheeler, Joseph L., and Herbert Goldhor. *Practical Administration of Public Libraries.* New York, Harper & Row, 1962.

CHAPTER 5

REFERENCE SERVICES

INTRODUCTION

In this chapter we will discuss the types of reference service, the purpose of reference work, and the role of the library technician in a reference department. The main goal of reference service is to interpret the library's collection for the patron. Achievement of this goal may require explaining how to use the card catalog or a reference tool, answering questions ranging from simple directional types to complex research types, or giving a tour of the library. The library will usually do whatever needs to be done to answer a question, within the limits of its resources and the competency of its staff. The only reason for the existence of reference services is to give information to the library's patrons. This work requires a special outlook and a real desire to serve people; not every library technician (or for that matter, not every librarian) is suited for reference work.

ROLE OF THE LIBRARY TECHNICIAN

The library technician's role in reference service is not as clearly defined as his role in circulation work and in such technical services as acquisitions, cataloging and preparation of materials. In reference service there is no consensus as to how much responsibility can be assumed by the library technician.[1] Conservative, moderate, and liberal views exist, ranging from one which allows little or no role for the library technician in reference services to one which gives him a major role. Each library develops the role it will allow its library technicians to assume depending on the philosophy of the librarians and, to some extent, on the type of library and the type of patrons served.

Some responsibilities which the library technician might assume are: staffing information desks, answering directional and ready reference questions, and arranging interlibrary loans. Most directional questions ("where do you keep periodicals?") and ready reference questions ("how long is the Mississippi River?") can be answered by trained and experienced library technicians. In fact, some information desks might be staffed with clerks or student assistants if it has been determined that few questions asked there require even a library technician. Surveys have shown that in some libraries up to 95 percent of all questions asked are either directional or of the ready reference type. Allowing the library technician to be the patron's first contact will free the librarian from this time-consuming task, which can usually be handled as well by less highly trained staff. Except in certain special circumstances it is probably unwise for a reference department to insist that the patron's first contact always be with a librarian.

The major objection to an expanded role for library technicians is the concern that the quality of reference service will deteriorate. Of course, such deterioration is no more a certainty or even a probability than it is in the fields of medicine and law when paramedics and para-legal personnel are properly used. The selection of staff for reference work is the crucial element in maintaining quality service, and care must be exercised in selecting both librarians and library technicians.

The most specific objection to library technicians in reference service is that they may attempt to answer questions beyond their ability or training. They may delay too long before referring the questions to a librarian, or they may even give a superficial answer and not consult a librarian at all.[2] Although it is possible that poor service may be given occasionally, with well-trained and carefully-selected library technicians quality reference service can be maintained and even improved, because the librarian has been freed from the more routine duties.

The author holds a liberal view of the role of the library technician in reference services. The librarian cannot abandon his responsibilities for providing the library's patrons with quality service. But the librarian also has a responsibility to make the best use of the skills and training of both librarians and the non-professional staff. He should see that work performed by the librarian is at a professional level and that his talents are not wasted on duties which could be performed by well-trained non-professionals.

TYPES OF QUESTIONS IN REFERENCE

For our purposes, here, we will classify the great variety of questions asked in a reference department into four categories: 1) directional and ready reference, 2) general questions on specific topics, 3) research, and 4) reader's advisory. We will be most concerned with ready reference and directional questions because they are the most frequently asked and because the other types should be referred to a librarian.

Directional questions only require that the patron be directed to a specific location or to the location of the reference tool which he feels will answer his question. Typical questions are: "Where is the card catalog?," "On which floor do you keep current periodicals?," "Where are the restrooms?" All of these questions can be answered with simple directions. The patron can either be told the location, have it pointed out, or be taken there by the staff member. At a well-staffed information desk or reference desk, questions of this sort will be handled by a non-professional, thus allowing the librarian to make better use of his professional training.

The answers to ready reference questions are usually short, factual, and easily located in standard reference sources or in the library catalog.[3] This type of question normally will require little reflection and the library technician should be able to think of a possible source almost immediately. Typical questions might be: "How long is the Mississippi River?," "What was the population of New York City in 1960?," "What books does the library have by (or about) John Steinbeck?"

In actual practice, of course, distinctions between different types of reference questions are not always so easily made. In fact, general reference and research questions, which are discussed below, may start off as directional or ready reference types. For this reason it is essential for the library technician to analyze each question carefully and refer it to a librarian if there is any doubt about what the patron needs.

A general reference question is one which requires several sources to obtain an answer. Answers may be found in sources other than reference materials, and usually do include resources found throughout the collection. Typical questions are: "What materials do you have for a paper on Steinbeck?," "What were the causes of World War II?" Obviously these questions cannot be answered by one or two reference sources. Questions of this sort should be referred to a librarian.

Another category of question is the research question. There may be little difference between a research and general reference question except in the number of sources consulted and the depth of the answer. There may be no definitive "answer" to a research question, and the librarian can only offer a number of references to materials on the subject. The resources of several libraries might be consulted by telephone inquiry or by interlibrary loan if local resources are inadequate. Research questions are always handled by librarians. It is possible, however, that the library technician might help in answering a research question by searching certain sources pre-selected by a librarian and by doing some of the legwork involved.

Another kind of question is the reader's advisory type. Here the patron is seeking material on a particular topic and is interested in suggestions on the "best book" on the subject. Typical questions are: "What is a good science fiction novel?," "What is the best bibliography on Walt Whitman?," "What is a good biography of Harry Truman?" Again this kind of question should be referred to the librarian. In larger libraries a separate reader's advisory department with its own librarian may be established independently of the reference department. In smaller libraries the reference department will handle reader's advisory questions. Answering this kind of question requires skills often quite different from those needed to answer the other kinds of questions discussed above.

In actual reference work it is usually difficult to categorize questions. Nonetheless, the library technician must analyze every question as well as he can in order to give the best service. This skill can be acquired through experience, hopefully under the direction of a skilled reference librarian.

LIMITS OF REFERENCE SERVICE

All libraries place some limits on the reference services they offer. Each library must establish a policy based on its resources, staff, the clientele served, and the purpose of the library. The limits on reference services are usually established by the library's administration and not unilaterally by the reference department. A staff manual or special reference manual will clearly define the limitations of the library's service.

Reference service limits vary greatly among libraries. In a public library the reference service may refuse to answer questions to help patrons do crossword puzzles or to answer contest questions. Restrictions may also be placed on how much help will be given to students working on school projects. An academic library may give limited reference service to students from other institutions. It may also refuse to do translations for students or faculty. In a special library, however, translating may be a common service. Interlibrary loan service for research questions might be restricted to graduate students and faculty. And no library will give either legal or medical advice, but would refer the patron to a local legal aid service or medical society. The library technician must be aware when the patron is seeking medical or legal advice and turn the question over to a librarian or suggest one of the local services mentioned above.

Regardless of the reference service policy in a library, there are always exceptions to the policy. Such exceptions should be made by the librarian. A public library which might not be willing to devote four hours time researching a question for a student may spend four days answering the same question asked by a city councilman. An academic library might normally encourage a student to do as much of his own work as possible. However, the president of the institution would not be encouraged to find the answer himself! The library staff would do the necessary work and give the president an answer, not instructions on how to find it. In a school library the teachers and principal may receive more in-depth service than that given to individual students. Librarians cannot ignore political reality.

REFERENCE TECHNIQUES

The use of "old-fashioned common sense" is the basis for good reference technique. Nearly every book on reference service lists a set of techniques for handling questions, but most are based on common sense and respect for the other person. Some of the more important techniques are discussed below.[4]

All questions should be treated as if they were equally important, since the patron probably would not ask a question unless it was important to him. It is not up to the library staff to decide what is or is not important as long as the question is within the limits of service offered by the library. The librarian may decide to limit the time and staff that can be given to an inquiry, but the library technician would usually not make this decision.

The patron should be made to feel at ease. Patrons are often intimidated and are afraid of making themselves look foolish. The person sitting at the information or reference desk should look approachable—as if he is there to serve the patron. It is unfortunate that patrons begin an inquiry with, "I am sorry to bother you, but . . ." When the library technician is so busy doing something else that a questioning patron does indeed disturb him, the patron's timidity is reinforced. A person surrounded by work hardly presents the idea that he is there to serve the patron. Many jobs can be performed at slow periods, but the library technician at the reference desk should not seem too busy to answer questions. A smile and a pleasant word will go a long way to put the patron at ease, especially since many patrons are reluctant to ask a question in the first place.

The person manning the reference desk should listen carefully to the patron's question in order to determine exactly what the patron wants—unfortunately patrons often are unclear when asking for the information they desire. One must remember that the question is important to the patron or he would not bother to ask it. During the process of listening to the question, the listener should be trying to determine if the question is directional, ready reference, or one that should be referred to a librarian.

Another reference technique is to treat questions as a private matter between the patron and the library staff member. The patron's inquiry is not the concern of other patrons or even other staff, unless it is necessary to refer the question. The discussion required depends on the nature of the question and the use of common sense. A patron who asks a question is, in a way, placing himself in an "inferior" position. This may be the feeling that makes some patrons reluctant to approach library staff with any question, and library personnel must be careful to avoid giving the impression of being "superior." Since many patrons do not like to be placed in the position of having to ask another person for help, library personnel must keep this possibility in mind when they deal with patrons. Except for blatant rudeness, few things will discourage a person faster than the feeling that he is being patronized. There is no place in a public services operation—or in any part of a library operation—for a person who consistently shows that he thinks of himself as "superior."

Whenever the library technician is on duty at an information or reference desk, he should be aware of the back-up system available for questions he cannot answer. After carefully listening to the patron's question, the library technician must make a speedy decision as to whether he can (or believes he can) answer the question. Depending on the nature of the question, this decision should be made within a minute. If the library technician is unable to think of the answer or a source to find the answer within a minute, then help should be sought or the question should be referred to a librarian. It is poor service to keep patrons waiting unnecessarily. However, it is assumed that the patron will not mind waiting while library personnel find the answer to his question. The important objective here is to get a fast start initiating a search for the answer.

A final skill of reference work is to know when patrons want to be helped. It is good policy to ask patrons if they need help, but if the answer is "no" then help must not be forced on the patron. Help given against the patron's will may be worse than no help at all as far as the library-patron relationship is concerned.

QUESTION ANALYSIS AND SEARCH

Once the library technician has been asked a question, he must decide whether it is a directional, ready reference, or general reference question. If it is a directional or ready reference question, he must then choose a course of action which will quickly lead to an answer or to a referral to a librarian.

The first thing that must be determined is the subject of the question. Generally the subject can be found in the question itself. "What do you have on World War II?" or "What was the date of the Normandy Invasion?" It might be necessary, however, to question the patron to find out more specifically what he is looking for. For the first question above the library technician should probably ask if the patron is interested in a specific aspect of World War II or just in general works on the war. Depending on the patron's answer the library technician might refer to the subject entries in the card catalog or call for a librarian's help. Determining the exact information needed by the patron and the scope of the question are the first and perhaps most important steps in coming up with an answer.

While he is determining the exact subject of the question, the library technician must also try to perceive the patron's purpose or his reason for needing the information. A question on atomic physics from a high school student or even a college freshman may be a ready reference question which could be answered satisfactorily in an encyclopedia article. A similar question from a physicist or professor may require an entirely different approach and would probably be a question referred to a librarian. To provide material either too simple or too complex for a particular patron will delay his search and thus give less than the best service. Through on-the-job experience it becomes easier to judge a patron's needs. In an academic library or special library this task may be somewhat easier because of the restricted clientele; it will be more difficult in a public library, which caters to a much larger number of patrons with a wider range of abilities and needs.

It is important for the library technician to realize that the procedures for analysis discussed above are equally important for either answering a question or referring a question. The main goal in reference work is to provide the patron with the best and speediest service possible. The effectiveness of a library technician in reference service will be determined by his ability to analyze a question, decide exactly what has been requested, and either attempt to find the answer himself or quickly refer the patron to someone who can.

ORGANIZATION OF REFERENCE COLLECTIONS

The physical organization of a reference department can take one of several forms. The three most popular are: 1) central or general reference, 2) divisional reference, and 3) departmental reference. The organization used in a library will depend on many factors, the more important ones being 1) philosophy of the librarians, 2) physical layout of the library, 3) size of the library's collection, 4) abilities of available staff, 5) type of library and type of patron, and 6) financial resources for collection development.

A central or general reference department organization brings all the reference materials together in one physical location in the library. Some of the arguments for this organization are: 1) the patron and reference staff can locate materials more easily because they are all together rather than shelved in several locations; 2) because so many subjects are interrelated (e.g., history and literature, biology and chemistry), it will be easier to do reference work if the related reference material is all kept together; 3) there is a savings of book funds because it is not necessary to purchase duplicate materials such as some indexes, yearbooks and dictionaries; and 4) it is possible to make better use of staff by concentrating personnel on one service point rather than having to staff several service points.

Nearly all small libraries and most medium-sized libraries will use a central or general reference type organization. Usually the considerations of book budget and staffing rule in favor of central reference.

Division reference organization brings together all the reference materials for a particular group of related subjects. A divisional reference organization may divide the collection into social sciences, humanities, and natural sciences, or any other arrangement best suited to the library. Some of the arguments in favor of divisional reference organization are: 1) a smaller reference collection is easier for both the patron and the library staff to use; 2) the reference

Figure 1
Reference Questions

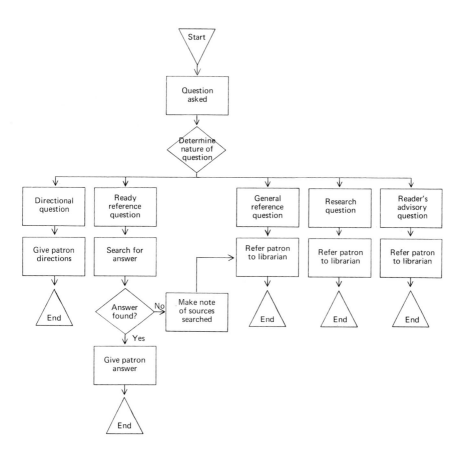

materials and the general collection (non-reference) materials on a particular subject will be physically close, thus allowing easier access to both types of material; 3) if a divisional card catalog is established, it will be smaller than the general catalog and easier for the patron to use; and 4) librarians who are subject specialists can better utilize their talents when they work in their area of subject specialization.

In larger libraries there may be departmental libraries in addition to either a central reference collection or divisional reference collections. The collection in each of these departmental libraries is usually restricted to one subject area (such as physics, chemistry or education), and each department may have a reference collection and offer reference service of its own. The advantages of this organization are, of course, the same as those stated for divisional reference organization.

Before the discussion of the organization of reference collections ends, a few words should be said about information desks. In small libraries the information desk and reference desk may be one and the same. In larger libraries an information desk may be physically separate from the reference desk. Several reasons for having a separate information desk are: 1) to give the patron an immediate easily found contact point, 2) to save the patron's time by directing him to the proper place, and 3) to serve as a "filter" for directional questions and some ready reference questions rather than having these handled at the reference desk. If the information desk is staffed by library technicians it can take a significant workload away from the librarian.

Figure 2
Central or General Reference Organization

Figure 3
Divisional Reference Organization

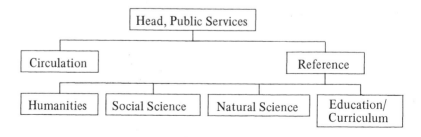

Figure 4
Departmental Reference Organization

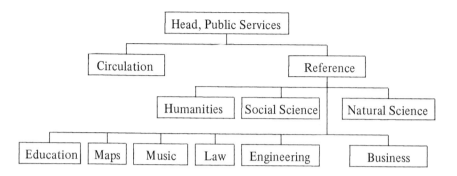

FOOTNOTES

1. Refer to the Bibliography for Chapter 1 for articles on the role of library technicians.

2. Refer to Chapter 1, page 20, for a discussion of the ethical responsibilities of working in a library and particularly of working directly with the public.

3. Chapters 10 through 23 will discuss some standard reference tools.

4. A good, easy-to-read book on techniques of handling patrons is Sarah L. Wallace's *Patrons Are People: How to Be a Model Librarian*, rev. and enl. ed. Chicago, American Library Association, 1956.

BIBLIOGRAPHY

Bunge, Charles A. "Library Education and Reference Performance: A Preliminary Report of a Study," *Library Journal* 92:1578-81 (April 15, 1967).

Cheney, Frances Neel. *Fundamental Reference Sources.* Chicago, American Library Association, 1971.

Crum, Norman J. "The Librarian-Customer Relationship: Dynamics of Filling Requests for Information," *Special Libraries* 60:269-77 (May-June 1969).

Foskett, D. J. *Information Service in Libraries,* 2nd ed. Hamden, Conn., Archon Books, 1967.

Geller, Evelyn. "Think Session at High John: Report of a Three-Day Conference on Library Service to the Disadvantaged," *Library Journal* 93:2963-71 (September 1, 1968).

Harris, Katherine G. "Reference Service in Public Libraries," *Library Trends* 12:373-89 (January 1964).

Hutchins, Margaret. *Introduction to Reference Work.* Chicago, American Library Association, 1944.

Katz, William A. *Introduction to Reference Work.* New York, McGraw-Hill, 1969. 2v.

"Library Service to Undergraduate College Students: A Symposium," *College and Research Libraries* 17:143-55 (March 1956).

Moore, Everett T. "Reference Service in Academic and Research Libraries," *Library Trends* 12:362-72 (January 1964).

Mount, Ellis. "Communication Barriers and the Reference Question," *Special Libraries* 57:575-78 (October 1966).

The Present Status and Future Prospects of Reference/Information Service. Chicago, American Library Association, 1967.

"Reference Encounter: How Reference Work Should Be Taught," *Library Journal* 90:1818-24 (April 15, 1965).

"A Reference Roundup," *Library Journal* 92:1582-85 (April 15, 1967).

Rothstein, Samuel. *The Development of Reference Services Through Academic Traditions, Public Library Practice and Special Librarianship.* Chicago, American Library Association, 1955.

Rothstein, Samuel. "Reference Service: the New Dimension in Librarianship," *College and Research Libraries* 22:11-18 (January 1961).

Rowland, Arthur Ray, editor. *Reference Services.* Hamden, Conn., Shoe String Press, 1964.

Shores, Louis. *Basic Reference Sources.* Chicago, American Library Association, 1954.

Smith, Dorman H. "A Matter of Confidence," *Library Journal* 97:1239-40 (April 1, 1971).

"Statement of Service to Library Users," *ACRL News* 27:21-22 (April 1966).

Taylor, Robert S. "Question Negotiation and Information Seeking in Libraries," *College and Research Libraries* 29:178-94 (May 1968).

Vavrek, Bernard. "The Reference Librarian as a Technician," *RQ* 7:5-8 (Fall 1967).

Wallace, Sara Leslie. *Patrons Are People: How to be a Model Librarian.* Rev. and enl. edition. Chicago, American Library Association, 1956.

Wheeler, Joseph T., and Herbert Goldhor. *Practical Administration of Public Libraries.* New York, Harper & Row, 1962.

Wynar, Bohdan. *Introduction to Bibliography and Reference Work: A Guide to Materials and Sources.* 4th rev. edition. Littleton, Colo., Libraries Unlimited, 1967.

Wynar, Bohdan. "Reference Theory: Situation Hopeless But Not Impossible," *College and Research Libraries* 28:337-42 (September 1967).

CHAPTER 6

REFERENCE SOURCES: THE LIBRARY CATALOG

INTRODUCTION

The catalog is the most important and useful reference source in the library. The catalog is a systematic list of the books and other materials in the library's collection. All library staff should be generally familiar with the catalog, and those who work directly with the public must have a detailed knowledge of it. The library technician in public service work must know how to use the catalog and how to instruct others in its use, be knowledgeable about the type of information that can be found in the catalog and what cannot be found there, be aware of the main rules for entry, and be familiar with the filing rules used to arrange the catalog.

THE CATALOG

The library catalog is built according to certain basic theories whose goal is to make it helpful for all users.[1] A properly developed and maintained catalog will enable a user to find material if he knows either

    (1) the author,
    (2) the title, or
    (3) the subject

and to show the holdings in a library

    (4) by a particular author,
    (5) on a particular subject, or
    (6) in a particular kind of literature (poetry, drama, fiction)

and to

    (7) describe materials adequately for easy identification and location of the correct title, edition, etc.

THE CARD CATALOG

Since the most popular format for a library catalog in the United States is the card catalog, we will concern ourselves with it, except for a brief description of several other types of catalogs.

The card catalog consists of 3-by-5 inch cards filed in alphabetical order. The cards are filed in trays or drawers. A 60-drawer catalog means that there are 60 removable drawers housed in one physical unit. Normally, card catalogs come in 2, 4, 6, 8, 10, 15, 30, and 60 drawer units. Each drawer can hold approximately 800 to 1,000 cards without overcrowding. Each drawer is labeled to show the exact alphabetical sequence of cards filed inside.

The popularity of the card catalog is due to certain inherent qualities, the more important of which are:

(1) Flexibility
    (a) The cards can be arranged in any way suitable to a library, alphabetically or numerically by call number.
    (b) The catalog can be in dictionary format or divided format.
    (c) The catalog can be kept current by adding or removing new cards.
(2) Ease of Use
    (a) The card catalog is relatively easy to use if the user takes the time to read a few instructions or to ask for help.
    (b) Guide cards, cross-references, and consistency in the forms of authors' names and subject headings make the card catalog an efficient tool for the experienced user.
(3) Cost to Produce and Maintain
    (a) No catalog is inexpensive, but if an up-to-date catalog is necessary, production and maintenance of the card catalog costs less than other kinds.
    (b) Printed and computer-produced cards requiring a minimum of in-library preparation are readily available.
    (c) Reproduction of catalog cards by Xerox, multilith, etc., is relatively easy and inexpensive.
    (d) Individual cards or sets of cards can be added or removed as material is added or withdrawn from the collection.
    (e) Maintenance consists mostly of adding or removing cards from the catalog. Other maintenance includes keeping cross references and subject headings current.

There are many criticisms of card catalogs, but no other format has consistently shown itself to be superior. The main criticism of the card catalog is that as the collection grows the catalog becomes larger and more complex and possibly more difficult to use.

ARRANGEMENT OF ENTRIES IN A CATALOG

The library's catalog must be arranged according to some plan. The particular arrangement will be dictated by the evaluation of library needs as made by the librarian. The five most common possibilities for catalog arrangement are:

(1) author-catalog listing only author entries
(2) title-catalog listing only title entries
(3) author/title-catalog listing author and title entries and all other entries except subject entries
(4) subject-catalog listings only subject entries
(5) dictionary-catalog listing all entries interfiled together

The two most commonly used arrangements are the dictionary catalog and the divided catalog, which consists of (3) and (4) above.

The dictionary catalog has all entries (author, title, subject, and other added entries) interfiled in one alphabetical order. Some difficulties with the dictionary catalog are: 1) filing becomes complex as the catalog grows, 2) catalog users may find a larger catalog difficult to use, and 3) many users may fail to distinguish between an author entry and a subject entry—i.e., an entry for a work *by* an author from an entry for a work *about* an author.

The divided catalog is an attempt to overcome some of the difficulties encountered with the dictionary catalog. The divided catalog usually has two parts: 1) author/title and other added entries, and 2) subject entries. The complexity of filing in a divided catalog is lessened to some extent. Because of the less complex filing and because each part of the catalog is smaller than in a dictionary arrangement, many people find the divided catalog easier to use. Signs identifying which part of the catalog is the author/title and which part is the subject are essential, since otherwise patrons may not realize which part of the catalog they are using. Another problem with the divided catalog is the

Figure 1
Signs on a Divided Catalog

AUTHOR/TITLE CATALOG	SUBJECT CATALOG
BOOKS IN THIS CATALOG CAN BE LOCATED BY AUTHOR AND GENERALLY BY TITLE.	ALL SUBJECT HEADINGS ARE CAPITALIZED. BOOKS ARE ARRANGED BY SUBJECT MATTER ONLY. FOR HELP WITH HEADINGS CONSULT THE LIBRARY OF CONGRESS LIST AT THE CATALOG SERVICE DESK.

necessity to check two files instead of one. In a dictionary catalog all the books by Hemingway and about Hemingway would be filed together. In a divided catalog the books by Hemingway would be filed in the author/title catalog and the books about Hemingway would be filed in the subject catalog.

THE CATALOG CARD

The catalog card is the basic component for entering information in the catalog. The standard size of the card is 3 by 5 inches. Each card serves as an access point in the catalog for a particular item. Each item in the library will have a *set* of cards in the catalog. Every card in the set will be similar except for the headings for the different entries typed on the top line of each card. The main entry card, however, will not have any heading typed on the top line. Figure 2 illustrates the information given on a catalog card, and Figure 3 shows a complete set of cards with headings typed and ready to be filed in a catalog.

Some libraries use Wilson or LJ (*Library Journal*) card sets. These provide less detailed cataloging information and usually have a brief descriptive annotation (Figure 4).

Figure 2
Main Entry Card with Its Components

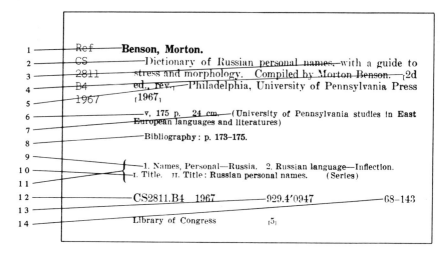

1. The author (main entry)

2. Title

3. Subtitle

4. Edition statement

5. Imprint—place of publication, publisher, publication date

6. Collation—pagination, illustrations (if any), size in centimeters

7. Series statement

8. Notes of interest or more detailed description of the item, including any special features

9. Subject headings—note that these are preceded by arabic numbers

10. Other added entries—note that these are preceded by roman numbers

11. Tracings—all of the subject headings and added entries listed at the bottom of the card

12. Library of Congress classification number and author number

13. Suggested Dewey Decimal Classification number

14. Library of Congress card number—used when ordering sets of cards

Figure 3
Complete Set of Catalog Cards with Entry Headings

Main Entry	**Hipple, Byron Thomas, 1913–** Fiscal policy and the public social services; a study of State-local fiscal relations in New York ₍by₎ Byron T. Hipple. ₍Albany, Graduate School of Public Affairs, State University of New York₎ 1965 ₍i. e. 1966₎
Added Entry: Subject	PUBLIC WELFARE - NEW YORK (STATE) - FINANCE. **Hipple, Byron Thomas, 1913–** Fiscal policy and the public social services; a study of State-local fiscal relations in New York ₍by₎ Byron T. Hipple. ₍Albany, Graduate School of Public Affairs, State University of New York₎ 1965 ₍i. e. 1966₎
Added Entry: Subject	GRANTS-IN-AID - NEW YORK (STATE) **Hipple, Byron Thomas, 1913–** Fiscal policy and the public social services; a study of State-local fiscal relations in New York ₍by₎ Byron T. Hipple. ₍Albany, Graduate School of Public Affairs, State University of New York₎ 1965 ₍i. e. 1966₎
Added Entry: Subject	INTERGOVERNMENTAL FISCAL RELATIONS - NEW YORK (STATE) **Hipple, Byron Thomas, 1913–** Fiscal policy and the public social services; a study of State-local fiscal relations in New York ₍by₎ Byron T. Hipple. ₍Albany, Graduate School of Public Affairs, State University of New York₎ 1965 ₍i. e. 1966₎
Added Entry: Title	Fiscal policy and the public social services **Hipple, Byron Thomas, 1913–** Fiscal policy and the public social services; a study of State-local fiscal relations in New York ₍by₎ Byron T. Hipple. ₍Albany, Graduate School of Public Affairs, State University of New York₎ 1965 ₍i. e. 1966₎
Added Entry: Series	Public affairs monograph series (Albany) Monograph no. 2 **Hipple, Byron Thomas, 1913–** Fiscal policy and the public social services; a study of State-local fiscal relations in New York ₍by₎ Byron T. Hipple. ₍Albany, Graduate School of Public Affairs, State University of New York₎ 1965 ₍i. e. 1966₎ xv, 143 p. illus., maps. 22 cm. (Public affairs monograph series. Monograph no. 2) 1. Public welfare—New York (State)—Finance. 2. Grants-in-aid—New York (State) 3. Intergovernmental fiscal relations—New York (State) I. Title. (Series: Public affairs monograph series (Albany) Monograph no. 2) HV98.N7H5 361.609747 66–65352

Figure 4
Wilson Card

---

792   Barnes, Grace
       On stage, everyone ₁by₁ Grace Barnes ₁and₁ Mary Jean
       Sutcliffe.   Macmillan (N Y) 1961
       401p illus

              First published 1954. The 1961 edition has been brought up to date
       and scenes from best present-day plays have been added
              In this handbook for teachers of drama courses in secondary schools
       the methods and materials have been organized around acting projects.
       Emphasis is placed upon the role of educational dramatics in personality
       development

       1 Amateur theatricals   2 Drama in education   I Jt. auth.   II Title   792

       61W14,297   (W)   The H. W. Wilson Company

TYPES OF MAIN ENTRIES

There are several types of main entries other than the usual "author"
entry. The library technician should be familiar with different possibilities for
entering material in a catalog.

(1) An individual or single author (Figure 5).

Figure 5

Storr, Richard J
       The beginnings of graduate education in America ₁by₁
       Richard J. Storr. New York, Arno Press, 1969 ₁°1953₁

       ix, 195 p. 24 cm. (American education; its men, ideas, and in-
       stitutions)

       Bibliography : p. 135–152.

       1. Universities and colleges—U. S.—Graduate work.   I. Title.
       (Series)

       LA228.5.S75   1969   378.15′53′0973   72–89239
                                                                 MARC

       Library of Congress   70 ₁7₁

---

(2) A work of shared authorship (Figure 6).

Figure 6

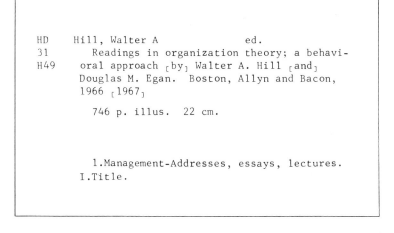

DD
256.3
M3

Manvell, Roger, 1909–
  The men who tried to kill Hitler ₁by₁ Roger Manvell
& Heinrich Fraenkel. ₁1st American ed.₁ New York,
Coward-McCann ₁1964₁

  272 p. illus., ports. 23 cm.

  Bibliography : p. 263–265.

  1. Hitler, Adolf, 1889–1945—Assassination attempt, July 20, 1944.
2. Anti-Nazi movement. ɪ. Fraenkel, Heinrich, 1897– ɪɪ. Title.

DD256.3.M3   943.086   64–25769

Library of Congress   ₁7–1₁

(3) Works produced by editors or compilers (Figure 7).

Figure 7

```
HD      Hill, Walter A                ed.
31         Readings in organization theory; a behavi-
H49     oral approach ₍by₎ Walter A. Hill ₍and₎
        Douglas M. Egan.  Boston, Allyn and Bacon,
        1966 ₍1967₎

           746 p. illus.  22 cm.



           1.Management-Addresses, essays, lectures.
        I.Title.
```

(4) Title entry (Figure 8).

Figure 8

The **Englishwoman** in Russia ₍by₎ a lady. New York, Arno Press, 1970.

    316 p. illus. 23 cm. (Russia observed)

    Reprint of the 1855 ed.

    1. Russia—Social life and customs.   ɪ. A lady.

DK32.E58 1970   914.7'03   77–115534
ISBN 0–405–03024–X   MARC

Library of Congress   71 ₍4₎

(5) Corporate authors—e.g., institutions and societies, government bodies, business and conferences (Figure 9).

Figure 9

Scottish Library Association.
    Scottish libraries, a triennial review, 1963–65; general editor: Moira Burgess, contributers: Moira Burgess, R. N. Beer, D. W. Doughty. Alloa, Scottish Library Association, 1966.

    59 p. front., illus. 22 cm. 7/6

                                          (B 66–21442)

    1. Libraries—Scotland.   ɪ. Burgess, Moira, ed. ɪɪ. Title.

Z791.S36   021.00941   66–68481

Library of Congress   ₍3₎

It is essential that a library technician working with the catalog be aware of the various kinds of main entries. A situation in which "the blind are leading the blind" is of little value to the patron. The library technician should make every effort to familiarize himself with some basic cataloging rules governing main entries. While a discussion of these rules is beyond the scope of this text, useful cataloging texts are cited in the bibliography at the end of this chapter.

ADDED ENTRIES

Added entries are made to give the material additional access points in the catalog. The most common added entries are for joint authors, titles, series, illustrators, and translators (Figures 10-12).

Figure 10
Added Entry—Joint Author

Ifejika, Samuel Udochukwu, jt. auth.

Nwankwo, Arthur Agwuncha, 1942–
    Biafra: the making of a nation, by **Arthur Agwuncha Nwankwo** and Samuel Udochukwu Ifejika.   New York, Praeger Publishers ₁1970, ᶜ1969₁

    xii, 361 p. illus. 22 cm. 8.95

    1969 ed. has title: The making of a nation: Biafra.
    Includes bibliographical references.

    1. Nigeria—Politics and government. 2. Nigeria—History—Civil War, 1967–1970.   I. Ifejika, Samuel Udochukwu, 1942–   joint author. II. Title.

    DT515.62.N85   1970   966.9′05   70–108559
                                                            MARC

    Library of Congress   70 ₁7₁

Figure 11
Added Entry—Series

The American Negro, His History and Literature

Universal Races Congress, *1st, London, 1911.*
    Papers on inter-racial problems.   Edited by G. Spiller. New York, Arno Press, 1969.

    xvi, 485 p. 24 cm. (The American Negro, his history and literature)

    Reprint of the 1911 ed., with new introductory material.
    Bibliography: p. 463–477.

    1. Race problems—Congresses.   I. Spiller, Gustav, ed. II. Title. (Series)

    HT1505.U6   1911de   301.45   70–94136
                                                            MARC

    Library of Congress   70 ₁4₁

Figure 12
Added Entry—Title

The many Americans shall be one

HN
59
S3
Salisbury, Harrison Evans, 1908–
  The many Americans shall be one ₍by₎ Harrison E. Salisbury. ₍1st ed.₎ New York, W. W. Norton ₍1971₎
   204 p. 22 cm. $6.50

   1. U. S.—Social conditions—1960– 2. Social history—1945–

 I. Title.

 HN59.S3   309.1'73'092   70–144093
 ISBN 0–393–05437–3   MARC

 Library of Congress   71 ₍4₎

    Familiarity with the kinds of added entries made for an item can be of
great help when using the catalog. Questions like "What books do you have in
the Rivers of American Series?" or "Do you have any books illustrated by
Norman Rockwell?" can be answered by reference to the catalog.[2]

SUBJECT ENTRIES

    A subject entry may be a name, place, object, word, or phrase appropriate
to describe the topic or topics of a work. When a subject heading is typed on a
card, it is distinguished from other entries by being typed either in capital
letters or in a different color. In a dictionary catalog this differentiation is
necessary to distinguish the subject entries from other entries. In a divided
catalog, of course, the subject is filed in a separate catalog; nevertheless, it is
common practice either to capitalize or to use different colors for subject
entries regardless of the type of catalog being used.
    Below are examples of some common subject headings (Figures 13-15).

Figure 13
Subject Heading—Corporate Body

U.S. INFORMATION AGENCY

E
744.5
D5
Dizard, Wilson P
  The strategy of truth; the story of the U. S. Information
Service. Washington, Public Affairs Press ₍1961₎

 213 p. 24 cm.
 Includes bibliography.

  1. U. S. - Information Agency. 2. U. S. Information Service.
 3. U. S.—Relations (general) with foreign countries. I. Title.

 E744.5.D5   327.73   61—8441 ‡

 Library of Congress   ₍62q5₎

Figure 14
Subject Heading–Person

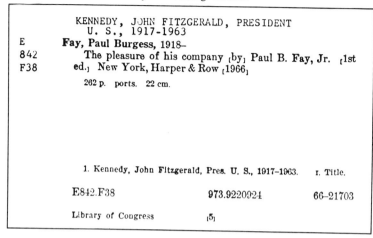

```
          KENNEDY, JOHN FITZGERALD, PRESIDENT
            U. S., 1917-1963
  E     Fay, Paul Burgess, 1918–
  842       The pleasure of his company [by] Paul B. Fay, Jr. [1st
  F38     ed.] New York, Harper & Row [1966]
            262 p.  ports.  22 cm.




          1. Kennedy, John Fitzgerald, Pres. U. S., 1917-1963.    I. Title.

          E842.F38                    973.9220924           66–21703

          Library of Congress           [5]
```

Figure 15
Subject Heading–Descriptive Phrase

```
  Q        WOMEN AS SCIENTISTS
  130
  Y63    Yost, Edna, 1889–
           Women of modern science. Illustrated with photos. New
         York, Dodd, Mead [1959,]1962
           176 p.  illus.  21 cm.




          1. Women as scientists.    I. Title.

          Q130.Y63                    925               59—6874 ‡

          Library of Congress           [59r30]
```

Subject headings may have subdivisions which give them a specific focus.
There are three basic types of subdivisions:

(1) Form: shows the material is in a specialized format such as an
abstract, dictionary, or periodical (Figure 16).
(2) Geographic: used to limit the subject to a geographical or political
area (Figure 17).
(3) Chronological or period: used to restrict the time period covered by
a particular work (Figure 18).

Figure 16
Subject Heading with Form Subdivision

```
              PHILOSOPHY - DICTIONARIES
Ref    Urmson, J      O        ed.
B           The concise encyclopaedia of Western phil-
41     osophy and philosophers.  The contributors:
U7     J.L. Ackrill [and others]  New York, Hawthorn
1960   Books, Inc. [1960]
```

Figure 17
Subject Heading with Geographic Subdivision

```
              POLITICAL PARTIES - GREAT BRITAIN
JN     Allen, A.   J.
1037        The English voter.  London, English Uni-
A59    versities Press [1964]

            18 p.  tables.
            Bibliographical footnotes.
```

Figure 18
Subject Heading with Chronological Subdivision

```
              U.S.—HISTORY—COLONIAL PERIOD
E
198    Parkman, Francis, 1823-1893.
P34         A half-century of conflict.  With a new introd. by Samuel
1962   Eliot Morison.  New York, Collier Books [1962]
            478 p.  18 cm.  ([Collier books] BS94)
```

Libraries use standard lists of subject headings rather than simply selecting subjects at random. Standard lists are essential in order to maintain consistency and uniformity in the catalog. The two most widely used standard lists are *Subject Headings Used in the Dictionary Catalogs of the Library of Congress* (7th ed. and supplements) and *Sears List of Subject Headings* (10th ed.).[3]

The library technician should become familiar with the list used in his library and should know how to use it. A copy of the list will often be placed near the catalog for public use, and the library technician must be knowledgeable enough to answer simple questions asked by patrons regarding the list.

REFERENCES

The two basic types of references used in a catalog are "see" references and "see also" references.

A "see" reference is a direction in the catalog guiding the user from a name or subject not used to the form used (Figures 19, 20).

Figure 19
"See" Reference from Form of Name Not Used to Form of Name Used

Moncrieff, Charles Kenneth Scott

See

Scott-Moncrieff, Charles Kenneth, 1889-1930

Figure 20
"See" Reference from Subject Not Used to Subject Used

ELECTRIC ACCOUNTING MACHINES

See

ACCOUNTING MACHINES

A "see also" reference is a direction in the catalog to other forms of an entry or other subject headings where more information might be found (Figures 21, 22).

Figure 21
"See Also" Reference

National Education Association of the United States.
Dept. of Audio Visual Instruction

See also

National Education Association of the United States.
Division of Audiovisual Instructional Service

Figure 22
"See Also" Reference for Subject Heading

ACCOUNTING MACHINE

See also

BOOKKEEPING MACHINE

FILING

Most libraries use the *A.L.A. Rules for Filing Catalog Cards* (2nd ed.) or its abridged edition, as a guide for filing in the catalog. In this text we will discuss only a few general rules to familiarize the reader with filing. The library technician who works with the catalog and helps patrons use the catalog should study the *ALA Rules* and be aware of any local changes or variations. Not all libraries follow the *ALA Rules* exactly, or even use them all.

Ten basic rules are:

1) All entries are alphabetized *word-by-word*.

Word-by-word	Letter-by-letter
I met a man	Image of America
Image of America	I met a man
In the days of giants	Inca
Inca	In the days of giants

2) Names beginning with Mc and M' are filed as if they were spelled Mac.

3) All punctuation marks in the entry are ignored.

Life	Life, its true genesis
Life—a bowl of rice	Life! Physical and spiritual
"Life after death"	

4) All articles *within* the entry are regarded in filing.
   All *initial* articles are ignored.

The *man* of his time	Work for *a* man
A *man* of the time	Work for *the* beginner

5) Abbreviations are filed as if they were spelled out (Mister, Doctor, Saint, etc.)

   Doctor at sea
   Dr. come quickly
   Mr. Jones
   Mister Klein

6) Numerals in a filing entry are filed as though spelled out (1911 is filed as "nineteen eleven," 100 as "one hundred")

   One America
   100 American poems (one hundred)
   101 best games for teens (one hundred and one)
   100,000 watts (one hundred thousand)
   1,199 laughs (one thousand, one hundred and ninety-nine)

7) The filing of subject entries follows the filing rules for alphabetical order except when a subject has historical chronological subdivisions.

   U.S. – HISTORY – COLONIAL PERIOD
                      – KING WILLIAM'S WAR, 1689-1697
                      – REVOLUTION
                      – WAR OF 1812
                      – WAR OF 1898
                      – 20TH CENTURY

8) The same word spelled in different ways is filed as if spelled only one way.

   Color
   Colour harmony
   Color harmony test

9) In a dictionary catalog works *by* a person (author entries) are filed before works *about* the person (subject entries).

10) If there are several editions of a work, the latest edition is filed after earlier editions.

OTHER CATALOG FORMATS

As stated earlier, although we are mostly concerned with the card catalog, there are several other formats with which the library technician should be familiar.

The **book catalog** consists of entries listed on pages which are bound into a book. The *National Union Catalog* is an example of a book catalog. This format, once widely used, is making a comeback due to the development of sophisticated means of production, including high-speed computer print-outs.

Another format is the **sheaf catalog**, where each entry is made on a slip of paper and inserted in a loose-leaf binder.

In some libraries, the catalog might be on microfilm, magnetic tape, or magnetic discs. Some of these formats require complex machines to make them accessible for use.

FOOTNOTES

1. These rules were first developed by Charles Ammi Cutter in his *Rules for a Dictionary Catalog* (1876).

2. In individual libraries some types of added entries may not be used. It will be necessary to check with the cataloging department to see what is done in a particular library. For example, a library may not make added entries for translators or illustrators. It is important to know not only what is in the catalog, but what is not in it.

3. See Appendix C for an explanation of the format and symbols used in these two lists.

BIBLIOGRAPHY

Akers, Susan Grey. *Simple Library Cataloging.* 5th ed. Metuchen, N.J., Scarecrow Press, 1969.

American Library Association. *A.L.A. Rules for Filing Catalog Cards.* 2nd ed. Chicago, American Library Association, 1968.

Anglo-American Cataloging Rules. North American Text. Chicago, American Library Association, 1967.

Bloomberg, Marty, and G. Edward Evans. *Introduction to Technical Services for Library Technicians.* Littleton, Colo., Libraries Unlimited, 1971.

Dunkin, Paul. "Cataloging and Reference, the Eternal Triangle," *RQ* 3:3-6 (March 1964).

Haykin, David J. *Subject Headings; a Practical Guide.* Washington, Government Printing Office, 1951.

Piercy, Esther J. *Commonsense Cataloging.* New York, H. W. Wilson, 1965.

Sears, Minnie E. *Sears List of Subject Headings*, edited by B. M. Westby. With "Suggestions for the Beginner in Subject Heading Work" by B. M. Frick. 10th ed. New York, H. W. Wilson, 1971.

U.S. Library of Congress. Processing Department. *Subject Headings Used in the Dictionary Catalogs of the Library of Congress.* 7th ed. Washington, Government Printing Office, 1966.

Wynar, Bohdan S. *Introduction to Cataloging and Classification.* 4th rev. ed. Littleton, Colo., Libraries Unlimited, 1972.

CHAPTER 7

REFERENCE TOOLS: LIBRARY CLASSIFICATION

INTRODUCTION

Most libraries in the United States use one of two classification systems: Decimal Classification (Dewey) or Library of Congress Classification. In order to give the best service to patrons, the library technician should be familiar with the classification system used in the library. The classification system is a "shorthand" code to the library collection, and the better one knows the "shorthand" the more valuable one becomes in public service work.

PURPOSES OF CLASSIFICATION

The importance of classification varies from library to library, depending on the library's size and function. Classification is more important in a 500,000-volume collection than in a 5,000-volume collection. But, depending on the clientele served, classification may be more important in a small special library and less important in a larger, but more general, library. Considering these varying demands of size and function, it is possible to generalize only about those purposes of classification which would hold true for most libraries.

Three general purposes of a classification system are: 1) to arrange materials on the shelves in a known order, facilitating use of the collection; 2) to allow materials on the same subject to stand together on the shelves, with related materials nearby; and 3) to allow materials to be reshelved in a minimum amount of time.

In this text it is expected that the reader will become familiar with the broad outlines of two classification systems. No attempt will be made here to teach mastery of the skills necessary for assigning classification numbers.

One word of caution is in order for the library technician when directing patrons to subject areas. As a collection grows, the classification system tends to separate subjects treated from different points of view. It is absolutely necessary to be aware of this problem. Browsing in the stacks to locate books is common—because many patrons assume all books on a subject stand together—but the trained library technician should warn the patron that some books on the subject may be found in a different location. Below are some examples of possible classification numbers for railroading:

Subject	Decimal	LC
a) Technical Aspects of Building a Railroad	625.1	TF200
b) Economic Aspects of Railroading	338.476251	HE1613
c) Model Railroads	625.19	TF197
d) Railroad Laws	343.095	KF2271

All of these topics are concerned with railroading but, as can be seen, they do not have a common location.

DECIMAL CLASSIFICATION

The Decimal Classification was first developed in outline form in 1873 by Melvil Dewey. He hoped to devise a simple classification which could be used by all libraries. The first edition, published in 1876, was 42 pages long, of which only 12 pages were the classification schedules. The Decimal Classification is now in its 18th edition (1971) and consists of three volumes.

In the United States about 95 percent of the public and school libraries and over 50 percent of the college and university libraries still use the Decimal Classification, although college and university libraries are tending to reclassify from the Decimal Classification to the Library of Congress Classification. Nevertheless, no other classification system has proved itself sufficiently superior to the Decimal Classification—or as easily understood—to warrant replacing the Decimal Classification. It will continue to be used in most libraries (especially the smaller ones) where it has been used for years.

Outline of the Decimal Classification

The Decimal Classification is composed of 10 main classes, numbered from 0 to 9.

000—General Works	500—Pure Science
100—Philosophy	600—Technology
200—Religion	700—Fine Arts
300—Social Sciences	800—Literature
400—Language	900—History

Each of these main classes is further subdivided into 10 parts. For example, the Social Sciences (300) are subdivided as follows:

300—Social Sciences	350—Public Administration
310—Statistics	360—Social Welfare
320—Political Science	370—Education
330—Economics	380—Public Services and Utilities
340—Law	390—Customs and Folklore

Each of these subdivisions is itself subdivided into 10 parts. For example, Education (370) is subdivided as follows:

370—Education
371—Teaching, School Organization, Administration
372—Elementary Education
373—Secondary Education
374—Adult Education
etc.

There are never more than three digits in a Decimal Classification without a decimal. The decimal is used after the third figure: 917.3, 917.309. The numbers to the right of the decimal are further subdivisions for specific topics.

For additional information, see the bibliography at the end of this chapter, especially Marty Bloomberg and G. Edward Evans, *Introduction to Technical Services for Library Technicians* (Littleton, Colo., Libraries Unlimited, 1971).

Author Numbers

To distinguish between books with the same classification number, a unique author number (a book number) is assigned to each item. Special tables exist for assigning these numbers. (The *Cutter-Sanborn Three Figure Author Table* is one of the more popular ones used by libraries. Because this table was originally compiled by Charles Ammi Cutter, the numbers are often called "cutter numbers" rather than author numbers.) The classification number and the author number make up the call number:

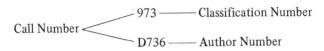

Call Number { 973 ———— Classification Number
D736 ———— Author Number

LIBRARY OF CONGRESS CLASSIFICATION

The Library of Congress Classification was developed originally to fit the needs of a specific collection. Consequently, the detail of each of the 28 separate schedules varies depending upon the material held and cataloged by the Library of Congress. Unlike the Decimal Classification, the Library of Congress Classification is the result of the work of many people.

This classification scheme, which is capable of much greater expansion than the Decimal Classification, is basically suited only to larger collections. Today the Library of Congress Classification is used mostly by college and university libraries and special libraries; almost no public libraries use the Library of Congress Classification.

Outline of the Library of Congress Classification

The Library of Congress Classification scheme comprises 29 volumes with over 7,000 pages. Each schedule covers a subject area. The schedules are:

A: General works, Polygraphy
B, pt. 1, B–BJ: Philosophy
B, pt. 2, BL–BX: Religion
C: History–Auxiliary Sciences
D: General and Old World History
E–F: American History
G: Geography, Anthropology, Folklore, Manners and Customs, Recreation
H: Social Sciences
J: Political Science
K: Law (only the KF schedule–Law of the United States–has been published)
L: Education
M: Music and Books on Music
N: Fine Arts
P–PA: Philology, Linguistics, Classical Philology, Classical Literature

PB–PH: Modern European Languages
PG, in part: Russian Literature
PJ–PM: Languages and Literatures of Asia, Africa, Oceania, America, Mixed Languages, Artificial Languages
PN, PR, PS, PZ: Literature (General), English and American Literature, Fiction in English, Juvenile Literature
PQ, pt. 1: French Literature
PQ, pt. 2: Italian, Spanish and Portuguese Literature
PT, pt. 1: German Literature
PT, pt. 2: Dutch and Scandinavian Literature
Q: Science
R: Medicine
S: Agriculture, Plant and Animal Industry, Fish Culture and Fisheries, Hunting Sports
T: Technology
U: Military Science
V: Naval Science
Z: Bibliography and Library Science

The Library of Congress Classification number always consists of at least two elements: a letter for the class (e.g., L for education) and a number representing a subdivision of the class. For example:

L–the class letter for Education
101–a subdivision covering yearbooks
U5–author number for country

DD–the subdivision for Germany
43–the subdivision for description and travel in Germany
B5–author number

Some classification numbers may consist of three elements:

N–the subdivision for Fine Arts
72–the subdivision for art in relation to other subjects
P5–the subdivision for photography as the other subject
D4–author number

Author Numbers

Library of Congress Classification numbers, like Decimal Classification numbers, require a unique author number to distinguish between books with the same classification number. A special table, not the "cutter table," is used to assign author numbers in the Library of Congress system. The classification number and the author number make up the call number:

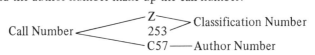

Call Number
Z
253 — Classification Number
C57 —— Author Number

BIBLIOGRAPHY

Akers, Susan Grey. *Simple Library Cataloging.* 5th ed. Metuchen, N.J., Scarecrow Press, 1969.

Bloomberg, Marty, and G. Edward Evans. *Introduction to Technical Services for Library Technicians.* Littleton, Colo., Libraries Unlimited, 1971.

Dewey, Melvil. *Decimal Classification and Relative Index.* 18th ed. Lake Placid, N.Y., Forest Press, 1971.

Immroth, John P. *A Guide to Library of Congress Classification.* 2nd ed. Littleton, Colo., Libraries Unlimited, 1971.

Institute on the Use of the Library of Congress Classification. *The Use of the Library of Congress Classification: Proceedings.* Chicago, American Library Association, 1968.

La Montagne, L. E. *American Library Classification with Special Reference to the Library of Congress.* Hamden, Conn., Shoe String Press, 1961.

U.S. Library of Congress. Subject Cataloging Division. *Classification. Class A–Z.* Washington, Government Printing Office, 1904– .

Wynar, Bohdan S. *Introduction to Cataloging and Classification.* 4th rev. ed. Littleton, Colo., Libraries Unlimited, 1972.

CHAPTER 8

REFERENCE WORK: BIBLIOGRAPHIC CITATIONS

INTRODUCTION

The ability to interpret the information given in footnotes and biblio-graphic entries is an essential skill for the library technician. This ability is important in all phases of library work, but especially so in reference, informa-tion desk work, interlibrary loan, and acquisitions.

Patrons often want to know whether a footnote or a bibliographic entry refers to a book or a periodical. Or the patron may need to know the meaning of *op. cit.* or *ibid.* Questions like these can be handled, for the most part, by a library technician with a basic knowledge of bibliographic citations. Occasionally a bibliographic citation may present problems that only a librarian can answer. The library technician must make judgments and refer problems to a librarian.

The purpose of this chapter will be to: 1) give examples of the more common types of bibliographic citations, 2) give the information generally included in a citation, and 3) give examples of the format of a citation. The material that follows is intended only as a basic introduction. Whole books are devoted to study of bibliographic citations. The library technician who works with a librarian compiling bibliographies or acting as a research assistant will need a more detailed knowledge of bibliographic citations than can be pre-sented here. The bibliography at the end of the chapter lists a number of books for further study.

FOOTNOTES

A footnote is a reference to a source of information used in the text of a work. Footnotes may, of course, give general information that would be in-appropriate in the text itself. However, our concern is with footnotes citing sources of information. Generally, one notes a footnote in the text by placing an arabic numeral at the end of the information or quote to be footnoted. The same number is then used before the footnote. For example:

Most of the procedures involved in the ordering process should be the responsibility of the library technician with aid and supervision from the librarian.[1]

The basic information included in a footnote for a book is 1) the name, or names, of the author not inverted, 2) the title of the work, 3) the name of the editor, compiler, or translator when required, 4) the edition if other than the first, 5) the place of publication, publisher and date of publication,[2] 6) the volume number if more than one volume, and 7) the page, or inclusive pages, referred to in the footnoted work. Some examples of footnotes for books are:

[3] Kellow Chesney, *The Anti-Society: An Account of the Victorian Underworld* (Boston: Gambit, 1970), p. 53.

⁴ J. Porkorny, "Druid," *Encyclopedia Americana,* 1965, IX, 350.

⁵ Georg Schneider, *Theory and History of Bibliography,* transl. by Ralph Robert Shaw (New York: Scarecrow Press, 1961), p. 10.

⁶ David M. Peterson and Marcello Truzzi, eds., *Criminal Life: Views from the Inside* (Englewood Cliffs, N.J., Prentice-Hall, 1972), p. 51.

A footnote for a periodical article includes the following information: 1) the name, or names, of the author (not inverted), 2) the title of the article, 3) the title of the periodical, 4) the volume number of the periodical and the date of the issue in which the article appears, and 5) the page or pages cited. Some examples of periodical footnotes are:

⁷ Everett T. Moore, "Reference Service in Academic and Research Libraries," *Library Trends* 12 (January 1964), p. 362.

⁸ Lars Schoultz, "Urbanization and Changing Voting Patterns: Colombia, 1946-1970," *Political Science Quarterly* 87 (March 1972), pp. 22-24.

⁹ Daniel R. Anderson and Joseph C. Todd, "Field Teaching as an Activist Strategy—Thoughts About Issues," *Peabody Journal of Education* 49 (April 1972), p. 205.

Two frequently used abbreviations which save time and space when several footnotes are made from the same source are *ibid.* and *op. cit.*

Ibid. is an abbreviation of the Latin word *ibidem*, which means "in the same place." This form is used only when footnotes for the same work follow each other with nothing between them.

¹⁰ David M. Peterson and Marcello Truzzi, eds., *Criminal Life: Views from the Inside* (Englewood Cliffs, N.J., Prentice-Hall, 1972), p. 51.

¹¹ *Ibid.* [a reference to the same work and same page]

¹² *Ibid.*, p. 53 [a reference to the same work, but to a different page]

Op. cit., meaning "in the work cited," is used to refer to a work already given a full bibliographic citation, but with intervening footnotes to other works.

¹³ Arthur Waley, *Chinese Poems* (London: Allen & Unwin, 1946), p. 50.

¹⁴ O. Edmund Clubb, *20th Century China* (New York: Columbia University Press, 1964), p. 75.

¹⁵ Waley, *op. cit.*, p. 51.

The use of *op. cit.* has been declining recently, but it still appears frequently enough to require knowledge of its meaning. It is often replaced by a shortened form of the title.

BIBLIOGRAPHY ENTRIES

A bibliography, for our purposes, is the listing of materials used in the preparation of a work, a listing of suggested readings (as is given at the end of

109

most chapters in this text), or a work listing writings on a particular topic. The bibliography entry for a book includes the following information: 1) the name, or names, of the author, with the first listed in inverted order to facilitate alphabetizing, 2) the title of the work, 3) the name of the editor, compiler, or translator when required, 4) the edition if other than the first, 5) number of volumes if more than one, and 6) the place of publication, publisher, and date of publication. Some examples of bibliography entries for books are:

Chesney, Kellow. *The Anti-Society: An Account of the Victorian Underworld.* Boston, Gambit, 1970.

Porkorny, J. "Druid," *Encyclopedia Americana*, 1965.

Petersen, David M., and Marcello Truzzi, eds. *Criminal Life: Views from the Inside.* Englewood Cliffs, N.J., Prentice-Hall, 1972.

Schneider, Georg. *Theory and History of Bibliography.* Translated by Ralph Robert Shaw. New York, Scarecrow Press, 1961.

Gates, Jean Key. *Guide to the Use of Books and Libraries.* 2nd ed. New York, McGraw-Hill, 1969.

Bibliography entries for periodical articles include the following information: 1) the name, or names, of the author, 2) the title of the article, 3) the title of the periodical, 4) the volume number of the periodical, and the date of issue, and 5) the inclusive pages of the article. Some examples of bibliography entries for periodical articles are:

Moore, Everett T. "Reference Service in Academic and Research Libraries," *Library Trends* 12 (January 1964), pp. 362-72.

Or, the variation as used in this text:

Moore, Everett T. "Reference Service in Academic and Research Libraries," *Library Trends* 12:362-72 (January 1964).

Schoultz, Lars. "Urbanization and Changing Voting Patterns: Colombia, 1946-1970," *Political Science Quarterly* 87 (March 1972), pp. 22-45.

Anderson, Daniel R., and Joseph C. Todd. "Field Teaching as an Activist Strategy—Thoughts About Issues," *Peabody Journal of Education* 49 (April 1972), pp. 205-210.

There are some abbreviations which are frequently used in bibliographic citations not only in books and periodicals but also in the indexes discussed in later chapters. Some of these abbreviations are:

comp.—compiler, compiled	pp.—pages
ed.—edition, edited, editor	pref.—preface
il.—illustrated	pseud.—pseudonym
introd.—introduction	rev.—revised
n.p.—no place of publication	tr.—translated, translator
n.d.—no date of publication	v., vol.—volume
p.—page	vols.—volumes

Unfortunately, there is no one method to handle bibliographic citations, and the reader will find many variations. The basic information given, however, generally remains the same, and only the format is different. For special bibliographic citations for microfilm, court cases, films, unpublished materials, or other special formats, the reader should refer to one of the manuals listed in the bibliography.

FOOTNOTES

1. Marty Bloomberg and G. Edward Evans, *Introduction to Technical Services for Library Technicians.* Littleton, Colo., Libraries Unlimited, 1971, p. 46.

2. Certain special materials, such as dictionaries and encyclopedias, are cited without reference to this information. See the example numbered footnote 4, p. 109.

BIBLIOGRAPHY

American Institute of Physics. *Style Manual for Guidance in the Preparation of Papers.* 2nd rev. ed. New York, American Institute of Physics, 1967.

American Psychological Association. *Publication Manual.* 1967 revision. Washington, American Psychological Association, 1967.

Campbell, William Giles. *Form and Style in Thesis Writing.* 3rd ed. Boston, Houghton Mifflin, 1969.

Chicago. University. Press. *A Manual of Style.* 12th ed. rev. Chicago, University of Chicago Press, 1969.

Conference of Biological Editors. *Style Manual for Biological Journals.* 2nd ed. Washington, American Institute of Biological Sciences, 1964.

Esdaile, Arundell. *Manual of Bibliography.* 4th rev. ed., by Roy Stokes. New York, Barnes & Noble, 1967.

Hurt, Peyton. *Bibliography and Footnotes: A Style Manual for College and University Students.* Rev. and enl. by Mary L. Hurt Richmond. Berkeley, University of California Press, 1963.

McKerrow, Ronald B. *An Introduction to Bibliography for Literary Students.* Oxford, Oxford University Press, 1928.

MLA Style Sheet. Compiled by William Riley Parker. 2nd ed. New York, Modern Language Association of America, 1970.

Schneider, Georg. *Theory and History of Bibliography.* Transl. by Ralph Robert Shaw. New York, Scarecrow Press, 1961.

Turabian, Kate L. *A Manual for Writers of Term Papers, Theses, and Dissertations.* 3rd ed., rev. Chicago, University of Chicago Press, 1967.

Uniform System of Citation, A: Forms of Citation and Abbreviations. 10th ed. Cambridge, Mass., Harvard Law Review Association, 1958.

CHAPTER 9

REFERENCE MATERIALS

INTRODUCTION

This chapter will serve as an introduction to the reference collection, the classes of reference materials, and the criteria for the selection of reference materials.

THE REFERENCE COLLECTION

The materials included in a reference collection vary among libraries. The fact that a work is in the reference collection in one library does not mean that every library will place it there. While there are many standard works listing recommended reference materials, there is little agreement among librarians as to which materials are essential to a collection. (The bibliography at the end of this chapter cites some of the standard lists of reference materials. For an interesting study on the lack of agreement on the relative importance of reference materials and what materials should be included in a basic reference collection, see Wallace J. Bonk, *Use of Basic Reference Sources in Libraries* (Ann Arbor, Mich., Campus Publisher, 1964). Bonk also has some interesting data on the reference materials that are considered basic by library schools and that are taught in reference courses.) The librarian, or librarians, responsible for developing and administering the reference collection will establish guidelines for including materials in the collection. These guidelines may include such things as:

1) Local needs. With experience every library finds that the recurrence of certain types of questions necessitates placing appropriate materials in the reference collection. For example, a history of a city might be placed in the reference rather than the general collection if it is frequently consulted for ready reference inquiries.

2) Usefulness in answering reference questions. This factor is judged by the experience of the librarians and library technicians who work with the collection. The degree to which a particular work is useful depends on the needs and purpose of a library.

3) Depth of coverage. A work whose purpose is to introduce subjects with brief introductory sections rather than to treat them in great depth might be placed in the reference collection. An example of this would be an encyclopedia or yearbook, which covers a number of subjects in brief articles or paragraphs.

4) Format. Some works are placed in a reference collection because they are intended to answer questions of fact and may not even be intended to be read *per se*. This would include such materials as atlases, books of mathematical tables, or telephone books.

5) Frequency of use. Some materials are placed in a reference collection simply because they are used frequently, and time is saved by keeping them physically close to a reference or information desk.

Generally, a reference work is not read at length but is consulted to locate facts or limited information on a subject. Reference materials do not circulate or, at least, do not circulate like general collection materials. Permission is often required to chårge out a reference work, and the circulation period is restricted to a limited time.

CLASSES OF REFERENCE MATERIALS

There are several classes of reference materials most helpful for answering ready reference questions. Some of these classes are: bibliographies or bibliographic guides, dictionaries, directories, encyclopedias, gazetteers and atlases, handbooks and manuals, indexes and abstracts, biographical sources, and yearbooks and almanacs.

Bibliographies are reference tools which list books and other materials. A bibliography may be a general list of books available for purchase, such as *Books in Print* (a trade bibliography), or it may be a list restricted to a specific subject such as Janet Ziegler's *World War II, Books in English, 1945-65.* The bibliography does not necessarily provide information on a subject, but directs the user to appropriate materials. Quite frequently entries listed in a bibliography or bibliographic guide will be annotated, thus assisting the user in selecting a given title according to its content.

Dictionaries are concerned with words and their definitions, spelling, pronunciation, syllabication, and origins. The dictionary may cover the words of a language in general, or it may be limited to special subjects. *Webster's Third New International Dictionary of the English Language* is a general dictionary of a language; *Black's Law Dictionary* is a dictionary limited to a specific subject.

A directory lists names of persons or organizations along with pertinent information about them. The directory may include addresses, telephone numbers, officers of an organization and/or a description of the organization. Examples are: local directories—telephone books and city directories; institutional directories—*The Handbook of Private Schools*; professional directories—*Directory of Medical Specialists*; and organizations—*Encyclopedia of Associations.*

Encyclopedias attempt to include information on almost all fields of knowledge. The information is usually presented in short articles varying in length from a paragraph to several pages. There are general encyclopedias covering all fields of knowledge—*Encyclopedia Americana*—and subject encyclopedias limited to more in-depth treatment of special fields—*McGraw-Hill Encyclopedia of Science and Technology.*

Gazetteers and atlases are primary sources of geographical information. An atlas contains a collection of maps and may be general or limited to a country or region. A general atlas would be the *Rand McNally New Cosmopolitan World Atlas*; a specialized atlas would be the *Rand McNally Commercial Atlas*, which concentrates on the United States. Because of constantly changing political divisions and geographic name changes, it is important that atlases and maps be current. A gazetteer lists names of towns, villages, rivers, mountains, lakes, and other geographic features. Supplemental information giving longitude and latitude and population statistics is usually included. An example of a gazetteer is the *Columbia Lippincott Gazetteer of the World.*

Handbooks and manuals serve as ready reference information sources in special limited areas of knowledge. The entries are usually concise and only a few lines in length. Some examples of handbooks are the *Handbook of Chemistry and Physics, Famous First Facts,* and *Emily Post's Etiquette: The Blue Book of Social Usage.*

Indexes and abstracts are systematic listings of materials which tell where the materials can be located. They are particularly important as sources to locate information in periodicals, serials, and pamphlets. Most of these materials are not accessible through the library catalog except by title. Examples of indexes are *The Reader's Guide to Periodical Literature* and the *New York Times Index.* There are also special indexes for difficult-to-locate material like songs—*Song Index*—or poetry—*Granger's Index to Poetry.*

Biographical sources give information about people. The biographical source may be limited to people in a particular field or country, or to only living people or only dead. The amount of information given about a person varies; it may consist only of brief factual information—*Who's Who*—or it may be an article several pages long—*Dictionary of American Biography.*

Yearbooks and almanacs contain miscellaneous facts and statistical information. These tools are useful in locating answers to a variety of ready reference questions. They contain recent statistical information and cover recent events. They are concise in their treatment of topics and serve as supplements to encyclopedias. Examples of yearbooks are the *World Almanac and Book of Facts, Statistical Abstract of the United States,* and encyclopedia-type yearbooks like the *Britannica Book of the Year.*

The library technician should remember that a reference book is potentially any book in the library used to answer a question. The reference collection, which may be only a small part of the library collection, is not the only place where an answer to a patron's question may be found. Normally a professional librarian becomes involved in reference work especially when it is necessary to go outside the ready reference collection to answer a question.

SELECTION OF REFERENCE MATERIALS

A librarian will be responsible for selecting materials for the reference collection. However, the library technician working in a reference department is in a good position to make suggestions for material to purchase, especially if the library technician is given responsibility for answering ready reference questions. Even if the library technician does not recommend a specific title, he can keep the librarian informed of materials that seem to be lacking or questions for which it was difficult to find answers. The librarian can use this information in evaluating the reference collection and attempting to correct weaknesses.

Many factors play a part in determining what materials are selected for the reference collection. Some of the more important ones are the purpose of the library (public, school, university, special, etc.), the kinds of patrons to be served, the library budget, the resources of other libraries in the area which are accessible in a reasonable time, and the evaluation of individual reference materials.

The last factor, evaluation of individual materials, will involve the library technician to the greatest degree. As material is received in the reference department, it should be examined and evaluated by everyone involved in reference work. When evaluating materials for purchase, or for their use after purchase, the librarian makes value judgments by asking certain basic questions. Among the most common points to be considered are:

1) Authority. What are the reputation and training of the author or editor? What are the sources of the data? Are they cited in the text? What is the publisher's reputation?

2) Aim and scope. What is the purpose of the work? Does it meet its stated goals? Is it more suitable for a particular age group, for the layman, or for the expert? What are its chronological or geographical limitations? What kind of question—factual, historical, statistical—will it answer? Will this work do something different from material already in the collection?

3) Currency. Is it necessary for this work to have the latest information, or is historical information sufficient? If this work purports to have the latest information, does it in fact?

4) Format. Is the material arranged alphabetically, topically, chronologically, or geographically? Are there sufficient cross references and an index? Is the binding strong enough for heavy use? Is the type easy to read? Are there illustrations of good quality, and are they in color?

While examining the reference works discussed in the following chapters, the reader should ask some of the critical questions suggested above.

BIBLIOGRAPHY

Barton, Mary Neill, and M. V. Bell, comps. *Reference Books.* 7th ed. Baltimore, Enoch Pratt Free Library, 1970.

Bonk, Wallace J. *Use of Basic Reference Sources in Libraries.* Ann Arbor, Mich., Campus Publishers, 1964.

Goggin, M. K., and L. M. Seaberg. "The Publishing and Reviewing of Reference Books," *Library Trends* 12:437-55 (January 1964).

Katz, William A. *Introduction to Reference Work.* New York, McGraw-Hill, 1969. 2v.

Murphey, Robert W. *How and Where to Look It Up: A Guide to Standard Sources of Information.* New York, McGraw-Hill, 1958.

Sager, Donald J. *Reference: A Programmed Instruction.* Columbus, Ohio Library Foundation, 1968.

Shove, Raymond H., and others. *The Use of Books and Libraries.* 10th ed. Minneapolis, University of Minnesota Press, 1963.

Taylor, Margaret. *Basic Reference Sources: A Self-Study Manual.* Prelim. ed. Metuchen, N.J., Scarecrow Press, 1971.

Walford, Albert John. *Guide to Reference Material.* 2nd ed. London, Library Association, 1966-70. 3v.

Winchell, Constance M. *Guide to Reference Books.* 8th ed. Chicago, American Library Association, 1967. Supplements.

Wynar, Bohdan S. *Introduction to Bibliography and Reference Work: A Guide to Materials and Sources.* 4th rev. ed. Littleton, Colo., Libraries Unlimited, 1967.

CHAPTER 10

REFERENCE MATERIALS: ALMANACS AND YEARBOOKS

INTRODUCTION

Chapters 10 through 24 will introduce the library technician to a select number of reference works. About 300 titles have been selected, with three goals in mind: 1) to meet the needs of library technicians whose primary responsibility will be to answer ready reference questions, 2) to introduce representative works of various kinds in a number of subject fields, and 3) to introduce the library technician to a core of reference works to serve as a basis for development as he gains experience.

The beginning student will be better off studying a limited number of reference works in detail rather than cursorily studying a great number. A library technician knowledgeable about 300 reference works will be more efficient and more successful in answering questions than one barely familiar with several times as many works. With experience, of course, knowledge of new reference works will come more rapidly.

The titles discussed in this text should be examined as well as read about in this text. Actually handling and studying each reference work is essential. Read the preface and introductory material, which explain how to use the work, what information it contains, and what information it does not contain. Knowing the latter can save much time in any search. Look up each title in the card catalog and see what call number and subject headings have been assigned to it. Go to the shelves and get an idea of what other kinds of material have a similar call number. Check the subject catalog to see what other materials have similar subject headings. Many types of reference materials are given form subdivisions and can be located by looking for them under the subject heading: ART–DICTIONARIES, ENGLISH LANGUAGE–DICTIONARIES, or U.S.–HISTORY–BIBLIOGRAPHY.[1]

One word of caution may be in order. The reference works for this text were selected for a specific purpose as stated earlier and are not the only ones in use.[2] One library may find a work most useful while another library never uses it. No selected list is ever "final" since new editions are always being published and better works become available to replace older ones.

There has been no attempt in this text to include any children's reference materials or any foreign language reference materials.

ALMANACS AND YEARBOOKS

These reference tools are valuable for brief factual information on a variety of subjects. Names, addresses, chronological listings of events, major developments in subject fields, brief biographical information, and statistical information of all types are found in these works.

World Almanac and Book of Facts. New York, World Telegram, 1868-1966;
   New York, Doubleday, 1960– . (Annual)
   This is one of the best known and must useful ready reference works. It
includes a variety of facts and statistical information on population, industry,
agriculture, sports, government, education, etc. Most of this information is
about the United States, but shorter sections are included for other countries.
A helpful chronology of events of the preceding year is included, as well as lists
of world leaders and rulers, city mayors, record holders, colleges, ships, etc.
A detailed index, in front of the book, allows easy access to the contents.

Information Please Almanac, Atlas and Yearbook. New York, Simon & Schuster,
   1947– . (Annual)
   An excellent supplement to the *World Almanac*. Most emphasis is placed
on facts and statistics on the geography, population, history, economy, education, etc., of the United States. Shorter and less detailed sections are devoted to
other countries. Much of the factual and statistical information is not in the
World Almanac. Short articles on current important events are included each
year. A detailed index facilitates its use. The format is good and the print is
easy to read.

*The Statesman's Yearbook: Statistical and Historical Annual of the States of
   the World.* New York, St. Martin's Press, 1864– . (Annual)
   An annual publication with detailed information about each country and
its government. A brief history of the country is given with relevant data on
area, population, religion, education, judicial system, finance, defense, agriculture, industry, commerce, etc. Information is given for international organizations–United Nations, UNESCO, etc. The good index facilitates the locating
of information. Includes select bibliographies for each country (and in some
cases for its political subdivisions) and for international organizations.

Whitaker, Joseph. *Almanack.* London, Whitaker, 1869– . (Annual)
   This is the British counterpart of the *World Almanac*. The emphasis is on
Great Britain with some information on other countries. Contains lists of public
officials and their salaries, members of Parliament, addresses of societies and
organizations, etc. A detailed index is helpful in locating information.

Britannica Book of the Year. Chicago, Encyclopaedia Britannica, 1938– .
   (Annual)
   Issued as a general supplement to the *Encyclopaedia Britannica*. A number
of articles cover the important events of the preceding year. A special feature is
a day-by-day chronological record of events for the preceding year. Special
supplements give current statistical data on a number of topics. Numerous
photographs are included. The index is detailed and covers the current year and
major articles from past yearbooks.

Americana Annual. New York, Americana Division, Grolier Corp., 1923– .
   (Annual)
   Issued as an annual supplement to the *Encyclopedia Americana*. Articles
are mainly concerned with events of the previous year. Has a day-by-day

chronological record of world events. Includes a variety of statistical information. Lists prominent persons who died during the year and has biographies of many living persons. The articles are concise and in a journalistic style. The index is detailed and covers the current year and four previous years. Numerous photographs are included. Areas covered include biographies, cities, economics, education, human welfare, medicine and health, religion, science, etc.

U.S. Bureau of the Census. *Statistical Abstract of the United States.* Washington, Government Printing Office, 1878– . (Annual)
A summary of important statistical data supplied by all the statistical agencies of the United States Government and by some private agencies. The statistics are arranged in 33 broad subject fields such as population, finance, vital statistics, railroads, commerce, immigration and naturalization, education, law enforcement, etc. The emphasis is on national statistics rather than state and local breakdowns. The statistics include current data and retrospective data for 15 to 30 years. A detailed index, which is arranged by subject, name, and profession, allows easy access to the data. A recent edition had over 1,200 tables and over 40 pages of index. A companion volume useful for statistics covering a greater time span is *Historical Statistics of the United States, Colonial Times to 1957* (Washington, Government Printing Office, 1960. Supplements). For local statistical data, see companion publications: *County and City Data Book* (Washington, Government Printing Office, 1962) and *Congressional District Data Book* (Washington, Government Printing Office, 1963).

United Nations. Statistical Office. *Statistical Yearbook.* New York, United Nations, 1949– . (Annual)
A compendium of world-wide statistics. Some of the subjects covered are agriculture, population, trade, education, manpower, forests, mining, communication, consumption, culture, etc. The latest statistics and those for several past years are given.

Facts on File, Weekly World News Digest with Cumulative Index. New York, Facts on File, 1940– . (Weekly)
Gives factual summaries of current news events. The coverage is worldwide and the information is taken from metropolitan newspapers. Summaries are recorded chronologically and arranged under such topics as Education and Religion, Sports, Obituaries, Arts and Science, etc. Indexes are issued bi-weekly and cumulated.

FOOTNOTES

1. The following form subdivisions are commonly used with subject headings: ABSTRACTS, BIBLIOGRAPHY, BIO-BIBLIOGRAPHY, DICTIONARIES, DIRECTORIES, HANDBOOKS, MANUALS ETC., INDEXES, STATISTICS, and YEARBOOKS.

2. Winchell's *Guide to Reference Books* (8th ed.) and its supplements list nearly 10,000 titles. Of course, only the largest libraries would have most of these titles. *American Reference Books Annual* lists and evaluates about 1,800 reference books published in this country each year.

CHAPTER 11

REFERENCE MATERIALS:
DICTIONARIES AND THEIR SUPPLEMENTS

INTRODUCTION

Dictionaries and their various supplements are as most people know concerned with words. Included here are some examples of dictionaries on current definitions, historical dictionaries, and specialized dictionaries on slang, acronyms, synonyms, and current usage.

UNABRIDGED DICTIONARIES

Funk & Wagnalls' New Standard Dictionary of the English Language. New York, Funk & Wagnalls, 1963.
    A popular unabridged dictionary with over 450,000 words included. The emphasis is on contemporary usage, spelling and pronunciation. The common usage is the first definition given. The introductory material gives basic rules for spelling, pronunciation, hyphenation, and compounding. Proper names are included and the appendix contains foreign words and phrases and population statistics. Illustrative quotations are given to show current usage.

Webster's Third New International Dictionary of the English Language. Springfield, Mass., G. & C. Merriam, 1961.
    Contains about 450,000 words, with some 100,000 being either new words or new meanings for old words added since the last edition. Stress is placed on current usage and meaning of words. Definitions are arranged chronologically. Many quotations from contemporary sources illustrate current usage.

The Random House Dictionary of the English Language. Unabridged ed. New York, Random House, 1966.
    Includes some 260,000 words with emphasis on current usage. All entries are in one alphabet for easier use. Contains special supplements and lists such as: "Signs and Symbols," four concise foreign-language dictionaries (French, Spanish, Italian and German), "Basic Manual of Style," "Major Dates in History," "National Parks of the United States," "Atlas of the World," "Gazetteer," etc. Supplements make it encyclopedic in scope.

ABRIDGED DICTIONARIES

Webster's Seventh New Collegiate Dictionary. Springfield, Mass., G. & C. Merriam, 1971.
    This is an abridged dictionary containing about 130,000 words. The definitions, spelling, etc., are based on *Webster's Third New International Dictionary.* Special supplements and appendices include abbreviations, proofreader's marks, forms of address, rules of grammar, lists of colleges and

universities, biographical names (over 5,000), and a gazetteer (over 10,000 names of places), among others.

HISTORICAL DICTIONARIES

New English Dictionary on Historical Principles. J. A. H. Murray, ed. Oxford, Clarendon Press, 1884-1933. 13v.

Some 414,825 words in use since 1150 are included in this monumental work. The purpose of the *NED* is to show the origin of words, their spelling, pronunciation, usage and meanings at different times in history. Some 2,000,000 quotations from over 5,000 authors are used to illustrate the historical development of the words from their origins to the present. The dictionary is also called the *Oxford English Dictionary* and is abbreviated *NED* or *OED*. It is also a useful tool for quotations and slang words.

Craigie, Sir William, and James R. Hulbert, eds. *A Dictionary of American English on Historical Principles.* Chicago, University of Chicago Press, 1936-1944. 4v.

This work is based on the *NED*. Its purpose is to trace the origin and development of English words in the American colonies and the United States. Definitions are illustrated by chronologically arranged quotations to show variations in usage over the years. The work is a valuable source for American folklore and customs. A common abbreviation for the work is *DAE*. A valuable supplement to the *DAE* is *A Dictionary of Americanisms on Historical Principles*, edited by Milford L. Mathews.

CURRENT USAGE

Fowler, Henry Watson. *A Dictionary of Modern English Usage.* 2nd ed. rev. Oxford, Clarendon Press, 1965.

A standard work on correct grammatical usage. Arranged alphabetically in dictionary form. Some of the areas covered are definitions of terms, proper and disputed spellings and plurals, the misuse of words and expressions and parts of speech. Stress is placed on current usage.

Evans, Bergen, and Cornelia Evans. *A Dictionary of Contemporary American Usage.* New York, Random House, 1957.

A witty yet scholarly treatment of contemporary American usage. The material is arranged alphabetically in dictionary form. Covers such topics as grammar, punctuation, word usage, idioms, literary concepts, and many others. Most topics are covered in brief articles.

SLANG

Wentworth, Harold, and Stuart Berg Flexner, comps. *Dictionary of American Slang.* Supplemented ed. New York, Crowell, 1967.

Contains over 21,000 definitions of slang words, jargon, and colloquialisms. Most entries give the date of first use and illustrate usage with quotations.

Some examples of the origins of terms used in the armed forces, business, and politics are given, as well as terms used by teenagers, the beat generation, the underworld, and so forth. The definitions are detailed and the arrangement is alphabetical.

Partridge, Eric. *Dictionary of Slang and Unconventional English.* 7th ed., rev. and enl. London, Routledge & K. Paul, 1970. 2v.
    A standard reference work for English slang terms. Gives definitions and the date of first usage. Includes "such Americanisms as have been naturalized."

SYNONYMS AND ANTONYMS

Webster's New Dictionary of Synonyms. New ed. Springfield, Mass., G. & C. Merriam, 1968.
    One of the best and most comprehensive synonym dictionaries. Illustrative quotations are given from both classical and contemporary sources. A history of synonyms is included.

Roget's International Thesaurus. 3rd ed. New York, Crowell, 1962.
    A standard work on synonyms. Arrangement is by category according to ideas. An index of words refers the user to the subject categories.

ABBREVIATIONS

Gale Research Company. *Acronyms and Initialisms Dictionary.* 3rd ed. Detroit, Gale Research, 1970.
    One of the more comprehensive works on abbreviations. The subtitle gives the sources for many of the entries, some of which are: aerospace, business and trade, education, labor, medicine, physiology, religion, science, societies, sports, and transportation.

CHAPTER 12

REFERENCE MATERIALS: ENCYCLOPEDIAS

INTRODUCTION

This type of reference material attempts to present general basic information in all fields of knowledge. The information is given in articles which vary in length from one paragraph to many pages. The encyclopedia serves as an excellent introduction to a topic, but it is not considered a definitive treatment. The serious student or reader will want to refer to other works after consulting an encyclopedia for introductory material.

The encyclopedias listed below are general, covering all subject fields. Specialized encyclopedias, which are limited in scope, are discussed in later chapters under the specific subject.

When examining the encyclopedias you will notice that they contain some of the same information as the almanacs and yearbooks discussed earlier. In each case the library technician, or librarian, will have to judge from the patron's question which source would be best for that particular patron.

GENERAL ENCYCLOPEDIAS

Encyclopedia Americana. New York, Americana Corp., 1903-04– . 30v.

A general encyclopedia with articles on subjects in all branches of knowledge. Some emphasis is placed on information about Amercan cities and towns, the United States and Canada in general, and the fields of science and technology. The *Americana* includes about 69,000 articles and a comprehensive index of 359,000 entries and cross references. Includes numerous illustrations, maps, and bibliographies. It is kept up to date through continuous revision. (See also the *Americana Annual*, Chapter 10.)

Encyclopaedia Britannica. Chicago, Encyclopaedia Britannica, 1768– . 24v.

A comprehensive encyclopedia with both short and lengthy articles on many subjects. Articles are by experts in their fields and are written to appeal to the expert as well as the general reader. Includes bibliographies, illustrations, and a separate atlas in the index volume. The index is comprehensive and allows good access to the material. The *Britannica* is kept up to date by continuous revision. (See also the *Britannica Book of the Year*, Chapter 10.)

Collier's Encyclopedia. New York, Crowell-Collier-Macmillan, 1950– . 24v.

A comprehensive encyclopedia with somewhat less coverage and detail than the *Americana* or *Britannica*. The style is popular and the work is aimed at the layman and college level. Contains some 25,000 articles, over 14,000 illustrations, and 1,400 maps throughout the text. The index volume has a study guide. All bibliographies are included in the index volume rather than at the end of each article. The bibliographies are especially useful as they list titles for readers at various levels from high school through college graduate. *Collier's* is kept up to date by continuous revision.

DESK ENCYCLOPEDIAS

Columbia Encyclopedia. Edited by William Bridgewater and Seymour Kurtz.
     3rd ed. New York, Columbia University Press, 1963.
     A one-volume encyclopedia with concise information on a wide range of
subjects with some emphasis on place-names and biographies of living people.
Bibliographies are included with some, but not all, articles. There is no separate
index, but there are 80,000 cross references to connect related subjects. Contains both illustrations and maps. Updated by incorporating new material in
the next printing run.

JUVENILE ENCYCLOPEDIAS

World Book Encyclopedia. Chicago, Field Enterprises, 1917– . 20v.
     One of the best-known juvenile encyclopedias. It aims to meet the general
reference needs of students from elementary through high school and to serve
as a general family encyclopedia. The newest and the most prominent feature
of the 1972 edition of the *World Book* is Volume 22, "Research/Guide Index."
This index, with more than 150,000 entries, supplements and complements an
elaborate system of cross references. The arrangement of articles in this encyclopedia is alphabetical, word-by-word. There are over 20,000 illustrations,
more than 10,000 of which are in color.

CHAPTER 13

REFERENCE MATERIALS:
BIOGRAPHICAL INFORMATION

INTRODUCTION

Biographical information can be found in many of the more general reference materials such as encyclopedias, almanacs, and dictionaries. However, the materials discussed below are devoted exclusively to biographical information and are more inclusive in their coverage than other sources. The texts usually include factual information like birthdates, birthplaces, vital statistics, memberships, jobs held, publications, addresses, etc.

The individual biographical reference works are usually limited in scope. Some are international in coverage; some are limited to persons in a particular country; others are limited to living persons or to persons no longer living; and some are limited to persons in a particular profession or occupation. Therefore, before searching for biographical information it is helpful to know the person's nationality, profession, and whether he is living or dead.

If the patron wants more detailed information on a person, he should be referred to the catalog to look for biographies or autobiographies on the person.

The materials discussed below are all general in nature. For specialized material on particular professions or groups of related professions, look in a library catalog under the subject entry.[1] For example, SCIENTISTS–BIOGRAPHY, or ARTISTS–BIOGRAPHY. The sources for national biography are restricted to the United States and Great Britain. For works on other countries, look in the library catalog under the particular country.[2] For example, CANADA–BIOGRAPHY, or FRANCE–BIOGRAPHY.

BIOGRAPHICAL INFORMATION–INTERNATIONAL

Biography Index: A Cumulative Index to Biographical Material in Books and Magazines. New York, H. W. Wilson, 1946– . (Quarterly)

A quarterly publication cumulated annually and in permanent triennial cumulations. No actual biographical information is given here, but references are made to articles, books, etc., where information is available. It indexes biographical information in current books in the English language and biographical information from over 1,500 periodicals. The index is in two parts: by name (giving dates, nationality, profession, and sources where biographical information can be found) and by profession or occupation. It is international in scope and includes both living and dead persons.

Current Biography. New York, H. W. Wilson, 1940– . (Monthly except August)

A monthly publication with an annual cumulation titled *Current Biography Yearbook.* It is international in scope and includes persons of various occupations and professions. Includes 300 to 400 biographies annually of people currently in the news. Articles are brief and include a portrait, address, birth date, occupation, list of writings, biographical sketch, and references to other bio-graphical sources. Each issue and the annual cumulation contain an index by name and an index by occupation or profession.

New York Times Obituaries Index, 1858-1968. New York, New York Times, 1970.
  Contains over 350,000 obituaries that have appeared in the *New York Times* since 1858. International in scope, including persons of all professions and occupations. All, of course, are not living. Reference is given to the issue, page, and column of the *New York Times* where the obituary appears. For persons who died after 1968, consult the *New York Times Index,* which is discussed in Chapter 19.

Webster's Biographical Dictionary. Springfield, Mass., G. & C. Merriam, 1972.
  A biographical dictionary listing over 40,000 names of persons from all nations and all periods. Includes people still living. Information is brief, ranging from several lines to a full page. Although international in scope, it is somewhat stronger in American and English names than foreign names. Special attention is given to pronunciation of names. Contains many special features such as lists of presidents, justices of the Supreme Court, rulers of various countries, popes, and others.

The New Century Cyclopedia of Names. Edited by Clarence L. Barnhart. New ed. New York, Appleton-Century-Crofts, 1954. 3v.
  Contains about 100,000 names of persons, places (real and legendary), characters from plays, mythology and literature, historical events, etc. Infor-mation varies in length from a few lines to half a page. Contains appendices including a chronological table of world history, a list of forenames with pro-nunciations, and lists of rulers. International in scope and includes both living and not living persons.

The International Who's Who. London, Europa Publications, 1935– . (Annual)
  Contains 10,000 to 15,000 names of prominent people in Europe, North and South America, Asia, Africa, and Australia. All fields of endeavor are covered, including banking, diplomacy, music, science, education, sociology, and many others. Biographies are brief and include nationality, profession, birthdates, education, publications, addresses, and other useful information. Most persons listed are living.

BIOGRAPHICAL INFORMATION–UNITED STATES

Who's Who in America: A Biographical Dictionary of Notable Living Men and Women. Chicago, Marquis, 1899– . (Biennial)
  The standard American biographical dictionary, which currently lists about 60,000 names of living Americans. Some select prominent foreigners and heads of state are included. The editors include "individuals who are of current national reference interest because of meritorious achievement in some reputable field or because of the positions they hold." The brief and factual entries

include place and date of birth, occupation, vital statistics, religion, political affiliation, publications, and addresses.

A related series of *Who's Who* with more limited geographical scope is produced by the same publisher. The reader should examine the volume relevant to his particular geographic area: *Who's Who in the East, Who's Who in the Midwest, Who's Who in the South and Southwest,* or *Who's Who in the West.* Another related work is *Who's Who of American Women,* which is national in coverage and supplements the information for women listed in *Who's Who in America.*

Dictionary of American Biography. New York, Scribner, 1928-1958. 20v. and
    Supplements.

This set is the standard scholarly biographical dictionary for America. To date there are about 15,000 separate biographies ranging from 500 words to 16,500 words in length. Persons who lived in the original 13 colonies or lands that became a part of the United States are included. Bibliographies accompany the articles. No living persons are included in this work. To be included the person need only to have distinguished himself in American history, whether his actions were "good" or "bad." Hence, John Wilkes Booth is included. The work is often called the *DAB.*

Who Was Who in America: A Companion Biographical Reference Work to
    Who's Who in America. Chicago, Marquis, 1942– .

These volumes include persons who have been removed from *Who's Who in America* because of death. The biographical material is essentially the same as in *Who's Who in America,* with some minor revision including addition of death dates and place of burial. Because sketches of persons previously included are deleted following their death, many libraries keep back years of *Who's Who in America.*

Presently there are five volumes of *Who Was Who in America: Who Was Who in America: Historical Volume, 1607-1896,* and four volumes for the periods 1897-1942, 1943-1950, 1951-1960, 1961-1968. These volumes are occasionally referred to as *Who's Who in American History.*

BIOGRAPHICAL INFORMATION–GREAT BRITAIN

Who's Who. London, Black, 1849– . (Annual)

This is the British counterpart to *Who's Who in America* and preceded it by some 50 years. It was one of the first works of its type and has served as a model for others. The entries are principally British, but some notables from other countries are included. Entries include name, degrees, titles, vital statistics, publications, addresses and other useful data. There are about 20,000 entries. The helpful section called "Abbreviations Used in This Book" explains those abbreviations used in the biographical entries which may be unfamiliar to the American reader. All persons included are living.

Dictionary of National Biography. Edited by Leslie Stephen and Sidney Lee.
    London, Smith, Elder, 1885-1901. 63v. Supplements. Reissued: Oxford,
    Oxford University Press, 1938. 22v. Supplements.

This set is the basic biographical dictionary for Great Britain. It includes material for persons from Great Britain, Ireland, and the colonies. The basic set includes about 29,000 articles, and the supplements bring the work up to 1960. Most biographies are about a page in length, though some are as long as 50 pages. Information given includes birth and death dates, profession, education, important events, vital statistics, bibliography of works by the person, and a bibliography of works about the person. No living persons are included. The set is often called the *DNB*.

Who Was Who: A Companion to Who's Who Containing the Biographies of Those Who Died. London, Black, 1897/1916– .

The subtitle explains the purpose of this work. It is the British counterpart of *Who Was Who in America.* The entries are revised to include the latest information and to supply a death date. Presently five volumes cover the periods 1897-1915, 1916-1928, 1929-1940, 1941-1950, 1951-1960. Each volume contains an explanation of abbreviations which would be unfamiliar to the American reader.

FOOTNOTES

1. An exception in this text are biographical works devoted to authors. Because of their importance and frequent use, they are included in Chapter 20, in the section on literature.

2. For a survey of biographical dictionaries for countries other than the United States and Great Britain, see Winchell's *Guide to Reference Books* (8th ed.), pp. 167-90, and its supplements.

CHAPTER 14

REFERENCE MATERIALS:
BIBLIOGRAPHIES AND BIBLIOGRAPHIC GUIDES

INTRODUCTION

A bibliography is a list of materials usually on a relatively restricted subject. The bibliography may list books, periodicals, documents, and audio-visual materials, or it may be restricted to only one or two types of materials. The bibliography may be comprehensive and attempt to list all materials on a subject, by an author, materials published during a specific period of time, in a particular language, or in a specific geographic area. Other bibliographies are restrictive and limit themselves to a select number of items.

Some bibliographies contain only brief descriptions for material including the author, title, publisher, date, and price. Others are annotated and give the information cited above plus a description of the contents of the work. The arrangement of a bibliography may be alphabetical by author, title, or subject, or a combination of these; chronological by date of publication; or by format of the material such as books in one section, periodicals in another, and non-print materials in another.

In this chapter we will discuss some examples of general bibliographies, a national bibliography, a library bibliography or bibliographic guide, and several trade bibliographies. These bibliographies are generally restricted to materials in English and published mostly in the United States and England.

With a few exceptions bibliographies on specific topics are not included in this text. The library technician will find subject bibliographies in a library through the catalog. The form subdivision BIBLIOGRAPHY is added to the subject heading to indicate this special kind of work. For example: U.S.–HISTORY–BIBLIOGRAPHY, ART–BIBLIOGRAPHY, MATHEMATICS–BIBLIOGRAPHY, or SHAKESPEARE, WILLIAM, 1564-1616–BIBLIOGRAPHY. Another way to locate subject bibliographies is to consult bibliographic guides (e.g., *American Reference Books Annual* or Winchell's *Guide to Reference Books*) and check to see what is listed for each subject.

GENERAL BIBLIOGRAPHIES

Bibliographic Index: A Cumulative Bibliography of Bibliographies. New York, H. W. Wilson, 1938– .

This is a semi-annual publication cumulated annually and in larger permanent cumulations. It lists bibliographies on all subjects including biographies and the scientific fields. Bibliographies included are: 1) separately published books, 2) those included in books, and 3) those in some 1,500 selected periodical titles if they have 40 or more items. The index is arranged alphabetically by subject with the bibliographies arranged by author within each subject. (See Figure 1.)

Figure 1
Entries for *Bibliographic Index**

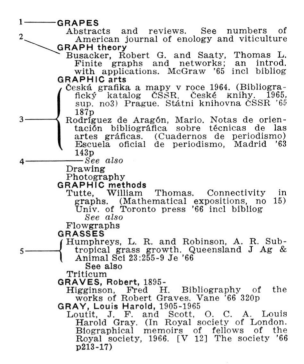

[1] Subject entry

[2] Entry for the book in which a bibliography on "Graph Theory" appears—author, title, publisher, date of publication, and bibliography

[3] Entries on a subject arranged in alphabetical order

[4] "See Also" reference to related subjects

[5] Entry for a periodical in which a bibliography on "Grasses" appears—authors, title of the article, title of the periodical where the article can be found, volume of the periodical, pages, and date of the periodical issue

American Reference Books Annual. Edited by Bohdan S. Wynar. Littleton, Colo., Libraries Unlimited, 1970– .

Published annually since 1970, *ARBA* provides a comprehensive reviewing service of reference books published in this country, plus a selected number of foreign reference books distributed in the United States by an exclusive agent. Each year some 1,800 titles are reviewed by 150 subject specialists. Works covered include bibliographies and bibliographic guides, encyclopedias, dictionaries, indexes, handbooks, almanacs, atlases, and other types of reference books. The materials are arranged in 40 sections subdivided by over 300 separate subject headings. Added to entries in *ARBA* are citations to reviews in leading library periodicals. All titles are indexed by author, title, and subject.

Barton, Mary N., and Marion V. Bell, comps. *Reference Books: A Brief Guide.* 7th ed. Baltimore, Enoch Pratt Free Library, 1970.

The present edition comments on 815 titles, either in the main entries or in the notes. The arrangement is by types of reference materials and by subject matter. All entries provide adequate bibliographical descriptions and good annotations. Of particular value for small libraries.

Winchell, Constance M. *Guide to Reference Books.* 8th ed. Chicago, American Library Association, 1967. Supplements.

The standard American guide to reference materials. The latest edition and its supplements list and annotate about 10,000 titles. Materials from many countries in different languages are included, but the emphasis is on American reference materials. The materials are arranged in five sections: General Reference Works, The Humanities, Social Sciences, History and Area Studies, and Pure and Applied Sciences. Each section is further divided into categories of special forms of material such as guides and manuals, encyclopedias, dictionaries, handbooks, biographical works, etc. The index includes author and subject entries, and some title entries. This is one of the most valuable reference tools, and the reader should be sure to examine it. Many libraries keep Winchell at the reference desk because it is so frequently used.

Public Library Catalog. Edited by Estelle A. Fidell. 5th ed. New York, H. W. Wilson, 1969. Supplements.

A list of basic books for a public library collection, covering all fields except fiction. It is a most helpful guide for medium or small public libraries. Books are arranged by subject and are indexed by subject, author, and title. Each title is given a short annotation. The basic volume lists about 11,000 titles, and each supplement lists about 3,500 titles. Related volumes useful for other types of libraries are *Senior High School Catalog, Junior High School Catalog,* and the *Children's Catalog.*

NATIONAL BIBLIOGRAPHIES

Publishers' Trade List Annual. New York, R. R. Bowker, 1873– . (Annual)

A collection of catalogs of over 1,600 American publishers. The last edition was in six volumes. The catalogs are arranged alphabetically by the name of the publisher. A supplementary section in the first volume provides a table of contents and listings of books of smaller publishers. The information provided varies among publishers. Valuable for determining in-print books for a publisher, prices, discounts, ordering information, and addresses. Indexed by author and title in *Books in Print*. Often called the *PTLA*.

Books in Print. New York, R. R. Bowker, 1948– . (Annual)
   A listing by author and title of American books currently in print and available for purchase. Volume 1 is an alphabetical list of authors and volume 2 is an alphabetical list of titles. The author volume gives the most complete information. The information given is author, title, publisher, date of publication, and price. In some cases the edition, translator, series, grade level, or other essential information is also given. A comprehensive list of American publishers is included in the second volume. The latest edition of *BIP* has over 200,000 titles listed. This work is an author-title index to the *Publishers' Trade List Annual*, which is discussed above. (See Figure 2.)

Figure 2
Entries in *Books in Print*

Briston, R. J. Stock Exchange & Investment Analysis, British. (Illus.). 1970. 12.00 (ISBN 0-8426-0100-7). Verry.
Bristow, ed. see Defoe, D.
Bristow, Allen P. Effective Police Manpower Utilization. (Illus.) 1969. 6.75. C C Thomas.
— Field Interrogation. 2nd ed. (Illus.). 1970. 7.50. C C Thomas.
Bristow, Allen P. & Gabard, E. Caroline. Decision-Making in Police Administration. (Illus.). 1961. 5.25. C C Thomas.
Bristow, Allen P. & Williams, John B. Handbook in Criminal Procedure & the Administration of Justice. rev. ed. (California Handbook Series in Police Science). (Orig.). 1966. text ed. 3.95 (47381). Glencoe.
Bristow, Allen P., jt. auth. see Gourley, G. Douglas.
Bristow, Allen P., jt. auth. see Roberts, Willis J.
Bristow, Allen P., ed. Police Supervision Readings. (Illus.). 1970. 24.75. C C Thomas.
Bristow, Eugene K., ed. & tr. see Ostrovsky, Alexander.
Bristow, Gwen. Calico Palace. 1971. Repr. pap. 1.25 (ISBN 0-671-78064-6). PB.
— —Calico Palace. 1970. 7.95 (ISBN 0-690-16608-7). T Y Crowell.
— —Celia Garth. 1959. 6.95 (ISBN 0-690-18348-8). T Y Crowell.

[1] Author	[6] Publisher
[2] Title	[7] Edition
[3] Illustrations included in the book	[8] Series
[4] Date of publication	[9] Reference to correct entry
[5] Price	

Subject Guide to Books in Print. New York, R. R. Bowker, 1957– . (Annual)

This is a companion set to *Books in Print.* It lists the books alphabetically by subject, using basically the subject headings and cross references used by the Library of Congress. Books not assigned subject headings by the Library of Congress are excluded: fiction, drama, poetry, and Bibles. Contains a list of publishers' addresses. Information on each book includes author, title, edition, publisher, price, and other useful information where pertinent. (See Figure 3.)

Figure 3

Entries in *Subject Guide to Books in Print**

```
        Turner, David R. Complete Guide to U. S. Civil
          Service Jobs. (Il., Orig). 6th ed. 1966. pap. 1.00.
          (pap. ISBN 0-668-00537-8). Arco.
1 ————CIVIL SERVICE REFORM
2 ————see also Corruption (In Politics); Patronage, Political
3 ————Fowler, Dorothy C. Cabinet Politician: The
          Postmasters General, 1829-1909. 1943. 12.95. (ISDN
          0-404-02542-0). AMS Pr.
        Hoogenboom, Ari. Outlawing the Spoils: A History of
          the Civil Service Reform Movement, 1865-1883. 1968.
          pap. 2.95. (pap. ISBN 0-252-78406-5). IB. U of Ill Pr.
        Notation Technique de Promotion au Merite. 1960.
          pap. 0.80. Pub Admin.
        CIVIL SUPREMACY OVER THE MILITARY
        Cavaioli, Frank J. West Point & the Presidency. 1962.
          pap. 2.50x. (pap. ISBN 0-87075-046-1). St Johns.
        Daalder, Hans. Role of the Military in the Emerging
          Countries. (Orig). pap. 1.25. Humanities.
```

[1] Subject heading.

[2] "See also" reference to related subjects.

[3] Author entry with bibliographic information to identify the work.

Paperbound Books in Print. New York, R. R. Bowker, 1955– . (Semi-annual)

A listing of in-print paperbound books issued by American publishers. Consists of separate author, title, and subject alphabetical listings. The subject index is divided into 26 major subject headings. A list of publishers' addresses and abbreviations is included. Each section—author, title, subject—gives the author, title, publisher, standard book number, and price for the book. A useful tool for helping locate relatively inexpensive books.

Publishers Weekly. New York, R. R. Bowker, 1872– . (Weekly)

A basic source for locating recently published books. Excluded are government documents, subscription books, dissertations, printings other than the first, and pamphlets of 49 pages or less. The books are arranged alphabetically by main entry, with the following information: title, publisher, date of publication, edition, price. Decimal and Library of Congress classification numbers, Library of Congress subject headings, Library of Congress card number, and brief descriptive notes are also provided. Each issue contains general information about the publishing industry. Special issues each year cover topics like children's books, trade statistics, university presses, and religious books.

---

*Figures 2 and 3 are reproduced by permission of R.R. Bowker (a Xerox company).

INTERNATIONAL BIBLIOGRAPHIES

Cumulative Book Index. New York, H. W. Wilson, 1898– . (Monthly)
Subtitled "A World List of Books in the English Language," this work attempts to be a complete international bibliography of books published in English. Not included are government documents, most pamphlets, many paperbound books, maps, music scores, and material of a local or ephemeral nature. The dictionary arrangement includes author, title, and subject entries in one alphabet. Valuable for its additional entries under series and translators. The most complete information is given with the author entries; it includes author's name and dates, title, series, edition, paging, price, publisher, date of publication, standard book number, and Library of Congress card number. Each volume contains a list of publishers and addresses. This work is referred to as *CBI.* (See Figure 4.)

LIBRARY CATALOGS–INTERNATIONAL IN SCOPE

U.S. Library of Congress. *The National Union Catalog: A Cumulative Author List Representing Library of Congress Printed Cards, and Titles Reported by Other American Libraries.* Washington, Government Printing Office, 1956– . (Monthly)
This monumental set is a main entry listing of books acquired and cataloged by the Library of Congress and hundreds of other cooperating libraries. Each entry is a reduced-size reproduction of a Library of Congress card with complete cataloging information, or a card submitted from other libraries with generally the same information, except that no classification number is provided. Location symbols are given for other libraries holding each item. Entries, which are for materials in all languages, include books, maps, atlases, periodicals, other serials, and pamphlets. Separate volumes are published for motion pictures (*Motion Pictures and Filmstrips*) and music (*Music and Phonorecords*). The entire work is usually called the *NUC.* (See Figure 5.)
The *NUC* is issued monthly with quarterly cumulations except for October, November and December. These three months are included in the annual cumulation. The annuals are cumulated quinquennially.
An important set used with the *NUC* is the U.S. Library of Congress' *A Catalog of Books Represented by Library of Congress Printed Cards, 1942-55* (191 vols.). The format is similar to that of the *NUC*, the main difference being the *NUC*'s inclusion of many other library holdings. Presently a work is in process which will make the *NUC* retrospective (before 1956) and show the holdings of other libraries. The set is titled *The National Union Catalog: Pre-1956 Imprints* and will be complete in 610 volumes. Because of its cost it is likely to be found only in larger libraries.
The *NUC* is valuable in acquisitions, cataloging, and reference for verification of information and for the historical notes and explanations for many entries.

Figure 4
Entries in the *Cumulative Book Index*

1 ——The limits of American capitalism. Heilbroner,
   R. L. pa $1.25 Harper
   The limits of science. Rousseau, P. 45s Phoe-
   nix house; Can$9.50. Dent
   The limner's daughter. Clarke, M. S. $3.95; lib
   bdg $3.77 Viking
   Lin, Yu-Kweng Michael, 1923-
   Probabilistic theory of structural dynamics.
   366p il $14.50 '67 McGraw   LC 67-10624
2 ——Lincoln, Abraham, 1809-1865
   Williams, T. H. Lincoln and his generals.
   pa $1.95 '67 Vintage
3 ———————————————Juvenile literature
   Cammiade, A. Lincoln and the American
   Civil war. $3.95 '67 Roy pubs; 15s Methuen
   Lindall, Edward, pseud.—See Smith, E. E.
4 ——Linder, Staffan Burenstam. See Burenstam
   Linder, S
   Lindgren, Astrid (Ericsson) 1907-
   Noy lives in Thailand; phot. by Anna Riw-
   kin-Brick. $2.95; lib bdg $2.94 '67 Macmil-
5 ——lan (N Y)———————————LC 67-2637
6 ——Lindgren, Barbro
   Hilding's summer; tr. from the Swedish by
   Annabelle MacMillan; il. by Stan Tusan.
   138 p $3.75 '67 Macmillan (N Y)

[1] Title entry—title, author's name, paper format, price, and publisher.

[2] Subject heading—entries listed under the subject alphabetically by author.

[3] Subdivision of the main subject "Lincoln, Abraham, 1809-1865." (If this were typed on a catalog card it would read "Lincoln, Abraham, 1809-1865–Juvenile Literature.")

[4] "See" reference from form of a name not used to the form used.

[5] Library of Congress card number—when available.

[6] Author entry—title, translation, illustrations, paging, price, year of publication, publisher.

Figure 5
Entries in the *National Union Catalog*

The National Union Catalog

Glagoleva, Elena Georgievna
    see Gel'fand, Izrail' Moiseevich. Functions
    and graphs. Rev. English ed. based on the 2d.
    Russian ed.   New York, Gordon and Breach
    [c1969]

Glaser, Anton, 1924–
    History of binary and other nondecimal numeration.
    Southampton, Pa. [1971]
    ix, 196 p. illus. 21 cm.
    Based on the author's thesis, Temple University, with title: His-
    tory of modern numeration systems.
    Includes bibliographies.
    1. Numeration—History.   I. Title.
    QA141.2.G55   513'.5   71-149293
    ISBN 0-9600324-1-X   MARC

Glassco, John, comp.
    The poetry of French Canada in translation, edited with
    an introduction by John Glassco. Toronto, Oxford Univer-
    sity Press, 1970.
    xxvi, 270 p. 18 cm. (An Oxford in Canada paperback, 20) 4.00
                                                                C•••
    1. French-Canadian poetry—Translations into English. 2. English
    poetry—Translations from French.   I. Title.
    PQ3914.Z5E54   841'.008   73-569139
    ISBN 0-19-540167-0   MARC

Glasser, Stephen A., ed.
    see Pension plans, deferred compensation,
    and executive benefits. New York, Practising
    Law Institute [1969]

CHAPTER 15

REFERENCE MATERIALS: ATLASES AND GAZETTEERS

INTRODUCTION

Atlases, gazetteers, maps, and guidebooks are primary sources for geographical information. In this chapter we will discuss some representative examples of these materials.

An atlas is a collection of maps. The maps may be topographical or topical (on subjects like population, political conditions, history, economics, and miscellaneous statistics). Atlases must be examined to discover exactly what kind of maps they contain. Never assume that only topographical maps are included.

Gazetteers give locations for places—cities, towns, lakes, rivers, historic sites, etc. There will usually be some description of the place, map coordinates, and statistical information such as population. There are also dictionaries of place names, which emphasize the historical origin of place names and the different forms they have assumed through the years.

Guidebooks, or travel guides, as they are often called, give descriptive information about cities and countries. Information provided for cities may cover museums, historic sites, restaurants, hotels, weather and temperature, shopping hints, and street maps.

Although we will not give any examples of individual maps, the library technician should be aware of the more important kinds of maps and sources for these maps. Nearly every library will have some general maps of the local area, the state, and special local maps such as bus or subway routes, school district boundaries, congressional district maps, and street guides.

The U.S. Geological Survey publishes a number of detailed topographic maps for each state in a series titled the *National Topographic Map Series*. Although not yet complete, the series will eventually cover all 50 states, Puerto Rico, Guam, American Samoa, and the Virgin Islands. Libraries will probably have the "quadrangle map" for the local area and perhaps the whole state. Many libraries will acquire the complete series. In any case library technicians should be aware of these maps and know which ones are available in their libraries.

The U.S. Coast and Geodetic Survey issues nautical charts covering rivers, harbors, lakes, and coastal areas. These charts are useful to boat owners, and many libraries purchase those of local interest. The same department also issues a number of aeronautical charts for the United States and foreign countries.

The U.S. Department of Agriculture publishes specialized agricultural soil survey maps for many areas of the country. Maps accompany the written report and are not available separately. Many libraries purchase these soil surveys for their local area.

The U.S. Army Topographic Command publishes a large number of detailed topographic maps for the United States and for other countries. Their great detail makes them especially valuable.

A great number of general topological and topical maps are issued by various other federal agencies, agencies of state and city governments, and private organizations. Automobile clubs and service stations are often good sources for road maps, city maps, and other material of local interest.

One other important map project on an international level is the *International Map*, sometimes called the "Millionth Map." The United Nations is coordinating this project, although the work is being done by many national agencies. When complete, this collection will cover the entire world.

Because of rapidly changing political and physical conditions, maps and atlases have their limitations. The library technician must keep these limitations in mind. For example, a ten-year-old atlas would be inadequate to determine political boundaries in Africa; a ten-year-old city map would not show the latest streets. When using geographic reference tools, it is necessary to be aware of the following points: 1) date of the atlas or map, 2) its scope—local, regional, or international, 3) whether an index or gazetteer is included, 4) the kinds of maps or other information in an atlas, and 5) how to interpret the maps—scale, color coding, and meaning of symbols.

In certain cases where current political changes have taken place, it may be necessary to consult the latest almanac, encyclopedia yearbook, or political handbook for maps rather than an atlas.

To locate other atlases in a library, look in the catalog under the subject heading ATLASES. Materials on maps can be found under the subject heading MAPS. Also the form subdivision MAPS is added to subject headings to denote this specialized material (e.g., U.S.—HISTORICAL GEOGRAPHY—MAPS, EUROPE—HISTORICAL GEOGRAPHY—MAPS, AFRICA—ECONOMIC CONDITIONS—MAPS, and U.S.—CLIMATE—MAPS). Gazetteers will be found under the subject GEOGRAPHY—DICTIONARIES, but the term GAZETTEERS is used as a subject subdivision under the names of countries, states, etc. (U.S.— GAZETTEERS, CALIFORNIA—GAZETTEERS).

ATLASES—INTERNATIONAL

The Times, London. *The Times Atlas of the World*. Edited by John Bartholomew. London, Times, 1955-59. 5v.

A standard set and one of the best world atlases. Each volume covers a section of the world: Volume 1, World, Australasia, and East Asia; Volume 2, Southwest Asia and Russia; Volume 3, Northern Europe; Volume 4, Southern Europe and Africa; Volume 5, The Americas. Each volume has its own gazetteer and index. Contains topographic maps and many special maps covering areas such as population, climate, communications, vegetation, soils, air routes, and many others. About 200,000 place names are given in the five volumes. Many city maps are included.

Many libraries have the excellent one-volume eidtion published in 1967, which was revised at that time to bring it up to date.

Goode's World Atlas. 13th ed. Chicago, Rand McNally, 1971.

One of the better small inexpensive world atlases. Since frequent revisions keep it up to date, it is therefore an excellent tool for finding the most recent information. The balance of maps is good, and no great emphasis is placed on the United States. Contains many thematic maps on economics, physical features, political divisions, climate, temperature, rainfall, vegetation, and resources and products. Many city maps are included. The index lists about 30,000 names with their pronunciations.

ATLASES–UNITED STATES

Rand McNally Commercial Atlas and Marketing Guide. Chicago, Rand McNally, 1876– . (Annual)
The emphasis in this atlas is on the United States, although some maps of foreign countries are included. Part one–about 80 percent of the pages–is devoted to the United States; part two covers every other country except Canada; and part three covers Canada. Each state has a separate map. Besides good detailed maps, the atlas contains statistics related to American economic conditions. Statistical and other related information given includes airline routes, population, retail sales, and population growth. There is a detailed index of cities, counties, transportation, banks, and post offices.

U.S. Geological Survey. *The National Atlas of the United States of America.* Washington, United States Department of the Interior Geological Survey, 1970.
One of the newest and most comprehensive atlases of the United States. Includes 765 maps on principal characteristics of the country including physical features, historical evolution, economic activities, socio-cultural conditions, and administrative subdivisions. The index contains about 41,000 place names. Some special topics treated by maps include earthquakes, solar radiation, seasonal winds, air pollution, battle sites, land use, ethnic population, and ZIP codes. There were many contributors to this atlas, including both government and private agencies.

ATLASES–HISTORICAL

Shepherd, William. *Historical Atlas.* 9th ed. New York, Barnes & Noble, 1964.
This atlas provides chronological coverage of world history from ancient Egyptian history (about 2000 B.C.) to 1964. The 226 pages of maps (there is no text) include maps of ancient and medieval kingdoms, war campaigns and battles, and geographic effects of treaties. Some specific topics covered by the maps include "Territorial Expansion of Rome," "Development of Christianity to 1300," "The Waterloo Campaign," "Campaigns of the American Revolution, 1775-1881," and "The World at War, 1939-1945."

GAZETTEERS AND GEOGRAPHICAL DICTIONARIES

Columbia Lippincott Gazetteer of the World. Edited by Leon E. Seltzer. New York, Columbia University Press, 1962.
A comprehensive gazetteer listing about 130,000 place names with over 30,000 cross references. Information given includes pronunciation, altitude, description, historical importance, natural resources, population, political

location, geographical location, etc. Contains entries for cities, villages, rivers, mountains, historic sites and other geographic features. There are no maps included, and information is generally provided in concise paragraphs.

The Times, London. *The Times Index Gazetteer of the World.* New York, Houghton Mifflin, 1966.
A comprehensive gazetteer listing about 345,000 place names and geographic features. Map references are given for approximately 200,000 names which appear in the *Times Atlas of the World.* The longitude and latitude coordinates given can be used not only with the *Times Atlas* but with any larger scale map which gives parallel and meridian lines. A good source for finding spellings for geographical terms.

Webster's Geographical Dictionary: A Dictionary of Names of Places with Geographical and Historical Information and Pronunciations. Rev. ed. Springfield, Mass., G. & C. Merriam, 1969.
A geographical dictionary listing over 40,000 place names and geographical names, providing information on population, location, altitude, geographical features, historical background. Includes about 200 maps, with information on both current terms (World War II, Korean War) and historic terms (Biblical and medieval).

GUIDEBOOKS

Hotel and Motel Red Book. New York, American Hotel and Motel Directory Corp., 1886– . (Annual)
A directory to hotels and motels in the United States and Canada, with information also on selected foreign cities. Includes the name of the hotel or motel, number of rooms, prices, address, phone number, and the manager's name.

TRAVEL GUIDES

These works are especially useful for the traveller. Each book is usually devoted to one country–Germany, France, etc.–or an area–Europe, South America, etc. Travel guides usually provide information on museums, historic sites, restaurants, hotels, weather and temperature, shopping specialities, etc. Some of the more important series are *Baedeker, Blue Guides, Nagel's Travel Guides,* and *Fodor's Modern Guides.* Each of these series includes books on a number of countries and areas. A popular guide limited to Europe is *Fielding's Travel Guide to Europe.* A series of over 100 volumes limited to the United States is the *American Guide Series.*

BIBLIOGRAPHY

Bagrow, Leo. *History of Cartography.* Rev. and enl. by R. A. Skelton. Cambridge, Harvard University Press, 1964.

Greenhood, David. *Mapping.* Rev. ed. Chicago, University of Chicago Press, 1964.

Le Gear, Clara E. *Maps: Their Care, Repair, and Preservation in Libraries.* Rev. ed. Washington, Library of Congress, 1956.

Raisz, Erwin. *Principles of Cartography.* New York, McGraw-Hill, 1962.

Ristow, Walter W. "Emergence of Maps in Libraries," *Special Libraries* 58: 400-419 (July-August 1967).

Tannenbaum, Beulah, and Myra Stellman. *Understanding Maps: Charting the Land, Sea, and Sky.* Rev. ed. New York, McGraw-Hill, 1969.

U.S. Department of the Army. *Map Reading.* Washington, Government Printing Office, 1956.

Walsh, S. Padraig, comp. *General World Atlases in Print, A Comparative Analysis.* New York, R. R. Bowker, 1966.

CHAPTER 16

REFERENCE MATERIALS:
DIRECTORIES AND HANDBOOKS

INTRODUCTION

Directories are lists of persons, institutions, businesses, or products; they provide such information as addresses, telephone numbers, officers of an organization, purpose or products of a business, etc.

Handbooks serve as ready reference information sources usually in well-defined areas of knowledge (such as stamps or coins), or for certain special forms of information, such as quotations or abbreviations.

Both directories and handbooks contain hard-to-find bits of information available in no other convenient source. The works discussed in this chapter are mostly general, can be used for a number of reasons, and are not narrowly restricted to one subject.

Directories and handbooks on specific subjects are discussed in later chapters. These works are supplemental to encyclopedias and almanacs and often include information not found or not easily found in either of these tools. To locate works on special topics, the library technician can use the library catalog. The form subdivision HANDBOOKS, MANUALS, ETC. is added to the subject heading. For example, PHYSICS–HANDBOOKS, MANUALS, ETC. or ECONOMICS–HANDBOOKS, MANUALS, ETC. Also, Winchell's *Guide to Reference Books* can be consulted to find handbooks and directories for most subjects.

HANDBOOKS–GENERAL

Benet, William Rose, ed. *The Reader's Encyclopedia.* 2nd ed. New York, Crowell, 1965.

An encyclopedic handbook with brief articles on many topics. Emphasis is on literature and the humanities. Includes information on authors, books, literary characters, musical compositions, plots of literary works, historical topics, art, philosophy and works of art. Entries are arranged in alphabetical order with many cross references.

HANDBOOKS–DATES

Douglas, George W. *The American Book of Days.* Rev. ed. New York, H. W. Wilson, 1948.

A day-by-day listing of holidays, festivals, anniversaries, religious holidays, birthdays of famous Americans, and other miscellaneous dates in American history. The index gives entries by subject or topic.

HANDBOOKS-ETIQUETTE

Miller, Llewellyn. *The Encyclopedia of Etiquette: A Guide to Good Manners in Today's World.* New York, Crown, 1967.
A comprehensive work on all aspects of etiquette. Topics covered include weddings, dining, dating, forms of address, business protocol and telephone manners. Contains illustrations and a detailed index.

HANDBOOKS-FIRST FACTS

Kane, Joseph N. *Famous First Facts.* 3rd ed. New York, H. W. Wilson, 1964.
A listing of famous "firsts" in the United States. The latest edition contains about 7,000 entries, including historical events, inventions, and discoveries. The entries are arranged alphabetically by subject; and the index includes personal names, dates, and geographical locations, allowing the user to locate information by several approaches.

HANDBOOKS-GOVERNMENT

United States Government Organization Manual. Washington, Office of the Federal Register, 1935– . (Annual)
The official handbook and guide to all branches of the United States government. Describes in detail the legislative branch, the agencies of the legislative branch, the judicial branch, the executive branch, and other commissions and committees of government. Information given includes chief officers, committee or commission members, a short history, statement of duties, and functions and addresses. Contains a number of useful organization charts.

U.S. Congress. *Official Congressional Directory.* Washington, Government Printing Office, 1809– .
An indispensable aid in locating information about Congress, members of Congress, and other governmental bodies. Sections include such topics as: biographical sketches of members of Congress, lists of Congressional delegations by state, committees of Congress and their membership, administrative assistants of members of Congress, latest election results, executive department personnel, independent agencies and their personnel, the judiciary with biographies of Supreme Court members and list of federal courts, District of Columbia government, lists of foreign diplomats and consuls in the United States, United States diplomatic and consular officers in foreign countries, and maps of Congressional districts. An index is included.

HANDBOOKS-LIBRARIES

The Bowker Annual of Library and Book Trade Information. New York, R. R. Bowker, 1956– . (Annual)
A compilation of statistics and topical articles on all aspects of libraries and the book industry. Materials are presented in four parts: "The Year's Work in Librarianship and Publishing," "National Library and Book Trade Develop-

ments," "Library and Book Trade Associations and Agencies," and "International Library and Book Trade Developments."

HANDBOOKS–OCCUPATIONS

Occupational Outlook Handbook. Washington, Bureau of Labor Statistics, 1949– . (Biennial)
Contains general descriptions of about 700 occupations, both professional and non-professional, for college graduates as well as non-college graduates. Information given on most occupations includes necessary training or qualifications, earnings, and where to find more information on the occupation. The handbook also lists major employers and describes working conditions and future employment trends. This work is supplemented and kept up to date by the *Occupational Outlook Quarterly.*

HANDBOOKS–PARLIAMENTARY PROCEDURES

Robert, Henry M. *Rules of Order.* New and enl. ed. Glenview, Ill., Scott, Foresman, 1970.
The standard handbook on parliamentary procedure. Includes parliamentary rules based on the practice of the U.S. Congress. Explains in great detail how to conduct a meeting, how to make motions, the order of business, and rules for nearly any situation that could arise in conducting a meeting.

HANDBOOKS–QUOTATIONS

Bartlett, John. *Familiar Quotations.* 14th ed., rev. and enl. Boston, Little, Brown, 1968.
One of the best known standard collections of quotations. Includes Biblical quotations and others from 2000 B.C. to modern times, arranged chronologically by author. Sources of quotations are given, along with historical notes tracing their origin. The index includes entries by author, key words of the quotation, and subject. Thus, each quotation has several entries.

Stevenson, Burton Egbert. *The Home Book of Quotations, Classical and Modern.* 10th ed. New York, Dodd, Mead, 1967.
A comprehensive work of over 50,000 quotations arranged alphabetically by subject. The source of each quotation is given if known. The index includes entries by author, key words, and subject. The author entry in the index includes some biographical information–full name, brief identification, and birth and death dates.

HANDBOOKS–STAMPS

Standard Postage Stamp Catalogue. New York, Scott Publications, 1867– . 2v. (Annual)
A comprehensive catalog of stamps issued by the countries of the world. Stamps of each country are illustrated (black and white), brief descriptions are given, and the value of principal stamps is cited.

DIRECTORIES—ASSOCIATIONS

Encyclopedia of Associations. Detroit, Gale Research, 1956– .
An alphabetical listing of national associations in the United States.
Includes all kinds of associations: trade, business, commercial, legal, military,
educational, cultural, fraternal, athletic, and labor, to name only a few. Information given includes the official name, address, officers, membership statistics, number of staff, founding date, publications, and functions and activities.
Contains lists of name changes and defunct associations. A second volume is a
listing by geographic location and index to executive offices, and a third volume
is a loose-leaf supplement with current information for new associations or new
listings.

DIRECTORIES—EDUCATIONAL INSTITUTIONS

Patterson's American Education. Mount Prospect, Ill., Education Directories,
    1904– . (Annual)
This comprehensive educational directory for the United States covers
public and private schools at all levels of education—elementary, secondary, and
colleges and universities. Public school systems are listed by state and by town
within the state. Includes names of school officials at the state, county, and city
levels, addresses of schools, and educational associations. An index includes
private schools and colleges and universities.

American Junior Colleges. 8th ed. Washington, American Council on Educa-
    tion, 1971.
An alphabetical list by state of public and private junior colleges, with the
addition of colleges in the Canal Zone, District of Columbia, Guam, and Puerto
Rico. Information provided for each school includes name, address, admission
requirements, enrollment, curriculum and special programs, history, fees,
teaching staff, student aid, special facilities, library collection, student life and
publications. Appendices list church-related colleges and special programs
offered by colleges.

American Universities and Colleges. 10th ed. Edited by Otis A. Singletary and
    J. P. Newman. Washington, American Council on Education, 1968.
A comprehensive list of institutions of higher education, excluding junior
colleges, arranged alphabetically by state. For each school the following types of
information are given: name, address, history, admission requirements, gradua-
tion requirements, fees, degrees offered, teaching staff by rank and department,
enrollment, special programs, library collection, student aid, publications, and
names of some higher administrators.

DIRECTORIES—MANUFACTURERS

Thomas' Register of American Manufacturers. New York, Thomas Publishing
    Co., 1905– . (Annual)
A comprehensive alphabetical listing of products manufactured in the

United States. Under each product is a list of manufacturers with their geographical location. There are alphabetical indexes to manufacturers and to trade names, and lists of chambers of commerce, business and commercial organizations, and other related bodies.

DIRECTORIES–TELEPHONE BOOKS

All libraries keep copies of the local telephone directory, and many libraries maintain collections of directories for major cities in the United States and major foreign cities. These directories are useful for locating or verifying names, addresses and, of course, phone numbers. The "yellow pages" serve as a guide to local businesses and manufacturers.

CHAPTER 17

REFERENCE MATERIALS: INDEXES

INTRODUCTION

Indexes tell where material can be located. The indexes themselves usually do not contain any information on a subject, but serve only as guides to locate material. The most common index is contained within a book. The library catalog is an index to the collection, and the call number is a direction to the exact location of the item.

In this chapter we will discuss some selected indexes to periodicals, newspapers, book reviews, and dissertations, plus two general interdisciplinary indexes. There are also indexes to specialized materials such as plays, poetry, songs, drama, pamphlets, and government documents, selected examples of which are discussed in later chapters.

To locate specialized indexes in the library catalog the form subdivision INDEXES is added to the subject heading. For example: PERIODICALS–INDEXES, CHEMISTRY–PERIODICALS–INDEXES, SONGS–INDEXES, and POETRY–INDEXES. Examples of specialized indexes can be found under the subject in Winchell's *Guide to Reference Works.*

It is essential to keep in mind that the types of indexes discussed in this chapter are often the only way to locate information in periodicals, newspapers, etc. The library catalog is of very limited value here. Because a subject heading is not in the catalog is no indication that the library does not have material on that subject. It is also important to remember that even if a subject is in the catalog, much more material may be found by using the other indexes.

In many libraries a large part of the collection is in periodicals rather than books, so periodical indexes take on even more importance. In some special science libraries 80 to 90 percent of the collection may consist of periodicals, and in such libraries the periodical indexes rather than the card catalog may be the most important reference tool.

It is also necessary to be aware that comparatively few periodicals are indexed. The major periodical indexes published by the H. W. Wilson Company—all of which are discussed below—index about 1,500 periodicals. It is estimated that over 100,000 periodical titles are published worldwide, and over 40,000 of these are published in the United States. Many periodicals issue their own indexes annually and cumulate them to cover many years. Two examples of these are the cumulative indexes for *Playboy* and for *National Geographic.*

At the end of the section on periodical indexes, two non-index items will be discussed—*Ulrich's International Periodicals Directory* and *Ayer's Directory of Newspapers and Periodicals.* These two, which combine bibliographical and directory-type information, are essential to anyone working with periodicals and newspapers. Because of their importance in using periodicals they are discussed here rather than in the chapter on bibliography.

PERIODICAL INDEXES–GENERAL

The Readers' Guide to Periodical Literature, 1900 to date. New York, H. W. Wilson, 1905– .

This work indexes about 130 titles of popular non-technical periodicals published in the United States. The titles indexed vary from time to time and it is necessary to check the latest issue to see what is currently indexed. The index is an alphabetical dictionary arrangement with author entries, as many subject entries as necessary, and sometimes title entries for each magazine article. The subject headings are based on Library of Congress headings. The entries include the title of the article, author's name, title of the periodical, volume number, inclusive paging of the article, and date of the periodical. If the article includes illustrations or bibliographies, this is indicated. The index is issued twice a month and monthly in July and August. These issues are cumulated quarterly and annually. (See Figure 1.)

An *Abridged Readers' Guide to Periodical Literature* is available for use in elementary schools and small public libraries. This smaller index includes about 40 periodicals selected from the 130 titles indexed in the unabridged edition.

Social Sciences & Humanities Index, 1907 to date. New York, H. W. Wilson, 1916– .

An index to about 200 scholarly American and English periodicals in the social sciences and humanities. It is necessary to check the particular volumes being used to see what periodicals are indexed, since the titles have varied over the years. The entries, arranged alphabetically by subject and title, include the author's name, title of the article, title of the magazine, volume number, inclusive paging of the article, date of the periodical, and illustrations and bibliographies if included. Until 1965 the title was *International Index.* Some subjects currently covered are anthropology, economics, geography, history, literature, philosophy, political science, religion, sociology, and theater arts.

PERIODICAL INDEXES–HUMANITIES

Art Index. 1929 to date. New York, H. W. Wilson, 1933– . (Quarterly)

An index of about 100 periodicals, annuals, and museum bulletins on all aspects of art. Both American and foreign publications are indexed. Some fields included are archaeology, architecture, sculpture, painting, art history, graphic arts, photography, ceramics, and landscape architecture. Articles are entered by author and under as many subjects as necessary. Entries give the author's name, title of the article, title of the periodical or annual, volume number, inclusive paging of the article, date of the periodical, and illustrations. Artists' exhibitions are included and indexed under the artist's name. Book reviews are included under the author's name.

Music Index. Detroit, Information Service, 1949– . (Monthly)

An index to about 200 periodicals on all aspects of music. Both American and foreign titles are included. Entries, which are alphabetical by subject and author, include the same kind of information as the *Art Index.* Some important books are indexed. Issued monthly with annual cumulations.

Figure 1
Entries in *The Readers' Guide to Periodical Literature*

BASKERVILLE, John
  Writing master turned master printer. P. W.
  Schmidtchen. il pors Hobbies 72-104-5 My '67
BASKETBALL fans
  Fans get the booby prize; partisan spectators
  at NBA pro playoffs. F. Deford. il Sports
  Illus 26-28-31 Ap 24 '67
BASKETBALL players
  See also
  Bradley, B.
BASKETBALL teams
  Fans get the booby prize; partisan spectators
  at NBA pro playoffs. F. Deford. il Sports
  Illus 26:28-31 Ap 24 '67
  Sweet revenge; W. Chamberlain with Phila-
  delphia 76ers. Time 89-40 My 5 '67
  Waiting made it sweeter; 76ers dethroned
  the Celtics. F. Deford. il Sports Illus 26:
  54-6 My 8 '67
BASKETS
  Budget basket; how to make a simple flower
9 ─── basket. M. M. Ridenour. il Home Gard 54:
  11 My '67
BASKING sharks. See Sharks
BASS fishing
  Bass are everywhere. W. Davis. il Outdoor
  Life 139:43-5+ My '67
  Midsummer's meal for a largemouth bass.
  R. H. Boyle. il Sports Illus 26:59-60 My 8
  '67
  Ponds upon ponds of bass. T. Janes. il Out-
  door Life 139:66-7+ My '67
BATES, Marston
  Naturalist at large. Natur Hist 76:14+ My
  '67
BATHROOM fixtures
  See also
  Plumbing
BATTLE fatigue. See Neuroses
BAUER, Erwin A.
  Adventuring westward. por Outdoor Life 139:
  49-51+ Ap; 50-3+ My '67 (to be cont)
BAVASI, Buzzie. See Bavasi. E. J.
10 ─── BAVASI, Emil Joseph, and Olsen, Jack
  Dodger story. Sports Illus 26:78-82+ My 15
  '67 (to be cont)
11 ─── BAYER, Ann
  Woman who gave of herself; story. Sat Eve
  Post 240:62-4 My 20 '67

MARKETS
  Great food markets of the world. il Life
  62:64-81 My 12 '67
  See also
  Paris—Markets
MARKETS, Municipal
  Great food markets of the world. il Life
  62:64-81 My 12 '67
MARKETS, Outdoor. See Street trades
MARRANOS. See Maranos
1 ─── MARRIAGE
  Can this marriage be saved? ed. by D. C.
  Disney. See issues of Ladies' home journal
  Innocent game that disrupts marriage. N.
  M. Lobsenz. il Redbook 128:64-5+ Ap '67
  Marriage in the modern world; address, July
  1966. D. Burke. Cath World 205-101-6 My '67
2 ─── Rational ethics says no. G. G. Grisez. Com-
  monweal 86:122-5 Ap 14 '67
  Social life of married couples: its pleasures
  and problems; survey findings. M. M. Hunt.
  il McCalls 94:67-9+ My '67
  You can make yourself sick. F. R. Schreiber
  and M. Herman. Sci Diges 61:24-5 Ap '67
  Young wife's world. H. Valentine. See issues
  of Good housekeeping
3 ─── *See also*
  Divorce
  Remarriage
MARRIAGE counseling
  Can this marriage be saved? ed. by D. C.
  Disney. See issues of Ladies' home journal
MARRIED women
4 ─── ─────Employment
  Do women really want the freedom they've
  won? G. Samuels. il Redbook 129:54-5+
  My '67
  Tomorrow's wife and mother. S. Hertz. Amer-
  ica 116:718-22 My 13 '67
MARS (planet)
  Contamination
  JPL scientists challenge sterilization goals. H.
  M. David. Tech W 20:32-3 My 1 '67
5 ─── MARSH, Tracy H.
6 ─── Unique salt and pepper shaker. Hobbies 72:
7 ─── 84 My '67
8 ───

---

[1] Subject heading	[7] Title of the periodical in which the article appears
[2] Entries for articles on "Marriage" arranged alphabetically by title	[8] Citation to the exact location of the article in the periodical—72:84 My '67 means Volume 72, page 84, May 1967 issue
[3] "See Also" reference to related subjects	
[4] Subdivision of the main subject "Married Women." (If this were typed on a catalog card, it would read "Married Women—Employment")	[9] "See" reference from a subject heading not used to the subject heading used
[5] Author entry	[10] Joint author entry
[6] Title of the article	[11] Note that the story will be continued in another issue

PERIODICAL INDEXES-SOCIAL SCIENCES

Public Affairs Information Service. *Bulletin*. New York, Public Affairs Information Service, 1915– . (Weekly)

A subject index to current periodicals, books, pamphlets, government documents, and special reports. Subjects covered by the indexed materials include political science, government, foreign affairs, economics, sociology, public administration, and other related fields. The entries are alphabetical by subject and contain the author's name, title of the article or book, year of publication for a book, standard periodical citation for articles, and prices for books. About 1,000 periodicals receive selective indexing. Some entries are annotated. Published weekly and cumulated five times a year, the last cumulation being the annual volume. This index is often referred to as *PAIS*.

Business Periodicals Index. New York, H. W. Wilson, 1958– . (Monthly)

An index to about 170 periodicals on every aspect of business. The entries are by subject and include the same type of bibliographic information as other Wilson indexes. Some of the subjects covered by the periodicals indexed are accounting, advertising, taxation, insurance, economics, auditing, marketing, office management and public administration. From 1913 to 1957 this material was included in the *Industrial Arts Index*, also published by H. W. Wilson.

Index to Legal Periodicals, 1909 to date. New York, H. W. Wilson, 1908– .

An alphabetical author and subject index to about 300 legal periodicals. Special sections on individual cases and book reviews are included. Issued monthly with annual cumulations and three-year cumulations. Entries include author's name, title of the article, periodical title, volume number, inclusive paging of the article, and date of the periodical.

PERIODICAL INDEXES-EDUCATION

Education Index, 1929 to date. New York, H. W. Wilson 1930– .

An alphabetical author and subject index to over 200 periodicals in all phases of education. Related material in sociology, psychology, and other social sciences is included. This is an especially important index in libraries serving teachers or in academic institutions with teacher training programs. Entries include author's name, title of the article, periodical title, volume number, inclusive paging of the article, date of the periodical, and bibliographies if included. Issued 10 times a year and cumulated annually.

PERIODICAL INDEXES-LIBRARY SCIENCE

Library Literature, 1921/32 to date. New York, H. W. Wilson, 1933–
(1921-1933, Chicago, American Library Association)

An author and subject index to about 180 periodicals on library science. Coverage is international, with citations for books, pamphlets, theses, dissertations, and microfilm materials. Entries contain author, title of article and periodical, volume number, inclusive paging of the article, date of the periodical, and bibliographies when included. Issued quarterly; cumulated annually and triennially.

PERIODICAL INDEXES–SCIENCE

Applied Science and Technology Index. New York, H. W. Wilson, 1958– . (Monthly)

An alphabetical subject index to over 200 periodicals in all fields of science. Some fields covered are aeronautics, automation, chemistry, electricity, industrial and mechanical arts, physics, geology, and metallurgy. Entries include the same information as other Wilson indexes. Issued 11 times a year with an annual cumulation. From 1913 to 1957 this material was included in the *Industrial Arts Index.*

Biological & Agricultural Index. New York, H. W. Wilson, 1964– .

An alphabetical subject index to about 150 English language periodicals covering all phases of biology and agriculture. Entries include the same information as other Wilson indexes. Issued monthly with annual cumulations. Continues the *Agricultural Index,* which was published from 1919 to 1964.

Engineering Index, 1885 to date. New York, Engineering Magazine, 1892-1919; New York, American Society of Mechanical Engineers, 1920-1934; Engineering Index, 1934– .

A comprehensive, alphabetically arranged subject index to materials on all aspects of engineering. Indexes about 1,500 periodicals in English and many foreign languages–society publications, government publications, conference papers, symposia publications, and other materials devoted to engineering. Entries contain title of the article, periodical title, volume and date of the periodical, inclusive paging of the article, and illustrations. Most entries have brief annotations. Issued monthly with annual cumulations. An author index is included.

PERIODICAL AND NEWSPAPER DIRECTORIES AND UNION LISTS

Ulrich's International Periodicals Directory. 14th ed. New York, R. R. Bowker, 1971. 2v. (Biennial)

A comprehensive list of over 50,000 periodicals published in the United States and over 100 other countries. The periodicals are arranged alphabetically by 223 subject headings and subheadings. A title and subject index is included in the second volume. Contains a list of periodicals no longer published and periodicals which have appeared since the last edition. Entries include most of the following: name of the periodical, title changes, sponsoring organization, year of first issue, subscription price, frequency, name of publications in which indexed, language of text, and a keyword annotation.

A related work useful in larger libraries is *Irregular Serials and Annuals,* 2nd ed., R. R. Bowker, 1972.

N. H. Ayer and Son's Directory of Newspapers and Periodicals. Philadelphia, Ayer & Son, 1880– . (Annual)

A comprehensive list of about 22,000 newspapers and periodicals mostly published in the United States with some foreign publications included. Entries are arranged alphabetically by state and then by city, but periodicals known only by title can be located through an index. Information given for each periodical or newspaper includes its name, frequency of publication, subscription price, editors, political or religious affiliation, circulation statistics, and other vital data. Includes statistical information about states and cities.

Union List of Serials in Libraries of the United States and Canada. 3rd ed. New York, H. W. Wilson, 1965. 5v.

An alphabetical list of serials—mostly periodicals—held by 956 libraries. Entries are made under the latest title, with references to earlier titles. The latest entry includes history of title changes, place of publication, publisher, and date of first publication. A list of libraries and their holdings of the title follow each entry. The fact that some 156,449 titles are listed makes this set a valuable bibliographic tool for interlibrary loan.

New Serial Titles: A Union List of Serials. Washington, Library of Congress, 1950— . (Monthly)

A comprehensive alphabetical list by title of new serials. The entries include the title, place of publication, publisher, and date of origin. Following the entry is a list of libraries and their holdings. Also includes cross references for title changes. Nearly 800 libraries currently cooperate in listing their holdings. Issued monthly with annual cumulations and five- or ten-year cumulations. A valuable tool for locating holdings of serials and for interlibrary loan.

GENERAL INDEX—BOOKS AND ANTHOLOGIES

Essay and General Literature Index, 1900-1933. Edited by M. E. Sears and M. Shaw. New York, H. W. Wilson, 1934. Supplements. New York, H. W. Wilson, 1937— .

An author and subject index to essays and articles found in collections. Some title entries are included. Covers all fields of knowledge—science, humanities, and social sciences. Each issue includes a list of the collections indexed. Issued semi-annually with annual cumulations. Each entry gives the author's name, title of the essay or article, edition of the collection in which the essay or article is printed, title of the collection, and inclusive paging of the essay or article. Over 200,000 essays and articles have been indexed since 1900. (See Figure 2.)

NEWSPAPER INDEXES

The New York Times Index, 1851 to date. New York, The New York Times, 1913— . (Semimonthly)

An alphabetical subject index to the contents of the *New York Times.* Includes many cross references. Entries, listed chronologically under each subject, include date published, page, and column. Most entries give a brief summary of the article. Useful for obituaries, book reviews, and movie reviews. Helpful as a guide to other newspapers once the date of the event is known.

Figure 2
Entries in *Essay and General Literature Index*

1———Bowie, Robert Richardson
2————Strategy and the Atlantic Alliance
3————*In* Kissinger, H. A. ed. Problems of
        national strategy p237-63
4———Bowman, Mary Jean
    The requirements of the labour-market and
        the education explosion
    In The World year book of education,
        1965 p64-80
Bowne, Borden Parker
        About
    Maurer, A. A. Idealism of the schools
    In Gilson, E. H. ed. Recent philosophy,
        Hegel to the present p588-603
Bowra, Sir Cecil Maurice
    Homer's age of heroes
    In Horizon Magazine. The light of the
        past p8-25
Boxing
    Guthrie, Sir T. Other public pleasures
    In Guthrie, Sir T. In various directions
        p201-21
Boy Scouts
    Guthrie, Sir T. Other public pleasures
    In Guthrie, Sir T. In various directions
        p201-21
Boyd, Grace
    The selection and evaluation of materials
        for a comprehensive reading program
    In Conference on Reading. Recent de-
        velopments in reading p187-92
Boyden, Roland William
    The breakdown of corporations
    In Hacker, A. ed. The corporation take-
        over p43-61

Condemned books
    Sinclair, U. B. Poor me and pure Boston
    In The Nation. One hundred years of
        The Nation p151-54
5————*See also* Censorship
Conditioned response. See Reinforcement
    (Psychology)
6—Conduct of life
    ⌠Chesterton, G. K. The spice of life
    │ *In* Chesterton, G. K. The spice of life,
    │   and other essays p161-67
    │Jones, W. T. The ethical life
    │ *In* Jones, W. T. The sciences and the
    │   humanities p224-61
7—⎨Woodward, W. H. The institucion of a
    │   gentleman and Queene Elizabethes
    │   Achademy
    │ *In* Woodward, W. H. Studies in edu-
    │   cation during the age of the
    ⌡   Renaissance, 1400-1600 p295-306
    Woodward, W. H. The institution of a
        nobelman, 1607
    In Woodward, W. H. Studies in edu-
        cation during the age of the
        Renaissance, 1400-1600 p306-22
    Woodward, W. H. Matteo Palmieri
    In Woodward, W. H. Studies in edu-
        cation during the age of the
        Renaissance, 1400-1600 p65-78
5————*See also* Courage; Culture; Ethics;
        Self-culture; Simplicity; Success
Coney Island, N.Y.
    Cummings, E. E. Coney Island
    In Cummings, E. E. E. E. Cummings:
        a miscellany, revised p149-53

[1] Author entry for the essay

[2] Title of the essay

[3] Author and title of the book
    in which the essay is included

[4] Pages in book on which the essay
    can be found

[5] "See also" reference to a related
    subject

[6] Subject heading

[7] A number of essays on the subject
    "Conduct of Life" arranged
    alphabetically by author of
    the essay

BOOK REVIEW INDEXES

Book Review Digest. New York, H. W. Wilson, 1905– . (Monthly)
A digest of book reviews arranged alphabetically by author. Includes a subject and title index in each issue. Reviews are included from about 75 periodicals. Each entry contains the author of the book, title, number of pages, price, and publisher. Following the entry is a brief description of the book and then quotations from book reviews and references to the periodicals where the reviews are found. References include the title of the periodical, volume number, page, and date of the periodical. The number of words in the review is also given. Issued monthly with annual cumulations. Lists about 5,000 fiction and non-fiction titles annually. (See Figure 3).

Book Review Index. Detroit, Gale Research Company, 1965– .
An alphabetical author index to book reviews in about 220 periodicals. The index tells where the review can be found, but does not include quotations from the review. Entries give the author of the book, title, title of the periodical where the review appeared, name of the reviewer, and the volume, date, and page of the periodical. Gives much broader coverage than the *Book Review Digest* and includes less popular titles, covering both fiction and non-fiction reviews in social sciences, humanities, library science, and juvenile literature.

DISSERTATION INDEXES

Dissertation Abstracts International. Ann Arbor, Mich., University Microfilm, 1938– . (Monthly)
An alphabetical subject index to doctoral dissertations accepted by selected universities. The entries include the author of the dissertation, title, a short abstract of the contents, order number, and number of pages. All dissertations can be purchased in microfilm or xerographic reproduction from University Microfilms. Since Volume 30, each issue has consisted of two parts: Section A—Humanities and Social Sciences; Section B—the Sciences and Engineering. Each issue has a keyword index. Volumes 1 through 11 were titled *Microfilm Abstracts*; Volumes 12 through 29, *Dissertation Abstracts.*

Figure 3
Entries in *Book Review Digest*

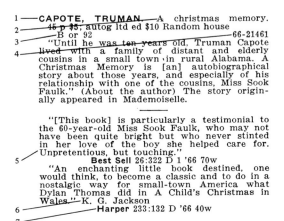

¹ Author of the book

² Title, paging, price, auto-
graphed limited edition,
price, publisher

³ Suggested Decimal Classification number

⁴ Library of Congress card number

⁵ Excerpt from the original
review in *Best Sellers*

⁶ Name of reviewer (if review is
signed)

⁷ Citation to where original review
is published—title of periodical,
volume number, page on which
review is located, date of the
periodical issue, and number of
words in the review

BIBLIOGRAPHY

Collison, Robert L. *Indexes and Indexing.* 3rd rev. ed. New York, De Graff, 1969.

Huff, William H. "Periodicals," *Library Trends* 15:398-419 (January 1967).

La Hood, Charles G. "Newspapers: Directories and Union Lists," *Library Trends* 15:420-29 (January 1967).

Metcalfe, J. W. *Subject Classifying and Indexing of Libraries and Literature.* New York, Scarecrow Press, 1959.

Mott, Frank Luther. *A History of American Magazines.* Cambridge, Harvard University Press, 1930-1968. 5v.

154

CHAPTER 18

REFERENCE MATERIALS: HUMANITIES

INTRODUCTION

In this chapter the library technician will be introduced to some specialized reference materials in subject areas which collectively are called the humanities. Unfortunately, information is not always stored and dispensed in neat little packages. Knowledge is becoming more and more interdisciplinary, a situation which makes reference work more complex. For example, there may be no easy dividing line between religion, mythology, philosophy, or even psychology, on certain points.

The subjects included in our discussion of humanities are philosophy, religion, mythology, literature, fine arts, and applied arts. For each subject several representative reference works have been selected. However, no attempt has been made to present the more specialized works within a subject, since these are best left to the librarian or to the experienced library technician. For example, we will discuss only some general reference books in music, while there are actually hundreds of reference books on music, many of which are limited to special subjects within the field (such as jazz, rock music, classical music, religious music, broadway musicals, or primitive music).

As suggested in the earlier chapters, the materials should be examined personally. One examination is worth a thousand descriptions. The library technician must know how to use the reference materials: a patron will be singularly unimpressed if the person helping him obviously does not know how to use a particular reference tool. The prefaces and other introductory materials provide explanations as to how to use the books, their special features, and their scope. Although it is better to know fewer titles well, rather than to have a vague hesitating familiarity with a greater number, one must still be aware of other materials on the shelves, to get a "feel" for what is available.

The titles discussed here are only representative samples, though hopefully the most useful titles. New materials are always being published, however, which are more up to date and perhaps more useful than older materials. In addition, individual library needs make some materials useful in one library while they are never used in another.

PHILOSOPHY

The Encyclopedia of Philosophy. Edited by Paul Edwards. New York, Macmillan, 1967. 8v.

A collection of nearly 1,500 signed articles covering all aspects of philosophy. The articles are primarily for the layman rather than the expert. Includes bibliographies, some with annotations, and much biographical material. The last volume has a detailed index. Worldwide in scope, and not limited to Western philosophy.

Urmson, James Opie. *The Concise Encyclopedia of Western Philosophy and Philosophers.* New York, Hawthorn, 1960.

This work includes brief articles on philosophers and the general terms and concepts used in philosophy. Written for the layman rather than the expert. Includes some portraits. Arranged alphabetically. A sampling of entries will include such terms as pragmatism, realism, universal, ethics, metaphysics, epistemology, and many others.

The Philosopher's Index. Bowling Green, Ohio, Bowling Green University, 1967– . (Quarterly)

An alphabetical author and subject index to about 100 periodicals in the field of philosophy. Emphasis is on American and British publications, but some other countries are included. Entries give the usual bibliographical information needed to locate the articles.

RELIGION

New Schaff-Herzog Encyclopedia of Religious Knowledge. New York, Funk & Wagnalls, 1908-1912. 13v.

A comprehensive alphabetically arranged work with articles on all aspects of religion and on most religions. The work is written from a Protestant viewpoint. Includes articles on the Bible, theology, denominations, sects, Biblical figures, church doctrines, religious controversies and biographical materials. Contains comprehensive but dated bibliographies. Supplemented by the *Twentieth Century Encyclopedia of Religious Knowledge* (Grand Rapids, Mich., Baker Book House, 1955, 2v.).

Sacramentum Mundi: An Encyclopedia of Theology. New York, Herder & Herder, 1968-1970. 6v.

A comprehensive encyclopedia of theology written from the Catholic viewpoint. Contributors are well-known scholars from all countries. Arranged alphabetically, with the addition of useful, up-to-date bibliographies.

New Catholic Encyclopedia. New York, McGraw-Hill, 1967. 15v.

A comprehensive alphabetically arranged collection of over 17,000 articles covering every aspect of the Catholic Church. Includes articles on art, literature, science, history, canon law, music, social work, and many other topics, with many biographical articles. Illustrations and bibliographies are included with most articles. A detailed index of some 350,000 entries allows easy access to information.

Encyclopaedia Judaica. New York, Macmillan, 1972. 16v.

A comprehensive encyclopedia containing articles on all aspects of Judaism. The arrangement is alphabetical, and the entries range in length from long paragraphs to entries like "Kabbalah," which is 160 pages long. Includes biographical materials with bibliographies of works by and about the authors. Other articles include bibliographical references. Over 8,000 illustrations and portraits are included, and the index (the first volume) contains some 200,000 subjects and entries. Special lists of "Israel Place Names," "Hebrew Newspapers and Periodicals," and "Synagogues" are included.

Strong, James. *The Exhaustive Concordance of the Bible.* New York,
    Abingdon-Cokesbury Press, 1894.
    A concordance to the text of the King James version of the Bible. Every word of the King James version is included, providing access to any Biblical passage. There are many other concordances available for different versions of the Bible.

Mead, Frank S. *Handbook of Denominations in the United States.* 5th ed.
    New York, Abingdon-Cokesbury, 1970.
    A handbook giving brief factual information on over 250 religious denominations. Includes a brief historical account of the religion, its doctrines, and statistical information.
    For detailed information on a particular denomination the library catalog should be checked under the title main entry or the subject entry for that denomination.

MYTHOLOGY

Frazer, Sir James, editor. *The Golden Bough: A Study in Magic and Religion.*
    3rd ed. London, Macmillan, 1955. 13v.
    A classic standard work on primitive religion, magic, customs and folklore. Some titles of individual volumes are "Taboo and the Perils of the Soul," "The Scapegoat," and ". . . the Fire Festivals of Europe and the Doctrine of the External Soul." Volume 12 consists of an extensive bibliography (with works in many languages) and a detailed index. Volume 13 is titled *Aftermath: A Supplement to the Golden Bough.*

Funk & Wagnalls Standard Dictionary of Folklore, Mythology, and Legend.
    Edited by Maria Leach. New York, Funk & Wagnalls, 1949-1950. 2v.
    A comprehensive dictionary with over 7,000 entries. The entries include gods, customs, festivals, folk songs, heroes, demons, rituals, vampires, animal folklore, etc. Entries range from short definitions to lengthy articles with bibliographies.

The Mythology of All Races. Edited by Louis Herbert Gray and others. Boston,
    Marshall Jones, 1916-1932. 13v.
    A major reference work presenting a comprehensive survey of mythology. Arranged by culture, some of the volumes are titled: "Greek and Roman," "Celtic," "Finno-Ugric, Siberian," "Semitic," "Indian," "Chinese," "North American," and "Latin American." Each volume has illustrations, bibliographies, and a table of contents. Volume 13 is a detailed name and subject index to the set.

LITERATURE—AMERICAN

Hart, James D. *The Oxford Companion to American Literature.* 4th ed., rev. and enl. New York, Oxford University Press, 1965.
An alphabetically arranged handbook with entries on a wide range of subjects relating to American literature. Entries include biographical material on authors, bibliographies for selected authors, and summaries of about 900 important novels, plays, stories, essays and poems. There is also information on literary schools, printers, magazines, literary awards, and many other topics. Includes non-literary topics which have influenced American literature.

Literary History of the United States. Edited by Robert E. Spiller and others. 3rd ed. rev. New York, Macmillan, 1963. 2v.
A general survey and bibliography of American literature from the colonial period to the present. Volume one is a series of articles presenting a comprehensive historical survey of American literature, with a select bibliography suitable for the non-specialist. The second volume is a series of bibliographic essays on all kinds of works relating to the history and development of American literature. Includes an index. A new bibliographical supplement was published in 1972.

Kunitz, Stanley J., and Howard Haycraft, editors. *American Authors, 1600-1900: A Biographical Dictionary of American Literature.* New York, H. W. Wilson, 1938.
A ready reference work with biographical essays on 1,300 American authors. Includes bibliographies listing works by and about each author and 400 portraits of various authors. Arranged in alphabetical order. Well-written biographies for the non-specialist.

LITERATURE—ENGLISH

The Cambridge History of English Literature. Cambridge, Cambridge University Press, 1907-1932. 15v.
A standard comprehensive historical survey of English literature from its beginnings to the end of the nineteenth century. The set is arranged in chronological historical order. Each volume includes detailed bibliographies and an index. Volume 15 is a general index to the entire set. Articles are scholarly and suitable for layman and specialist. Includes much biographical material.

Harvey, Sir Paul. *The Oxford Companion to English Literature.* 4th ed. rev. by Dorothy Eagle. New York, Oxford University Press, 1967.
A ready reference handbook with nearly 10,000 short articles on all aspects of English literature. Includes biographical sketches of authors, summaries of literary works, surveys of periods of literary history, and information on literary characters.

Kunitz, Stanley J., and Howard Haycraft, editors. *British Authors Before 1800: A Biographical Dictionary.* New York, H. W. Wilson, 1952.

An alphabetically arranged biographical dictionary of pre-nineteenth century English authors. Includes 650 biographies of selected important authors, with 220 portraits. Includes bibliographies of works by and about each author.

Kunitz, Stanley J., and Howard Haycraft, editors. *British Authors of the Nineteenth Century.* New York, H. W. Wilson, 1936.
A continuation of the previous work with the same kind of information for 1,000 authors. Includes 350 portraits.

LITERATURE–EUROPEAN

Columbia Dictionary of Modern European Literature. Edited by Horatio Smith. New York, Columbia University Press, 1947.
An alphabetically arranged handbook with entries on authors, important literary works and other topics relating to European literature. Some 1,167 articles, all written by specialists, are included. Contains articles on 31 literatures of Continental Europe. Articles include bibliographies, and the biographical sketches list the author's major works both in the original language and in English.

The Penguin Companion to Literature: Europe. Edited by Anthony Thorlby. Rev. ed. London, Penguin, 1971.
An alphabetically arranged dictionary of articles on important European authors. Includes writers, philosophers, scientists, literary characters, and literary schools important in European literature. Biographical entries include name, short biographical sketch, bibliographies of their writings and English translations, and critical comments. Includes an index of authors arranged chronologically by language. Restricted to Continental literature.

Kunitz, Stanley J., and Vineta Colby. *European Authors, 1000-1900: A Biographical Dictionary of European Literature.* New York, H. W. Wilson, 1967.
A ready reference book with short biographical articles on 967 important European authors. Includes novelists, poets, and others, such as historians and scientists who have affected European literature. Includes bibliographies of the author's works, translations of the works, and works about the author.

LITERATURE–CLASSICAL AND OTHERS

The Penguin Companion to Literature: Classical and Byzantine, Oriental and African. Edited by D. R. Dudley and D. M. Lang. Baltimore, Penguin, 1969.
An alphabetically arranged handbook of articles on important writers and others who have contributed to Classical, Byzantine, Oriental, and African literatures. Part one is devoted to the literature of ancient Greece and Rome; part two to Byzantium; part three to the Orient; and part four to African literature. Includes short biographical sketches, bibliographies, and recommended reading lists with each section.

Feder, Lillian. *Crowell's Handbook of Classical Literature.* New York, Crowell, 1964.

An alphabetically arranged handbook of Greek and Roman literature. Includes brief summaries of plays, histories, epics, and other individual works, plus brief biographical sketches of authors and literary characters, definitions of terms, and information on geographic locations. Bibliographic references and translations in English are cited. Entries range from a few lines to 24 pages on *The Odyssey.*

LITERATURE–GENERAL

Kunitz, Stanley J., and Howard Haycraft, editors. *Twentieth Century Authors: A Biographical Dictionary of Modern Literature.* New York, H. W. Wilson, 1942. Supplement, 1955.

A biographical dictionary including over 2,500 biographies of authors from all countries who are well known in English. Most biographies include portraits and bibliographical information. Written in popular style for the layman.

Contemporary Authors. Detroit, Gale Research, 1962– .

The subtitle of this work is "A Bibliographical Guide to Current Authors and Their Works." This reference tool, international in scope, attempts to include all published authors who write in English, without being selective. All persons included are living. Entries include name, birth date, personal information, education, degrees, office and home address, career information, memberships, writings, works in progress, avocational interests, and biographical works about the author. Most entries are written by the biographee.

Cassell's Encyclopaedia of World Literature. Edited by S. H. Steinberg. New York, Funk & Wagnalls, 1954. 2v.

A comprehensive encyclopedia which provides brief factual information on the authors and literatures of the world. The first part gives histories of some 80 different literatures such as Catalan, French, Russian, Eskimo, and Yiddish. Includes 555 articles on such general literary topics as science fiction, poetry, courtly literature, etc. Gives bibliographic references. Part two gives brief biographies of authors who died before August 1, 1914; part three covers authors who were alive after August 1, 1914. Includes bibliographies of works and translations into English.

Magill, Frank N., editor. *Cyclopedia of Literary Characters.* New York, Harper & Row, 1963.

Arranged alphabetically by the title of the literary work with the characters listed in order of importance. Includes 11,949 separate listings and 16,000 characters from 1,300 novels, plays and epics of all literatures. A short 100- to 150-word summary of major characters is given; minor characters are given shorter treatment.

LITERATURE—DRAMA

Gassner, John, and Edward Quinn, editors. *The Reader's Encyclopedia of World Drama.* New York, Crowell, 1969.

   This work is concerned with drama as literature. Includes information on writers, playwrights, plays, literary characters, dramatic theory, and other related topics. Some portraits are included. International in scope, with information on drama in all languages and literatures. Bibliographic references and translations into English are included.

Hartnoll, Phyllis, editor. *The Oxford Companion to the Theatre.* 3rd ed. New York, Oxford University Press, 1967.

   A handbook which provides brief summaries on authors, critics, historians, philosophers, literary characters, places, and historic events having an influence on drama or the theatre. Entries are arranged alphabetically. Articles on authors include bibliographies of their works.

Chicorel Theater Index to Plays in Anthologies, Periodicals, Discs and Tapes. New York, Chicorel Library Publishing Company, 1970— . In progress; 2v. to date.

   An index to help locate individual plays in some 500 anthologies. The arrangement is alphabetical with 9,200 author, title, editor, and anthology entries. Entries provide complete bibliographic information, including editor, title, publisher, price, and number of pages. Publishers' addresses are also given.

LITERATURE—POETRY

Granger, Edith. *Index to Poetry.* 5th ed., rev. and enl. Edited by William F. Bernhardt. New York, Columbia University Press, 1962. Supplement.

   Indexes poems in nearly 700 anthologies. Anthologies indexed in one edition are not necessarily included in the next edition, so many libraries keep all editions. Entries are by title and first line of the poem, but there is also an author and subject index. Information is provided which will help locate the anthology containing the poem.

LITERATURE—SHORT STORIES

Short Story Index, and Supplements, 1950-1963. New York, H. W. Wilson, 1953-1965. 4v.

   An index to nearly 90,000 short stories in some 6,000 collections published from 1949 to 1963, arranged alphabetically by author, title, and subject. A list of the collections indexed is given, with a bibliographic description covering author, title, publisher, and date.

LITERATURE—SPEECHES

Sutton, Roberta B. *Speech Index.* 4th ed., rev. and enl. New York, Scarecrow Press, 1966.

   This alphabetically arranged author, subject, and type-of-speech index to speeches in 259 collections covers speeches from about 1900 to 1965. A helpful guide to the speaker who must address almost any group on any occasion; political talks, toasts, introductions, and presentations are among the subjects included.

ART

Encyclopedia of World Art. New York, McGraw-Hill, 1959-1968. 15v.
   A set of well-written articles on all aspects of art throughout the world. The articles are by world-renowned art scholars, and bibliographies are included with many of them. Each volume contains numerous black and white and color plates of works of art. In art reference works the reproductions are often especially important. Art from all countries and in all historical periods is covered. Articles are arranged in alphabetical order and the last volume is a comprehensive index to the entire set.

The Oxford Companion to Art. Edited by Harold Osborne. Oxford, Clarendon Press, 1970.
   A handbook of definitions of art terms and brief biographical sketches of famous artists. Written as an introduction for the non-specialist. Includes extensive bibliographies. Specifically excluded areas of art are theatre, cinema, dance, and handicrafts.

MUSIC

Apel, Willi. *Harvard Dictionary of Music.* 2nd ed., rev. and enl. Cambridge, Mass., Harvard University Press, 1969.
   A dictionary of musical terms in all phases of musicology and of summaries of various musical works. Includes illustrations and bibliographic references. The arrangement is strictly alphabetical. No biographies are included.

Scholes, Percy Alfred. *The Oxford Companion to Music.* Edited by John Owen Ward. 10th ed., rev. and reset. New York, Oxford University Press, 1970.
   A comprehensive dictionary with definitions of musical terms in all phases of music. Also includes longer articles on special topics in music and about 1,500 biographies.

Ewen, David, comp. *Composers Since 1900: A Biographical and Critical Guide.* New York, H. W. Wilson, 1969.
   A biographical handbook of some 200 composers of all nations who have written since 1900. Both living and dead composers are included. Portraits, biographical references, and lists of major works are given for the composers. Selections were based upon the importance of a composer's works, general interest, and the frequency with which his works are played. A companion volume is also useful: *Great Composers, 1300-1900* (New York, H. W. Wilson, 1966). This work gives about 200 biographies with emphasis on European composers.

Ewen, David. *The New Encyclopedia of the Opera.* New York, Hill & Wang, 1971.

A general ready reference work giving a variety of information on operas. Summaries of the more important operas are included, along with major and minor characters. A list of major characters from minor operas is given. The articles on the sources of operas and on special topics are helpful.

DANCE

Chujoy, Anatole, and P. W. Manchester, comps. *The Dance Encyclopedia.* Rev. and enl. ed. New York, Simon & Schuster, 1967.

A comprehensive encyclopedic guide to all forms of the dance and other related subjects. Includes both short definitions and long scholarly articles. Bibliographic references are included.

TELEVISION

International Television Almanac. New York, Quigley Publishing Company, 1956– . (Annual)

A ready reference almanac containing a variety of information on all aspects of television and television personalities. Includes information on television stations, programs and their producers, stars, organizations, awards, codes, general statistical data, and many other features related to television. Covers television in the United States and some foreign countries.

MOTION PICTURES

Halliwell, Leslie. *The Filmgoer's Companion.* 3rd ed., rev. and expanded. New York, Equinox Books, 1970.

An encyclopedic handbook with over 6,000 entries arranged in alphabetical order, emphasizing American and British film-making and films. Definitions of terms and short summaries of film topics are included. Entries include actors, directors, composers, cinematographers and art directors; entries for actors, the most numerous type of entry, include stage name, real name, birth and death dates, and a list of films in which they appeared.

BIBLIOGRAPHY

Arnold, Charles Harvey. "Philosophy and Religion," *Library Trends* 15:459-77 (January 1967).

Asheim, Lester. *The Humanities and the Library: Problems in the Interpretation, Evaluation and Use of Library Materials.* Chicago, American Library Association, 1957.

Duckles, Vincent. "Music Literature, Music, and Sound Recordings," *Library Trends* 15:494-521 (January 1967).

Humphrey, James. "Architecture and the Fine Arts," *Library Trends* 15:478-93 (January 1967).

Preminger, Alex. "English Literature," *Library Trends* 15:522-49 (January 1967).

CHAPTER 19

REFERENCE MATERIALS: SOCIAL SCIENCES

INTRODUCTION

This chapter will serve as an introduction to some specialized reference materials in subject areas collectively called the social sciences. One subject included in this chapter, history, is sometimes considered better placed in the humanities. However, for our purposes its exact classification is of minor importance, since there is no easy dividing line and the social sciences tend to be interdisciplinary. Political science and history often overlap, education and educational psychology are obviously overlapping, and sociology is often difficult to separate from psychology or certain areas of economics. In the last example, for instance, the study of welfare economics may encompass social theory, economic statistics, political factors, and historical precedents.

Initially, however, the library technician need not be overly concerned with these complexities. The reference materials presented below should be studied with ready reference questions in mind.

The subjects included in our coverage of the social sciences are anthropology, archaeology, ethnic studies, education, history, geography, law, political science, psychology, business and economics, and sociology. Of the thousands of available materials, only a few basic ones are presented here, which it is hoped will be the most helpful for ready reference work.

GENERAL

International Encyclopedia of the Social Sciences. New York, Macmillan & The Free Press, 1968. 17v.

A comprehensive alphabetically arranged encyclopedia with articles on the following areas: anthropology, economics, geography, history, law, political science, psychiatry, sociology and statistics. Articles are scholarly and are written for the educated layman. Biographies are included for 600 key figures in the social sciences. Bibliographies follow each article. Volume 17 is an exhaustive index with complete references to page and volume number for each entry.

Gould, Julius, and William L. Kolb, editors. *A Dictionary of the Social Sciences.* New York, Free Press, 1964.

A general social science dictionary with some emphasis on terms in political science and sociology. Gives definitions and history of how terms have been used. Many terms with widely accepted definitions are excluded. British spelling is used.

ARCHAEOLOGY

The Concise Encyclopedia of Archaeology. Edited by Leonard Cottrell. New York, Hawthorn Books, 1960.

A compilation of articles on archaeology and biographies of archaeologists, written for the non-specialist. Also gives concise definitions of terms used in archaeology. Includes illustrations, some in color, and a bibliography for further reading. Little emphasis is placed on classical Greek and Roman archaeology.

ETHNIC STUDIES

Reference Encyclopedia of the American Indian. Edited by Bernard Klein and
    Daniel Icolari. New York, Klein, 1967.
    A general handbook divided in 17 sections, each covering a special topic related to Indians. Sections cover such topics as government agencies, museums, libraries, associations, reservations, schools, visual aids, government publications, magazines and periodicals, and a biographical "who's who." Each section is arranged either alphabetically or geographically. A bibliography is included and entries are listed alphabetically by author and by subject.

The Negro Handbook. Compiled by the editors of Ebony. Chicago, Johnson
    Publishing Company, 1966.
    A collection of essays on the Negro's contribution to life in the United States. There are 18 sections on such topics as population, civil rights, crime, education, the economy, armed forces, farms and farming, sports, statistical information, and biographical information.

Ploski, Harry A., and Ernest Kaiser, editors. *The Negro Almanac.* 2nd ed. New
    York, Bellwether, 1971.
    A comprehensive collection of information on the Negro in the United States. The book is divided into 32 sections devoted to such topics as historical review, historical landmarks, legal status, growth and distribution of population, black artists, jazz, black firsts, and soul food. Most sections include statistical information. Contains a detailed index.

Grebler, Leo, Joan W. Moore, and Ralph C. Guzman. *The Mexican-American
    People: The Nation's Second Largest Minority.* New York, Free Press,
    1970.
    This work is a socio-economic study of Mexican-Americans in the Southwest. It is not a reference book in the usual sense, but it can be a useful source for reference information. Includes 23 chapters under three general sections: "Historical Perspective," "The Individual and the Social System," and "Political Interaction." A statistical appendix, lengthy bibliography, and detailed index are included.

EDUCATION

The Encyclopedia of Education. New York, Macmillan, 1971. 10v.
    A comprehensive work containing 1,000 signed articles on all phases of education. It is international in scope, although its primary concern is with education in the United States. Bibliographies are included with the articles. The detailed index lists articles under as many subjects as necessary.

SPORTS

Menke, Frank G. *The Encyclopedia of Sports.* 4th rev. ed. South Brunswick, N.J., A. S. Barnes, 1969.
　　Covers almost every major and minor sport and recreational activity, with information on the history of the sport, its rules, and names of record-holders and records. Many statistics are included. Emphasis is placed on the United States.

HISTORY

Adams, James Truslow, editor. *Dictionary of American History.* 2nd ed. rev. New York, Scribner, 1940-1961. 6v.
　　Contains concise articles on both specific events and broader topics in American history. There are no biographies, but bibliographies are included with articles. Covers American history through 1960. Arranged alphabetically with a detailed index of over 250 pages.

Commager, Henry Steele. *Documents of American History.* 8th ed. New York, Appleton-Century-Crofts, 1968.
　　A collection of important historical documents relating to American history. Documents, preceded by a brief introduction and bibliographical references, are arranged chronologically and indexed by subject, name, and title. Some of the documents included are the Declaration of Independence, Constitution of the United States, The Atlantic Charter, and over 700 others. Also contains acts, treaties, Supreme Court decisions, speeches and other types of documents.

Morris, Richard B., editor. *Encyclopedia of American History.* Enl. and updated. New York, Harper & Row, 1970.
　　A collection of facts about American history and American institutions. The arrangement is both chronological and topical. Section I is a chronological listing of important events and facts. Section II is a topical chronological tracing of topics such as "The Expansion of the Nation," "Population and Immigration," and "The American Economy." Section III gives biographical sketches of a select number of notable Americans. A detailed index allows easy access to particular events or names, and many helpful maps, charts, and statistics are included.

Webster's Guide to American History: A Chronological, Geographical, and Biographical Survey and Compendium. Springfield, Mass., G. & C. Merriam, 1971.
　　A chronological listing by year and day of important facts and events in American history. Many charts and tables cover such events and topics as the Civil War, World War II, population, Indians, and natural resources. Special lists give information on presidential candidates, members of Congress, Supreme Court justices, drama awards, and many other topics. The biographical section is over 500 pages long.

Langer, William L. *An Encyclopedia of World History.* 5th ed., rev. & enl. Boston, Houghton Mifflin, 1972.

This chronological outline of ancient, medieval, and modern history covers events from the palaeolithic period to modern times. A detailed table of contents breaks down the outline into general periods of history, then by event or geographically. Includes maps and helpful genealogy tables. Appendices give lists of such things as "Roman Emperors," "Byzantine Emperors," "The Caliphs," "Roman Popes," and "Presidents of the United States." The index is a detailed listing of names, events, and subjects.

GEOGRAPHY

Monkhouse, F. J. *A Dictionary of Geography.* 2nd ed. London, Arnold, 1970.

This dictionary provides definitions for nearly 4,000 terms used in geography, with the emphasis on current usage in texts and periodicals. Definitions include statistical data where helpful (lists of longest rivers, highest mountains, etc.). Terms from related fields of oceanography, climate and weather, and cartography are included.

LAW

Black, Henry Campbell. *Black's Law Dictionary: Definitions of the Terms and Phrases of American and English Jurisprudence, Ancient and Modern.* Rev. 4th ed. by the publisher's editorial staff. St. Paul, Minn., West Publishing Company, 1968.

The standard law dictionary used in many American libraries. The arrangement is alphabetical. Definitions include quotations and citations of legal cases along with titles of books in which the cases can be found.

POLITICAL SCIENCE

Municipal Year Book. Washington, International City Managers' Association, 1934– . (Annual)

A handbook of current information on cities in the United States. Both topical essays and statistical information are included. A recent edition presents information in eight sections: city government; science, technology, and cities; public safety; counties; public manpower; municipal finance; bibliographic references; and directories to agencies. A good source for local financial and statistical information.

Book of the States. Lexington, Ky., Council of State Governments, 1935– . (Biennial)

A handbook of current information on the states of the United States. Includes a variety of statistical information and many topical articles. A recent edition presents information in seven sections: constitutions and elections, legislatures and legislation, judiciary, administrative agencies, finances, intergovernmental relations, and major state services (i.e., education, law enforcement, etc.). Also gives current state officials, official state flowers, birds, nicknames, songs, mottoes, etc.

Worldmark Encyclopedia of the Nations: A Practical Guide to the Geographic, Historical, Political, Social & Economic Status of All Nations, Their International Relationships, and the United Nations System. 4th ed. New York, Worldmark Press/Harper & Row, 1971. 5v.

A general survey of the nations of the world and international organizations. As the subtitle above indicates, the work is comprehensive in scope, attempting to cover all important aspects for each nation. Each of the five volumes covers a specific topic or geographic area: Volume 1, United Nations; Volume 2, America; Volume 3, Africa; Volume 4, Asia and Australasia; and Volume 5, Europe. For each country information is given on trade, industry, income, labor, migration, armed forces, flora and fauna, and population.

Yearbook of the United Nations. New York, United Nations, 1947– . (Annual)

A yearbook devoted to covering the year's activities of the United Nations and its specialized related agencies. Includes essay material on most topics with many documents of related interest. There are two parts to the yearbook, the first part covering the United Nations and the second part the specialized agencies. Voting records on resolutions are also included. The index includes entries for subjects, countries, and names.

PSYCHOLOGY

Psychological Abstracts. Washington, American Psychological Association, 1927– . (Bimonthly)

A comprehensive listing of books and periodical articles in English and foreign languages on all aspects of psychology. A short abstract in English is given for each entry. Material is grouped by special subjects such as "General," "Experimental Psychology," "Social Psychology," "Personality," and "Educational Psychology." Each issue has an author and subject index. Issued bimonthly with annual cumulations. A related work, *Psychological Index*, covers similar material from 1894 to 1935, when it ceased publication.

Drever, James. *A Dictionary of Psychology.* Rev. by Harvey Wallerstein. Baltimore, Penguin, 1964.

An alphabetically arranged dictionary with brief definitions for about 4,000 terms commonly used in psychology.

BUSINESS AND ECONOMICS

The McGraw-Hill Dictionary of Modern Economics: A Handbook of Terms and Organizations. New York, McGraw-Hill, 1965.

A combination dictionary of economic terms and directory of organizations concerned with economics. Part one gives definitions for some 1,300 terms used in economics and related fields. Part two is an alphabetical listing of about 200 public and private agencies, both American and foreign, concerned with economics and related fields. Definitions, written for the layman, include graphs, charts, and other explanatory material.

Encyclopedia of Business Information Sources. 2nd ed. Detroit, Gale Research Company, 1970. 2v.

A bibliography of materials on sources for business information. Includes references to books, periodicals, directories, handbooks, bibliographies, and organizations. The first volume is arranged alphabetically by subject or type of business such as "accident insurance," "steel industry," "zinc industry," etc., with references listed for each one. The second volume is arranged by geographic location and appropriate bibliographic references are listed for cities, towns, states, regions, and nations. This is a guide to help locate information; it does not itself contain the information.

Economic Almanac. New York, National Industrial Conference Board, 1940– .

A compilation of statistical information on every aspect of industry and commerce in the United States and Canada. The information is presented in nearly 600 tables in 22 topical sections. Some examples of these topical sections are: "Population," "Labor," "Material Resources," "Agriculture," "Transportation," "Personal Consumption and Savings," "Public Finance," and "International Economic Comparisons." A glossary of "terms frequently used in economic and business reports" is included. The table of contents is helpful in locating information, but there is also a detailed index.

Commodity Year Book. New York, Commodity Research Bureau, 1939– .

This compilation of statistical data for about 100 different commodities provides essential information on production, prices, imports, exports, and other information of importance to a particular commodity. Includes both current and retrospective data—the 1971 edition gives data from 1958 to 1971. Some examples of commodities treated are alcohol, coal, corn oil, glass, lard, iron and steel, honey, pork bellies, and soybean oil. A brief introduction precedes each commodity.

SOCIOLOGY

Sociological Abstracts. New York, Sociological Abstracts, 1952– .

An index and abstract to the periodical literature in all areas of sociology. International in scope with articles in the English language and over 20 foreign languages. All abstracts are in English. The entries are by major areas such as "Methodology and Research Technology," "Sociology: History and Theory," "Social Differentiation," "Sociology of Religion," and "Studies in Poverty." A recent volume used 27 major areas with 57 sub-sections under the areas. A complete bibliographic citation is given for each article and is followed by a short abstract. Author, periodical, and subject indexes are included.

Theodorson, George A., and Achilles G. Theodorson. *A Modern Dictionary of Sociology.* New York, Crowell, 1969.

A dictionary of terms and concepts used in sociology. Includes material from related fields such as cultural anthropology, psychology, statistics, political science, and philosophy. Emphasis is placed on current usage; if more than one definition is cited, the most relevant one is given first. Some bibliographic references are included. Designed for both undergraduate and graduate students.

Encyclopedia of Social Work. New York, National Association of Social Workers, 1929– . 2v. 1971 ed.

A collection of articles on topics relevant to social work and of biographies of prominent persons in the field. The arrangement is alphabetical with topical articles and biographies in one sequence. Bibliographies are included with many entries. Some typical entries are "Addiction: Alcohol," "Family Breakdown," "Crime and Delinquency," "Family and Population Planning," "Sexual Deviance," "Social Insurance," and many others. Appended are 52 special tables of statistics on "demographic and social welfare trends." A detailed index is found in Volume 2.

BIBLIOGRAPHY

Beckham, Rexford S. "Anthropology," *Library Trends* 15:685-703 (April 1967).

Brock, Clifton. "Political Science," *Library Trends* 15:628-47 (April 1967).

Coman, Edwin T. "Economics," *Library Trends* 15:601-615 (April 1967).

Daniel, Robert S. "Psychology," *Library Trends* 15:670-84 (April 1967).

Felland, Nordis. "Geography," *Library Trends* 15:704-709 (April 1967).

Forman, Sidney, and Ruby L. Collins. "Education," *Library Trends* 15: 648-69 (April 1967).

Hoselitz, Bert F., editor. *A Reader's Guide to the Social Sciences.* Rev. ed. New York, Free Press, 1970.

Lewis, Peter R. *The Literature of the Social Sciences: An Introductory Survey and Guide.* London, The Library Association, 1960.

McDonald, Gerald D. "American History," *Library Trends* 15:718-29 (April 1967).

Price, Miles O. "Anglo-American Law," *Library Trends* 15:616-27 (April 1967).

White, Carl M. *Sources of Information in the Social Sciences: A Guide to the Literature.* Totowa, N.J., Bedminster Press, 1964.

CHAPTER 20

REFERENCE MATERIALS: SCIENCE

INTRODUCTION

The reference materials presented in this chapter are concerned with the physical and applied sciences. The specialized subject areas covered here are biology, chemistry, earth sciences, engineering, mathematics, and physics.

When using science materials in particular, it is often essential to have the latest edition in hand. Although the materials discussed below are frequently updated, they tend to present a fairly stable body of basic scientific knowledge. The time-lag inherent in publishing a book means that books are not at the moment the best format for presenting the latest information. This time-lag must be remembered when using reference books in the sciences. Periodicals and abstracts tend to be more heavily used in the sciences, since these media are concerned with presenting the most current information. In fact, periodicals form a greater percentage of science collections than they do in the humanities or social sciences.

The emphasis in this chapter will be on dictionaries, encyclopedic treatments, and handbooks, all of which are meant to answer factual questions. Less emphasis is placed on abstracts and those materials more related to literature searches. Of course, some specialized scientific periodical indexes were discussed in an earlier chapter. Two important abstracts are described because every library technician should at least be aware of their existence and their physical location in the library—*Chemical Abstracts* and *Biological Abstracts.*

GENERAL

McGraw-Hill Encyclopedia of Science and Technology: An International Reference Work. 3rd ed. New York, McGraw-Hill, 1971. 15v.

A comprehensive encyclopedia with over 7,000 articles on all aspects of science and technology. Articles are arranged alphabetically by subject, and the last volume is an index which provides easy access to subjects covered. Includes illustrations, charts, and bibliographies. The articles, written for the layman rather than the expert, give general introductions to each branch of the sciences. Clinical medicine and biographical material are, however, excluded. Kept up to date between editions by the *McGraw-Hill Yearbook of Science and Technology.*

Van Nostrand's Scientific Encyclopedia. 4th ed. Princeton, N.J., D. Van Nostrand, 1968.

An alphabetically arranged encyclopedia with over 16,000 entries for terms and concepts used in all fields of science. Includes many illustrations. Written for both the layman and the scientist. Some of the areas of science covered are aeronautics, biochemistry, engineering, metallurgy, nuclear science and engineering, planetary exploration, and zoology. No biographical material is included.

BIOLOGICAL SCIENCES

Biological Abstracts. Philadelphia, BioSciences Information Service, 1926– .
(Semi-monthly)
   A comprehensive index and abstract to over 100,000 articles each year
found in some 5,500 periodicals, yearbooks, conference proceedings, and other
important reports. Periodicals from over 90 countries are included, and the
abstracts are in English regardless of the language of the article. Abstracts are
grouped into five basic areas (general biology, basic medical sciences, micro-
biology, plant sciences, and animal sciences), while a "Subject Classification
Outline" in each issue lists the special subdivisions covered. Each issue also has
an author index. One area excluded is clinical medicine.

Gray, Peter, ed. *The Encyclopedia of the Biological Sciences.* 2nd ed. New
   York, Van Nostrand Reinhold, 1970.
   Written for the nonspecialist and student, this encyclopedia has about
2,000 articles on all phases of the biological sciences. The arrangement is alphabetical with a detailed index. Some biographical articles are included for people
important in various fields of biology. Usefulness of the articles is enhanced by
illustrations, tables and diagrams (where appropriate), and bibliographies.

Henderson, I. F., and W. D. Henderson. *A Dictionary of Biological Terms.*
   8th ed. Princeton, N.J., Van Nostrand, 1963.
   Gives concise definitions for some 18,000 terms used in biology, botany,
anatomy, zoology, and other biological sciences. The derivation and pronunciation are given for each term, and the arrangement is alphabetical.

CHEMISTRY

Chemical Abstracts. Easton, Pa., American Chemical Society, 1907– .
   A comprehensive index and abstract to nearly 250,000 articles each year
found in over 9,000 journals published in the United States and nearly 100
foreign countries. The abstracts are in English regardless of the original language
of the article. Each issue has a table of contents with a topical breakdown of the
contents. Author and subject indexes are issued several times a year and cumulated
every five years—formerly every ten years.
   This work can be complex to use, and the library technician must be
thoroughly familiar with it before doing anything more than showing the patron
where it is located.

The Condensed Chemical Dictionary. 7th ed., completely rev. and enl. New York,
   Reinhold, 1966.
   An alphabetically arranged dictionary of chemicals. Each entry includes
the name of the chemical, chemical formula, physical properties, derivation,
grades, containers, uses, shipping regulations, and in some cases the trade name.

Handbook of Chemistry and Physics. Cleveland, Chemical Rubber Company,
   1913– .
   This handbook, which contains all kinds of chemical and physical data, is

divided into six major sections: Mathematical Tables, Elements and Inorganic Compounds, Organic Compounds, General Chemistry, General Physical Constants, and Miscellaneous. A detailed table of contents lists the contents of each section, and an index is useful for locating more specific information.

EARTH SCIENCES

The McGraw-Hill Encyclopedia of Space. New York, McGraw-Hill, 1968.
A general encyclopedia with articles on space, space exploration, and space travel. The work is divided into nine sections such as the rocket, artificial satellites, space navigation and electronics, man in space, and astronomy and astrophysics. Includes many illustrations. Written in popular style for the nonspecialist and student.

American Geological Institute. *Dictionary of Geological Terms.* Garden City, N.Y., Doubleday, 1962.
A dictionary containing over 7,500 terms used in geology and related sciences. An abridged version of a more comprehensive dictionary. Intended for use by nonspecialists, teachers, and students of geology.

ENGINEERING

Potter, James H., editor. *Handbook of the Engineering Sciences.* Princeton, N.J., Van Nostrand, 1967. 2v.
A comprehensive handbook with topical articles and definitions of terms in every area of engineering. Includes such fields of engineering as civil, space, aeronautical, electrical, industrial, etc. The first volume covers the basic sciences and the second the applied sciences.

MATHEMATICS

The Universal Encyclopedia of Mathematics. New York, Simon & Schuster, 1964.
A mathematics encyclopedia written for the high school and college student. Part 1 is devoted to articles on topics, concepts, and methods in mathematics. The arrangement is alphabetical. Part 2 contains mathematical formulae for arithmetic, algebra, geometry, trigonometry, calculus, and other special functions. Part 3 contains mathematical tables for such things as roots, powers, logarithms, and trigonometric functions.

The International Dictionary of Applied Mathematics. Princeton, N.J., Van Nostrand, 1960.
A dictionary giving definitions and descriptions for some 7,000 terms and methods used in mathematics and the application of mathematics to 31 fields of physical sciences and engineering. The arrangement is alphabetical. A special index lists mathematical terms in French, German, Russian, and Spanish.

MEDICINE

Dorland's Illustrated Medical Dictionary. 24th ed. Philadelphia, Saunders, 1965.
A standard dictionary of medical terms used in many libraries. Entries
include spelling, pronunciation, etymology, and a concise definition. Illustrations, plates, and tables enhance the usefulness of the dictionary and help make
some definitions more meaningful.

PHYSICS

Encyclopaedic Dictionary of Physics. New York, Macmillan, 1962-1964. 9v.
Supplements. New York, Pergamon Press, 1966– .
A comprehensive encyclopedic dictionary with over 20,000 topical articles.
The arrangement is alphabetical with an author and subject index. The first supplemental volume is a multilingual glossary of terms in English, French, German,
Spanish, Russian, and Japanese. Articles cover all aspects of physics as well as
such related fields as biophysics, mathematics, astronomy, geophysics, chemistry, etc. No biographical information is included. Most articles give bibliographical references and cross references to articles on related subjects. Primarily
for the specialist and graduate student.

The International Dictionary of Physics and Electronics. 2nd ed. Princeton,
N.J., Van Nostrand, 1961.
A dictionary of terms, concepts, and physical laws in the fields of physics
and electronics. Useful for both specialists and nonspecialists. Some preliminary
articles on the history and principles of physics are included. The arrangement is
alphabetical. An index of terms in French, German, Russian, and Spanish is
included.

Handbook of Physics. Edited by E. U. Condon and H. Odishaw. 2nd ed. New
York, McGraw-Hill, 1967.
An encyclopedic treatment of physics arranged in nine sections, each
with a number of chapters on specialized topics. Some examples of the broader
sections are mathematics, mechanics of particles and rigid bodies, electricity and
magnetism, optics and nuclear physics. Each chapter has a bibliography.

PHOTOGRAPHY

The Focal Encyclopedia of Photography. Rev. ed. New York, McGraw-Hill,
1969.
This alphabetically arranged encyclopedic dictionary provides articles and
definitions of terms on all aspects of photography. Contains biographical information, 1,750 illustrations, and bibliographical references for further reading.
Some examples of entries are chromatic aberration, churches, C.I.E. standards,
line of beauty, over-run lamp, and zoo praxiscope.

ASTRONOMY

Rudaux, Lucien, and G. De Vaucouleurs. *Larousse Encyclopedia of Astronomy.*

2nd ed. New York, Prometheus Press, 1962.
A general encyclopedic treatment of all phases of astronomy. Information is presented in four sections: general information, the sun and the planets, the stars and astronomical instruments. Includes many illustrations and some color plates. Written for the layman and student.

BIBLIOGRAPHY

Atherton, Pauline. "Physics," *Library Trends* 15:847-51 (April 1967).

Bamber, Lyle E. "Biology," *Library Trends* 15:829-35 (April 1967).

Blanchard, J. Richard. "Agriculture," *Library Trends* 15:880-95 (April 1967).

Brodman, Estelle, and Miwa Ohta. "Medicine," *Library Trends* 15:896-908 (April 1967).

Jenkins, Frances Briggs. *Science Reference Sources.* 5th ed. Cambridge, Mass., M.I.T. Press, 1969.

Lohwater, A. J. "Mathematical Literature," *Library Trends* 15:852-67 (April 1967).

Mellon, M. G., and Ruth T. Power. "Chemistry," *Library Trends* 15:836-46 (April 1967).

Neu, John. "The History of Science," *Library Trends* 15:776-92 (April 1967).

Phelps, Ralph H. "Engineering," *Library Trends* 15:868-79 (April 1967).

Shipman, Joseph C. "General Science," *Library Trends* 15:793-815 (April 1967).

CHAPTER 21

REFERENCE MATERIALS:
SPECIALIZED NON-BOOK MATERIALS

INTRODUCTION

In this chapter we will discuss some important sources for locating non-book materials. Specifically, we will cover bibliographic sources for pamphlets, overhead transparencies, motion cartridges, films, filmstrips, video tapes, records, tapes, globes, art prints, and microfilm.

While the book is still the most used item in libraries, non-book materials are playing an increasingly important role in disseminating information. We have already discussed some important indexes to the most popular non-book materials: periodicals and newspapers. Maps, another popular non-book item, have also been discussed. Other non-book materials found in libraries are manuscripts, flyers, clippings, annual reports, posters, prints, charts, music scores, pictures, photographs and post cards.

Before discussing the reference sources, it will be useful to give a brief introduction to some of the more commonly used non-book materials.[1]

NON-BOOK MATERIALS
Films

Motion pictures, filmstrips, and slides are used in many libraries. In some academic libraries the library may handle only a small portion of this film material with the audiovisual department handling the rest. In some libraries the "software" (i.e., the films) is available in the library, while the "hardware" (i.e., the projectors) is available in the audiovisual department. In other libraries, both "software" and "hardware" are available in the library. In still other libraries the "software" is available in the library and the patron makes his own arrangements for the "hardware." The library technician should be familiar with what is available and what is not available to the patron because the film media, unlike the book, require a variety of equipment to make them useful. Some of the equipment necessary to utilize even a modest film collection are 8mm projectors, 16mm projectors, wall screens, filmstrip projectors, filmstrip viewers, rear projectors for 8mm cartridges, slide projectors, speakers, and overhead projectors. Special viewing rooms must also be made available for in-library use of the material. The library technician working with films should be familiar with the equipment so that he will be able to operate it, to give instructions to patrons on how to use it, and to make minor repairs.

Films will normally be stored in special containers and placed in cabinets or shelves. The classification system used for films may be different from the system used for the book collection. If the book classification scheme is not used, the films may be shelved by title, by subject, by accession number, or by some other local scheme. In any case the library technician should be familiar with the physical location of film materials, what is available, and how it is classified. If films are available on a rental basis, it will be necessary to be familiar with the fee schedule and the procedures for renting the material. And, like books, films must be examined regularly for damage so that repairs can be made or the film replaced.

Records and Tapes

Records and tape recordings are one of the most common of library resources. While music recordings usually comprise the majority of most collections, libraries may also have recordings of plays, poetry readings, speeches, and interviews. Oral history is a rapidly developing area and many libraries, especially larger libraries, are building large collections. Local oral history projects, conducted by library staff or local historians, may consist of interviews with local people: early settlers, elected officials, etc.

Records and tapes, like films, require special equipment to make them useful—record players, headphones, amplifiers, tape recorders, and cassette players. Because of rapidly advancing technology the library staff must keep up with late developments and how they may affect the usefulness of the current equipment. The library technician should be familiar with the library's equipment in order to operate it, to explain the oeration to patrons, and to make minor repairs.

Records and tapes are usually shelved in a separate area, using specialized shelving and cabinets. The classification system may be considerably different from the one used for books. Instead of Dewey or Library of Congress classification, records and tapes may be arranged by subject, title, composer, accession number, or some other local scheme. Because of its simplicity, the accession number arrangement is one of the more popular systems in use.

Microfilm

Microfilm is playing an increasingly important role in developing library collections. This situation is particularly true in academic libraries, which require highly specialized research materials. Libraries faced with lack of space and money have started to purchase more microfilm because of its great space-saving quality and relatively low cost compared to books and bound periodicals. Unfortunately, there is often considerable reluctance on the part of patrons to use microfilm. This reluctance is due to several factors: 1) the extra work involved in using microfilm-readers, 2) the relative discomfort involved in using poor microfilm-readers for long periods of time, 3) the necessity of using microfilm only in the library,[2] and 4) the ingrained preference for the book or periodical format.

Because of the variety of microfilm formats, libraries must purchase a number of different kinds of microfilm-readers or else avoid purchasing certain types of microfilm. For example, the 1972 edition of *Guide to Microforms in Print* lists microfilms in the following formats: reel microfilm (16mm, 35mm, and 16mm cartridges); micro-opaque cards (3" x 5", 4" x 6", 5" x 8", and 6" x 9"); microfiche (3" x 5", 9cm x 12cm, and 4" x 6"); shelf microfiche (a bound volume with text on 4" x 6" microfiche); and ultramicrofiche (4"x 6" with 3,200 pages per sheet). Unfortunately, this lack of standardization has been expensive for libraries, since microfilm-readers cost from a few hundred dollars to several thousand dollars. The most common formats for microfilm are 16mm and 35mm reels, microfiche (a sheet form of microfilm usually in 3" x 5" and 4" x 6" sizes), and microcard (microfilm on 3" x 5" cards). Each format requires special microfilm-readers. Most microfilm is available as either negative or positive film; negative microfilm is light print on a dark background, and positive microfilm is dark print on a light background.

Like records and films, microfilmed materials may be classified in a system different from the book collection. Microfilm is stored in special cabinets fitted for either reels, cards, or fiche. Microfilm-readers will be nearby, usually in a semi-dark room suitable for microfilm reading. The library technician who works with microfilm should be thoroughly familiar with the operation of the microfilm-readers, and should be able to give clear instruction to patrons on how to use the readers. In an area where reader resistance is great, every effort must be made to make microfilm easy to use. Nothing would discourage a patron more than to see a library staff member fumble for five minutes trying to prepare microfilm for use.

Art Prints

Art prints are purchased by many libraries and made available for long-term loans with or without charge. Prints may be framed or unframed depending on the purpose they serve. A variety of prints covering various periods of art history will usually be purchased, with some emphasis on those periods of most interest to the community being served. If the prints are available on a rental basis, the library technician should be aware of the fees and the procedures for charging out prints.

Prints are often kept in alphabetical order by artist or by subject. Although some special classification schemes are available, they are generally used only in larger collections. As with other special materials, the library technician should know how prints are organized and where they can be found.

Television and Video Tape

The use of video tape to record special programs can make television programs a new non-book material available to library patrons. Films and special programs, both recreational and educational, can be recorded on video tape for playback on demand. Through the use of such video tape collections in some academic libraries, previously recorded lectures or special television programs can be played by students at their convenience either on special television sets in the library or even at home. It is possible that in the near future libraries will have extensive collections of video tapes for patrons to charge out for home use.

Catalog Entries

The entries made in the library catalog for non-book materials may differ from those made for books. Sometimes special color cards are made for non-book materials. If separate catalogs are set up for special materials, there may be no entries in the general catalog. In some libraries main entry cards are placed in the catalog, but no added or subject entries are made. These variations have developed over the years, partly because library catalogers have tended to think of non-book materials as being somewhat less important than books. It is necessary for the library technician working at the reference desk or information desk to know exactly what can be found in the catalog. If there are no entries for records or vertical file material, it would be a waste of time to search for information in the catalog. Below is an example of how various kinds of materials are entered in one library's catalogs:

Table 1
Catalog Entries for Library Materials

Material	Main Catalog	Floor Catalogs	Special Catalogs
Books	Full set of cards	Main entry and title entry	—
Periodicals	Full set of cards	Main entry and title entry	—
Curriculum Materials	—	—	Full set of cards
Maps	Main entry	—	Full set of cards
Microfilm— Books	Full set of cards	Main entry and title entry	—
Microfilm— Periodicals	Full set of cards	Main entry and title entry	—
Records and Tapes	—	—	Full set of cards
Vertical File	Subject entry	—	—
Films and Filmstrips	Main entry	—	Full set of cards
Art Prints	Main entry	—	Main entry
Music Scores	—	—	Full set of cards
Documents (Non-depository)	Full set of cards	—	—

The library technician should be aware of patron reactions to the use of non-book materials and their special equipment, taking special note of the attitudes toward the use of microfilm if the materials are also available in book or periodical form. Since one of the important factors determining the acquisitions policy of a library is patron use of materials, reports of patron reactions— positive or negative—can be helpful in planning future acquisitions.

A full discussion of the many kinds of non-book materials and their special problems is beyond the scope of this text. The library technician assigned to work with these special materials should refer to some of the books and articles cited in the bibliography at the end of this chapter.

Figure 1
Catalog Card for a Disc Recording

```
Simon, Paul Frederic, 1941-
   Bridge over troubled water. [Phonodisc] Colum-
bia KCS 9914. [1970]

   2 s. 12 in. 33 1/3 rpm. microgroove. stereo.
Popular songs; the composer and Arthur Garfun-
kel, with instrumental acc.
Words of the songs on slipcase.


   1.Music, Popular (Songs, etc.)-U.S. .I.Gar-
funkel, Arthur Ira.  II.Title.
```

Figure 2
Catalog Card for a Motion Picture

```
It's not just you, Murray (Motion picture). New
   York University, Dept. of Television, Motion
   Pictures, and Radio, 1964.

   14 min., sd., b&w, 16 mm.



   1.Success.  I.New York University. Dept. of
Television, Motion Pictures, and Radio.
```

180

Figure 3
Catalog Card for Reel Microfilm

Bernard, John, 1756–1828.
    Retrospections of America, 1797–1811. Edited from the
manuscript by Mrs. Bayle Bernard, with an introd., notes,
and index by Laurence Hutton and Brander Matthews.
New York, Harper, 1887 [^c1886]

    (American culture series : 93 : 4)

    Microfilm copy (positive) made in 1960 by University Microfilms,
Ann Arbor, Mich.
    Collation of the original : xiii, 380 p. illus., ports.

    1. U. S.—Soc. life & cust. 2. Theater—U. S.   I. Bernard, Mrs.
Bayle, ed. II. Title.

Microfilm 01291 reel 93, no. 4 E   Mic 60–7512

Library of Congress   [1]

Figure 4
Catalog Card for a Map

Maps Denoyer-Geppert Company.
G   Pacific area in World War II, 1941-1945.
3205s Edited by Edgar B. Wesley. Chicago, 1965.
WA34
1965   col.map 74 x 108 cm. "Map WA 34."
N4
     Equatorial scale: 300 miles to the inch.

     1.World War II-Maps. I.Wesley, Edgar B.
II.Title.

Figure 5
Catalog Card for a Piece of Equipment

```
8 mm Motion Picture Projector. (Equipment)

For information ask at Circulation Desk.
```

REFERENCE MATERIALS
General

Audio Visual Market Place. New York, R. R. Bowker, 1969– .
(Annual)
A comprehensive directory of producers, distributors, and manufacturers of audiovisual hardware and software. Includes special lists of associations, periodicals, etc., relating to all phases of the audiovisual industry.

Pamphlets

Vertical File Index, 1935 to date. New York, H. W. Wilson, 1936– . (Monthly)
An annotated list of non-book materials. Includes "pamphlets, booklets, brochures, leaflets, circulars, folders, maps, posters, charts, mimeographed bulletins, and other inexpensive materials . . ." (Preface). Most of the material is free or inexpensive. Entries are arranged alphabetically by subject and by title under the subject. There is also a title index. The following information is given with each entry: title, author, series, edition, paging, illustrations, date, publisher, address, price, and a brief annotation. Also keep in mind that the Public Affairs Information Service *Bulletin* (*PAIS*) is also a good source for locating pamphlet materials. (See Figure 6.)

Films, Filmstrips, Overhead Transparencies, and Video Tapes

National Information Center for Educational Media. *NICEM Indexes.* New York, R. R. Bowker; Los Angeles, NICEM, 1969– .

Figure 6
Entries in *Vertical File Index*

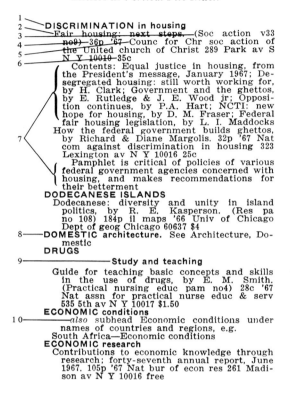

¹Subject heading

²Title of material

³Series

⁴Paging and date of publication

⁵Publisher and address (or at least place where material can be purchased)

⁶Price

⁷Annotation describing contents of the material

⁸"See" reference from a subject heading not used to the subject heading used

⁹Subdivision of the main subject "Drugs" (if this were typed on a catalog card it would read "Drugs–Study and Teaching")

¹⁰"See also" reference to related materials

Figure 6
Entries in *Vertical File Index*

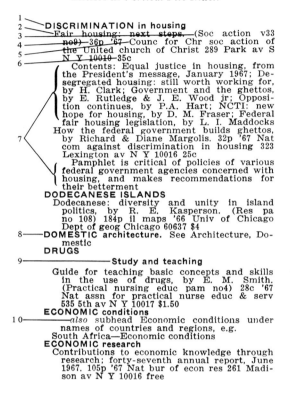

[1] Subject heading

[2] Title of material

[3] Series

[4] Paging and date of publication

[5] Publisher and address (or at least place where material can be purchased)

[6] Price

[7] Annotation describing contents of the material

[8] "See" reference from a subject heading not used to the subject heading used

[9] Subdivision of the main subject "Drugs" (if this were typed on a catalog card it would read "Drugs–Study and Teaching")

[10] "See also" reference to related materials

The following NICEM publications cover films and filmstrips: *Index to Educational Overhead Transparencies* (3rd ed.), *Index to 8mm Motion Cartridges* (3rd ed.), *Index to 35mm Educational Filmstrips* (4th ed.), and *Index to 16mm Educational Films* (4th ed.).

These four indexes list about 165,000 films, filmstrips, and transparencies in all subjects. Indexed by title with a subject guide to locate material by specific subject. Information provided for each entry includes a physical description, number of frames in a filmstrip or length of a film, color or black and white, audience level, year of release in the United States, producer, and information needed to order. Contains a complete list of names and addresses of producers and distributors. New editions, which are issued frequently, supplement rather than replace older editions.

Educators Guide to Free Films. Randolph, Wis., Educators Progress Service, 1941– . (Annual). *Educators Guide to Free Filmstrips.* Randolph, Wis., Educators Progress Service, 1949– . (Annual)

The materials described in these guides are classified alphabetically by curriculum area. Examples of curriculum areas are art, business education, history, industrial arts, science, etc. Annotations for each entry include a description of the contents, time, and black and white or color. Each guide has a title index, subject index, and source and availability index.

American Film Institute. *The American Film Institute Catalog of Motion Pictures Produced in the United States.* New York, R. R. Bowker, 1971– . (In progress)

A monumental set to be completed in 21 volumes. It lists feature films, short films, and newsreels produced in the United States from 1893 to 1970. The entries are arranged alphabetically by title and include such information as the producer, date produced, sound, black and white or color, size, number of reels and feet, director, cast, and an annotation describing the plot of the film. A list of subjects covered by the film is given after the annotation. There are two indexes: a credit index of personal and corporate names, and a subject index.

National Information Center for Educational Media. *NICEM Indexes.* New York, R. R. Bowker; Los Angeles, NICEM, 1969– .

The *Index to Educational Video Tapes* (2nd ed.) lists over 9,000 tapes on all subjects. The arrangement of entries is alphabetical by title and by subject. Each entry provides a description of the content, as well as information on audience level, length, producer and distributor codes, series, broadcast quality, tape size, and date released in the United States. A separate section lists producers and distributors, with their addresses.

Records and Tapes

Schwann Record & Tape Guide. Boston, W. Schwann, 1949– . (Monthly)

A catalog of currently available records and tapes. Includes listings for about 45,000 records, 8-track cartridges, and cassettes. New listings are incorporated in each issue. Special topical sections list records and tapes on classical music, electronic music, collections, musicals, movies, TV shows, current popular music, jazz, and jazz anthologies. Entries provide information on performances, orchestra, record label (manufacturer) and code number. A semi-annual supplement lists records and tapes not in monthly issues and is more comprehensive. Former title: *Schwann Long Playing Record Catalog.*

Educators Guide to Free Tapes, Scripts, and Transcriptions. Randolph, Wis.,
   Educators Progress Service, 1955– . (Annual)
   This guide includes cassettes, videotapes, stereo tapes, scripts, and transcriptions. Arranged by curricular area such as aerospace education, fine arts, language arts, science, etc. Includes title, subject, and source and availability indexes.

National Information Center for Educational Media. *NICEM Indexes.* New
   York, R. R. Bowker; Los Angeles, NICEM, 1969– .
   Two specialized indexes are devoted to audio tapes and educational records: *Index to Educational Audio Tapes* (2nd ed.) and *Index to Educational Records.* These list over 38,000 separate tapes and records. Entries include title, audience level, length of playing time, speed, number of tracks for tape, and the code for the producer and distributor. Arrangement is alphabetical by title and by subject. Includes a list of producers and distributors with addresses and other ordering information.

Art Prints

United Nations Educational, Scientific and Cultural Organization. *Catalogue of
   Color Reproductions of Paintings Prior to 1860.* Paris, UNESCO, 1950– .
   Catalogue of Color Reproductions of Paintings, 1860-1963. Paris,
   UNESCO, 1949– . Editions from time to time.
   Lists of over 1,000 famous prints available for purchase. A black and white reproduction of each print is included. Information given for the original work includes artist's name, dates, title of painting and date, medium, size, and current location. For the reproduction the following kinds of information are given: printing process, size, UNESCO archives number, publisher, and price in local currency. A list of publishers and their addresses is also included.

Microforms

Guide to Microforms in Print. Washington, Microcard Editions, 1961– .
   (Annual)
   A guide to currently available microfilm published in the United States. All microformat materials are included—reel microfilm, micro-opaque cards, microfiche, and ultramicrofiche. The arrangement is alphabetical, with books entered by author and journals by title. Entries give author and/or title, date of publication in original form, publisher of the microfilm, and price. A directory of publishers gives addresses and phone numbers.

FOOTNOTES

1. Government documents will be discussed in Chapter 22, and the vertical file in Chapter 23.

2. Because of new technological advances, there are now good portable readers available which will allow out-of-library use. These smaller microfilm readers may be checked out along with the microfilm, and the patron may take both out of the library.

BIBLIOGRAPHY

American Library Association. Audio-Visual Committee. *Guidelines for Audio-Visual Services in Academic Libraries.* Chicago, Audio-Visual Committee of the Association of College and Research Libraries and the ALA Audio-Visual Committee, 1968.

American Library Association. Public Library Association. Audiovisual Committee. *Guidelines for Audiovisual Materials and Service for Public Libraries.* Chicago, American Library Association, 1970.

Anderson, Herschel. *Audio-Visual Services in the Small Public Library.* Chicago, American Library Association, 1969.

Asleson, Robert F. "Microforms: Where Do They Fit?" *Library Resources and Technical Services* 15:57-62 (Winter 1971).

Barnes, Christopher. "Classification and Cataloging of Spoken Records in Academic Libraries," *College & Research Libraries* 28:49-52 (January 1967).

Brown, Robert M. "The Learning Center," *AV Communication Review* 16: 294-300 (Fall 1968).

Bryant, Eric Thomas. *Music Librarianship: A Practical Guide.* London, James Clark, 1959.

Hicks, Warren, and Alma May Tillin. *Developing Multi-Media Libraries.* New York, R. R. Bowker, 1970.

Irvine, Betty Jo. "Slide Collections in Art Libraries," *College & Research Libraries* 30:443-45 (September 1969).

Irvine, Betty Jo. "Slide Classification: A Historical Survey," *College & Research Libraries* 32:23-30 (January 1971).

Johnson, Jean Thornton, and others. *AV Cataloging and Processing Simplified.* Raleigh, N.C., Audiovisual Catalogers, 1971.

Kujoth, Jean Spealman, ed. *Readings in Nonbook Librarianship.* Metuchen, N.J., Scarecrow Press, 1968.

Kula, Sam. *Bibliography of Film Librarianship.* London, The Library Association, 1967.

Lewis, Ralph W. "User's Reaction to Microfiche: A Preliminary Study," *College & Research Libraries* 31:260-68 (July 1970).

"Microbooks: A New Library Medium," *Publisher's Weekly* 198:48-50 (November 9, 1970).

Miller, Shirley. *The Vertical File and Its Satellites: A Handbook of Acquisition, Processing and Organization.* Littleton, Colo., Libraries Unlimited, 1971.

Morgan (R. A.) Company. *Microform Readers for Libraries.* Library Technology Reports, May 1970. Chicago, American Library Association, 1970.

Mueller, Earl G. *The Art of the Print.* Dubuque, Iowa, W. C. Brown, 1969.

Pearson, Mary D. *Recordings in the Public Library.* Chicago, American Library Association, 1963.

Peterdi, Gabor. *Printmaking: Methods Old and New.* Rev. ed. New York, Macmillan, 1971.

Pickett, A. G., and M. M. Lemco. *Preservation and Storage of Sound Recordings.* Washington, Library of Congress, 1959.

Piercy, Esther J. *Commonsense Cataloging: A Manual for the Organization of Books and Other Materials in Schools and Small Public Libraries.* New York, H. W. Wilson, 1965.

Stone, C. Walter, ed. "Library Uses of the New Media of Communication," *Library Trends* 16:179-299 (October 1967).

"Ultramicrofiche Library Series: Encyclopaedia Britannica," *Library Journal* 94:937-38 (March 1, 1969).

Veaner, Allen B. *The Evaluation of Micropublications: A Handbook for Librarians.* Chicago, Library Technology Program, American Library Association, 1971.

Williams, Bernard J. S. *Miniaturised Communications: A Review of Microforms.* London, The Library Association; Hatfield, The National Reprographic Centre for Documentation, 1970.

Zachert, Martha J. "The Implications of Oral History for Librarians," *College & Research Libraries* 29:101-103 (March 1968).

CHAPTER 22

REFERENCE MATERIALS: GOVERNMENT DOCUMENTS

INTRODUCTION

Government documents[1] are among the most useful materials in a library, but they are often the most difficult to find and to process. In this chapter we will try to accomplish two goals: to present a brief general introduction to government documents, and to present some basic reference materials on current documents issued by the United States government, state governments, and the United Nations.

There will be textual references to some major retrospective indexes to United States documents. However, no descriptions of these materials will be given, since it is beyond the scope of this text to cover United States documents published before 1895. The emphasis in this chapter will be on sources for current materials.

The library technician should make every effort to see how documents are handled in several libraries, and particularly in a library that is a depository for United States government documents. First-hand experience, even for just a few hours, in a depository collection or other large collection will make the following description of documents more comprehensible.

It will be helpful, before a discussion of government documents, to define what is meant by the term. There is probably no single definition that is entirely satisfactory; put most simply, however, government documents are publications issued by or authorized for issue by a governmental body and paid for with public funds. The governmental body may be at the federal, state, or local level, or may be an international organization such as the United Nations.

UNITED STATES GOVERNMENT DOCUMENTS

The United States government is one of the world's largest publishers. Government documents are published on every conceivable subject and are not at all restricted to laws and statistical data. In a large documents collection material can be found in various areas of the humanities, social sciences, and the sciences—particularly in the sciences and social sciences. In some recent years the Superintendent of Documents has offered over 12,000 separate documents for sale. The Government Printing Office (GPO) was established in 1861 to handle government printing, which until that time had been contracted out to private printers. In 1895 the office of Superintendent of Documents was established to handle the sale and distribution of documents. The office of the Superintendent of Documents is part of the Government Printing Office. Despite the large volume of documents available from the Superintendent of Documents, it has been estimated that an even greater number are printed and processed by individual government agencies and must be purchased directly from the agency.

As early as 1813 the United States government deposited selected documents in various libraries throughout the country. The depository system in existence today was established in its basic form by the Printing Act of 1895, which also established the Superintendent of Documents office. There have been several modifications since then, and as of 1970 nearly 1,900 libraries and institutions are eligible to be government document depositories. As a depository a library is eligible to receive free copies of all government publications issued by the Government Printing Office except those meant for official use only, those classified for security reasons, those which would be of little or no interest to the public, and those which must be self-sustaining (such as the *National Union Catalog*).

There are several kinds of depository libraries: 1) full depositories where all eligible documents are sent to the library, 2) selective depositories which receive only a limited number of documents, and 3) regional depositories which acquire all eligible documents and provide interlibrary loan and reference services for other libraries and institutions.

Libraries that are not depositories must purchase their documents from the Superintendent of Documents or from a dealer specializing in government documents. It is often possible to receive certain documents by requesting them from local congressmen or senators.

Government documents are organized in a number of ways depending on the number acquired and how they are to be used. Some possible ways to organize government documents are listed below.

1) Documents may be classified or arranged using the Superintendent of Documents Classification System.[2] This is a special classification system which organizes the documents by the issuing agency and not by subject matter. Depositories, which acquire a large number of documents, would use this system to make their processing a more manageable job. The Superintendent of Documents Classification numbers are pre-assigned and easily located on depository shipping lists and in the *Monthly Catalog*. Documents classified under this system would be in a separate collection and would probably have to be located through a special catalog or the *Monthly Catalog*.

2) Some documents may be classified using the Superintendent of Documents Classification System—perhaps the less used items—and some with the book collection, using either the Decimal Classification or the Library of Congress Classification. Under this system some documents would still be in a separate collection and would be located through a separate catalog or the *Monthly Catalog*, while others would be shelved with the general collection.

3) All documents may be classified using the same classification system that is used for the book collection, and may then be shelved with the books.

4) All documents may be classified as in 3) above, but shelved in a separate collection. Above the first line of the call number a designation like "Doc" would indicate that the material was shelved in a separate area. Some frequently used materials might be shelved with the reference collection; in that case they would not have the special designation.

5) Some pamphlet-sized documents,[3] which might be less useful if classified either in a document collection or with the book collection, may be placed in the vertical file.

The *Monthly Catalog*, which is the main reference tool for current documents, will be described later in this chapter. There are several other books, however, that are essential for locating older government documents. The library technician should look at these books and be aware of their physical location in the library:

Poore, Benjamin Perley. *A Descriptive Catalogue of the Government Publication of the United States, September 5, 1774-March 4, 1881.* Washington, Government Printing Office, 1885.

Ames, John G. *Comprehensive Index to the Publications of the United States Government, 1881-1893.* Washington, 1905. 2v.

U.S. Superintendent of Documents. *Catalog of the Public Documents of Congress and of All Departments of the Government of the United States for the Period from March 4, 1893 to December 31, 1940.* Washington, Government Printing Office, 1896-1945. 25v.

The library technician who works with government documents or in a depository library which has older documents will want to familiarize himself with these reference materials. However, since they are fairly complicated, the assistance of an experienced librarian will be necessary in learning how to use them.

The library technician who works regularly with United States government documents will want to become generally familiar with the organization of the United States government. Documents fall into three general classes: executive, legislative, and judicial. The executive documents include those issued by the Office of the President, the 11 executive departments (Department of State, Department of Defense, etc.) and the various independent offices and establishments. Legislative documents include the records and debates of both houses of Congress and the reports and hearings of the various Congressional committees. Documents from the judicial branch consist mostly of laws and reports of court decisions by the Supreme Court, the Tax Court, etc.

STATE AND LOCAL DOCUMENTS

A second major source for government documents lies in the publications of city, county, and state governments. Public libraries usually have some of the more important city and county documents such as city charters, building and zoning codes, and local ordinances. At the state level, publications such as "Blue Books,"[4] codes of laws, and reports of various departments may be acquired by all but the smallest libraries.

State and local documents are organized in a variety of ways, as discussed earlier in this chapter. States like California have their own classification systems that can be used to organize their documents. Some states operate a depository system and one copy of every important state document is sent to selected libraries (such as those at state colleges and state universities). The state library is the most likely source for complete holdings of state documents. It is often the state library which receives copies of documents issued by all state agencies and which runs whatever depository system the state may have.

There is no one reference work that lists all publications at the local and state levels. For city, county and other local documents it is necessary to depend on the efforts of the local libraries to acquire and index these materials. Many states issue lists of their publications. The Library of Congress issues the *Monthly Checklist of State Publications*, which is discussed below. Like United States government documents, many state and local documents may be bought either directly from the issuing agency or from a central sales agency such as the state library.

UNITED NATIONS AND OTHER INTERNATIONAL ORGANIZATIONS

A brief mention should be made of the documents published by the United Nations and some of its specialized agencies. Most libraries acquire selected publications from the United Nations, the United Nations Educational, Scientific, and Cultural Organization (UNESCO), the World Health Organization, and the Food and Agriculture Organization of the United Nations (FAO). These materials are usually cataloged and shelved with the book collection. However, those libraries which acquire most of the United Nations publications may use the special U.N. Symbol Series System and maintain a separate collection.

The library technician who works with United Nations documents should be familiar with the physical location and the use of the *United Nations Documents Index*. For a general introduction to United Nations documents, see the book by Brenda Brimmer, *A Guide to the Use of United Nations Documents*, cited in the bibliography at the end of this chapter.

Working with United Nations documents is quite complex. The library technician's role in this area may be limited to answering directional questions and explaining how to use the *United Nations Documents Index*. In most libraries these documents are cataloged and can be found in the catalog under the appropriate main entries. The library technician must be aware of how these documents are handled in his particular library.

REFERENCE MATERIALS–UNITED STATES GOVERNMENT DOCUMENTS

U.S. Superintendent of Documents. *Monthly Catalog of United States Government Publications.* Washington, Government Printing Office, 1895– . (Monthly)

An index and bibliography of current government publications. The arrangement is alphabetical by the issuing department or bureau. Restricted, administrative, and "processed" (i.e., mimeographed, dittoed, etc.) documents are excluded. Each issue contains complete instructions on how to use the work and how to order documents. Entries for each document give the full title, personal author if appropriate, date of publication, paging, price, depository status, Library of Congress catalog card number, and Superintendent of Documents classification number. Each issue has an index, cumulated annually, which includes subject entries, personal author entries, and title entries. This publication is found in most libraries and serves as a bibliographic record and buying guide for government publications. It is the basic document source in most libraries in the United States and, to a degree, it does for documents what *Books in Print* and *Cumulative Book Index* do for books. (See Figure 1.)

Index

MONTHLY CATALOG, JANUARY–DECEMBER 1970

NOTE.—*Entries appear in this Index under subjects or titles. Bulletins, circulars, etc., having no specific subjects are entered under the issuing office only. Index citations are to entry numbers in the catalog.*

1—Lasers :
  airborne laser-radar studies of lower at-
    mosphere, 2104
  biological effects of laser radiation, USSR
    study, 12633
  communications today and tomorrow,
    USSR study, 18092
  electrical noise in GaAs diode lasers,
    12888
  frequency stabilization, investigation, 2063
2——fundamentals and experiments, 18314
  laser breakdown of copper vapor, 11679
  laser-generated plasma as spectroscopic
    light source, 18222
  laser heating of ionized helium, 12792
  laser irradiation, use in coal investiga-
    tions, 4475
  laser materials, ARPA–NBS program of
    research, 7576, 11737
  laser power and energy measurements,
    961
  laser radars, USSR study, 7370
  plasma, noise characteristics and ampli-
    tude stabilization, investigation, 14826
  sodium line, with NA+ and H− recom-
    bination, USSR study, 18094
  space qualified laser, design, 16946, 18186
  spaceborne laser altimeter, optical altime-
    ter receiver systems study and design,
    5901
  used for laser transmissometer calibrator,
    evaluation, 15340
  visibility measurement for aviation use,
    18378
  see also Ruby lasers.
Lash Italia (SS) :
  launching (remarks), 14757
Lasker, Reuben, experimental sea-water
  aquarium, 3708

Van Houten, Robert, fast breeder reac‹
  control, shield, and reflector materials ‹
  velopment, summary report, 10756
Van Keulen, Gail, selling in Yugoslav
  15723
3—Van Pelt, W. F., laser fundamentals a‹
4—experiments, 18314
Van Sickle, Charles C., forest resources ‹
  Mississippi, 4213
Van Sickle, Dale E., radiation-initiated em‹
  sion oxidation, 4893
Van Wert County, Ohio, community prof‹
  12476
Van Wyen, Adrian O., naval aviation ‹
  World War I, 1022
Vapor generators, use with dichlorvos to c‹
  trol drosophila in wineries, 6288
Vapor-phase deposition, *see* Vapor plating
Vapor plating, thermionic converter w‹
  chloride vapor deposited tungsten emit‹
  (110) and collector of molybdenum dep‹
  ited on niobium, characteristics, 18192
Vapor pressure :
  gold, interlaboratory measurements, an‹
    sis, 6003
  relationship of water vapor pressure ‹
    concentration of anomalous compon‹
    in mudified water, USSR study, 7400
  vapor-compression vacuum freezing pro‹
    evaluation on brackish water, 14593

[1] Subject heading
[2] Title of a specific document
[3] Author entry
[4] Item number (18314)–not a page number

192

U.S. Superintendent of Documents. *Selected United States Government Publications*. Washington, Government Printing Office, 1928– . (Bi-weekly)

An annotated list of 50 to 60 popular publications chosen from current *Monthly Catalogs*, plus some older but still useful items. All items are in print and available for purchase. Each entry includes title, date of publication, paging, price, and a catalog number for ordering.

U.S. Superintendent of Documents. *Price Lists*. Washington, Government Printing Office, 1898– .

Topical lists of government documents available for purchase. Examples of subjects covered by the lists are "Maps," "American History," "Laws," "Soils and Fertilizers," "Navy," and "Consumer Information." Lists are revised frequently and include current material as well as older material. Some annotations are included along with prices and other information needed to order the documents. Items on these lists have previously appeared in the *Monthly Catalog* or on the *Selected* lists. Only the form of presentation is different. (See Figure 2.)

Figure 2

Entries in a *Price List of Government Documents*

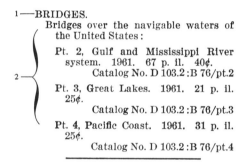

¹ Subject heading

² Titles of documents, date of publication, price, catalog number (same as Superintendent of Documents Classification Number)

U.S. Library of Congress. Processing Dept. *Monthly Checklist of State Publications*. Washington, Government Printing Office, 1910– . (Monthly)

A compilation of state documents received by the Library of Congress. The arrangement is alphabetical by state, and entries include information such as title, issuing body, other cataloging information, and some prices. An annual subject and author index is issued. Since 1963 the June and December issues include a list of periodicals published by the states.

Mechanic, Sylvia. *Annotated List of Selected United States Government Publications Available to Depository Libraries.* New York, H. W. Wilson, 1970.

A list of 500 selected items arranged in alphabetical order by issuing agency. Each item is annotated and represented by a reproduction of a Library of Congress card. Special sections explain the Superintendent of Documents classification system, list depository libraries, and provide an extensive bibliography.

Pohle, Linda C. *A Guide to Popular Government Publications: For Libraries and Home Reference.* Littleton, Colo., Libraries Unlimited, Inc., 1972.

Contains 2,000 annotated entries, listing government publications of wide appeal under more than 100 subject categories. The emphasis is on topics of current interest (civil rights, minorities, environmental problems, political and intellectual dissent, etc.). Most of the publications included were published within the last four years and are either moderately priced or free. Includes an analytical index.

Wynkoop, Sally. *Government Reference Books 68/69: A Biennial Guide to U.S. Government Publications.* Littleton, Colo., Libraries Unlimited, 1970.

A comprehensive guide to reference books published by the U.S. government and its agencies. Entries provide Superintendent of Documents classification number, price, and LC card number. Selection is based on considerations of practical value to general reference collections and the needs of special libraries. Ordering information is provided in an appendix, and there is an author-title-subject index. The second biennial edition, covering 1970/1971 titles, will be released in 1972.

Wynkoop, Sally. *Subject Guide to Government Reference Books.* Littleton, Colo., Libraries Unlimited, Inc., 1972.

A retrospective guide to more than 1,000 essential reference books published by the Government Printing Office. Material is arranged under broad subject categories, and a detailed index provides access to all entries through personal authors, titles, and subjects.

FOOTNOTES

1. This text will use the term "government documents," but they are often called "government publications," "public documents," or just "documents." While there is a technical difference between a "document" and a "publication," it is not important for our purposes here.

2. The Superintendent of Documents Classification System can be used only for United States government publications. The other methods of organization can be used for any kind of document.

3. In present usage a pamphlet is a publication of 49 pages or less, bound in a paper cover.

4. "Blue Books" are handbooks of state governments and include information like state insignia, government leaders, and general information on the departments and agencies of state governments. An example of a "blue book" is the *California Blue Book*. The library technician should check to see what is published in his state.

BIBLIOGRAPHY

Boyd, Anne M. *United States Government Publications*. 3rd ed. rev. with corrections. New York, H. W. Wilson, 1952.

Brimmer, Brenda, and others. *A Guide to the Use of United Nations Documents, Including Reference to the Specialized Agencies and Special U.N. Bodies.* Dobbs Ferry, N.Y., Oceana Publications, 1962.

Dale, Doris Cruger. *The United Nations Library: Its Origin and Development.* Chicago, American Library Association, 1970.

Jackson, Ellen. *Subject Guide to Major United States Government Publications.* Chicago, American Library Association, 1968.

Kling, Robert E. *The Government Printing Office.* New York, Praeger, 1970.

Sacramento Workshop on U.S. Government Publications. *U.S. Government Publications: Acquisitions, Processing and Use; Proceedings of Three Workshops.* Sacramento, Calif., California State Library, 1967.

Schmeckebier, Lawrence F., and Roy B. Eastin. *Government Publications and Their Use.* 2nd rev. ed. Washington, Brookings Institution, 1969.

Shaw, Thomas Schuler, ed. "Federal, State and Local Government Publications," *Library Trends* 15:3-194 (July 1966).

Shore, Philip. "An Evaluation of U.S. Document Bibliography," *Library Resources & Technical Services* 4:34-43 (Winter 1960).

United Nations. Dag Hammarskjold Library. *List of United Nations Document Series Symbols.* New York, United Nations, 1970.

Wilcox, Jerome K., ed. *Manual on the Use of State Publications.* Chicago, American Library Association, 1940.

Wood, Jennings. *United States Government Publications: A Partial List of Non-GPO Imprints.* Chicago, American Library Association, 1964.

Wynkoop, Sally. *Government Reference Books 68/69: A Biennial Guide to U.S. Government Publications.* Littleton, Colo., Libraries Unlimited, 1970.

Wynkoop, Sally. *Subject Guide to Government Reference Books.* Littleton, Colo., Libraries Unlimited, 1972.

CHAPTER 23

LIBRARY COOPERATION
AND INTERLIBRARY LOAN

INTRODUCTION

Networks, sharing, centralized processing, regional centers, interlibrary loan, and interlibrary cooperation are some of the terms the library technician will be reading about and hearing about in coming years. Libraries have cooperated for years, particularly in interlibrary loans, but in recent years the pressure for cooperative efforts has greatly increased. The volume of materials published every year makes it impossible for libraries to purchase more than a select number of items.[1] Even the largest university research libraries are not able to acquire everything published. Three factors enter into how much can be purchased by a library: 1) size of the budget, 2) physical space available to house the material, and 3) the need to acquire materials to meet the goals of the library. By sharing their collections libraries are able to make much larger resources accessible to their patrons. It is the goal of libraries to form a national network, thereby making the nation's library resources available to everyone.

In this chapter we will discuss several important concepts and methods used for achieving library cooperation, going into some detail with respect to the method which will most concern the library technician—interlibrary loan.

LIBRARY COOPERATION

In the most simple terms library cooperation is two or more libraries exchanging information and sharing their resources. This extended use of resources and information should result in better service for the patron. Since one of the tenets of our democracy is open and full access to information by all citizens, it follows that even the smallest library should have access to information no matter where it is located. While this ideal of information and collection sharing is not yet fully implemented, libraries at all levels are making efforts to meet the challenge as quickly as possible. Recent court decisions have held that local property taxes are an unfair base for school support, since community wealth then becomes the main factor in quality education. Educational opportunity based primarily on community wealth is antithetical to the idea of equal opportunity of education regardless of wealth. How these decisions might be applied to libraries remains to be seen. But it is certainly true at the moment that not all citizens have equal access to information, and that this accessibility is almost entirely dependent upon the financial ability of the taxpayers to support their library system.

One final thing to keep in mind is that library cooperation must be beneficial—or at least not detrimental—to the library's goals. When libraries enter into cooperative ventures they are aware of the possible results and the resources needed to make the project work. For example, a heavily used library might not want to expand its service area in a cooperative effort if the increased workload or collection use would lower the quality of service to all patrons. Cooperative ventures promise the possibility of better service, not necessarily less expense. Just because cooperation is possible does not mean that it should be done in every case. The problems of personnel, funds, and legal authorization are all areas which the librarian must study at length before final decisions can be made.

METHODS OF LIBRARY COOPERATION

There are probably thousands of cooperative projects currently in operation ranging from telephone calls between two libraries to national efforts involving computers and sophisticated telecommunication devices to communicate among many libraries. We cannot cover every cooperative method being used. We will discuss some of the more frequently used methods which the library technician will be most likely to encounter.

One way to share a library's resources is to give access to the collection to as many persons as possible. In Chapter 2 it was mentioned that a library card for a local library might also give the patron the right to use other libraries in the area. In some cases a patron registered in a public library can charge out materials from any other public library in the state. Colleges and universities allow non-students to use materials in the library and often establish borrowing privileges for special groups such as school teachers. Academic libraries in a given geographic area may make arrangements to allow students registered at one institution to borrow materials from other cooperating institutions. The California State University and College System, with 19 widely separated campuses, is currently developing a common student identification card which will allow a student registered at one campus to borrow materials from any of the 19 libraries. Opening the use of library collections to a greater number of potential users can be an effective method of library cooperation. The library technician must be aware of what his library is doing with respect to this kind of cooperation, especially if he is involved in circulation desk work.

Cooperative purchasing agreements can help insure that important materials are acquired by at least one library in a geographical area or in a given library system. Implicit, of course, in these agreements are some arrangements for sharing these materials. The sharing may involve either some form of interlibrary loan or the right to let anyone use the material in the library where the material is housed. For example, several libraries in a county may decide that there should be a complete set of the *New York Times* on microfilm available locally. Rather than purchase several sets, one of the libraries may agree to purchase a set and make it available to all. In return, each of the other libraries may agree to purchase important sets or works which they would then make available to the other libraries.

Another type of cooperative purchasing agreement concerns special collection development. If there are several colleges in an area, one may agree to develop a good Chinese history collection, another a science fiction collection, and yet another a Mexican art collection. This information would be communicated to the reference staffs who could refer patrons to the special collections for more advanced research. A special cooperative acquisitions program called the Farmington Plan has been in existence since 1942. The libraries that participate in this plan agree to purchase all possible materials in a special subject. The cataloging information is sent to the *National Union Catalog*, where it can be found by other libraries.

There are infinite possibilities for cooperative purchasing agreements depending on local needs and problems. Such cooperation can offer dollar savings by avoiding duplication, and the money saved can be used to purchase other materials.

In order to share materials libraries must know what is available and where it can be found. To make this information available, libraries can cooperate by developing lists of holdings for individual libraries and union lists containing the holdings of several libraries. We have already discussed three major holdings lists which are national in their coverage: *National Union Catalog, Union List of Serials in the Libraries of the United States and Canada,* and *New Serials Titles.* By using these works a library can locate material in any number of libraries throughout the country. On a smaller scale libraries can compile lists of their book or periodical holdings and make them available to other libraries. The more commonly compiled holdings list is for periodicals. Libraries entering into this kind of cooperation each compile a list of their periodical holdings and current subscriptions. Then each library exchanges lists with the others. Every library in the network can then know the holdings of other libraries and arrange for interlibrary loans or be able to tell the patron exactly where to find the material. In some places, regional bibliographic centers have been established, and libraries send their acquisitions information to the center. Any library in the system can communicate directly with the center to locate material in other libraries. Depending on the sophistication of the network, interlibrary communication may be by mail, telephone, teletypewriter (TWX), or computers and cathode ray tubes (CRT).

Another kind of cooperative network involves answering reference questions or locating a source that can supply the answer. The simplest network of this kind might take place within a library. If a question cannot be answered at the information desk, it will be transferred to the reference desk. This is a form of network used to direct the patron to a source which can best give an answer to his question. An expansion of this kind of network might involve referring a reference question from a branch library to the main library, to a regional reference service or state library, and then to the Library of Congress or other national library such as the National Library of Medicine. An example of an information network of this type is the *Medical Literature Analysis and Retrieval System* (MEDLARS). Questions involving a literature search can be sent to the National Library of Medicine or one of several centers around the country equipped to perform a search of medical literature. Libraries are currently working on other kinds of networks to enable quick retrieval of the best sources of information. These networks can be linked by mail, telephone, teletype, or computer.

For years libraries have formed systems for cooperative acquisitions and cataloging. Not only is it usually more economical, but it also allows for production of holdings lists for several libraries, which can be useful for locating material in the immediate geographic area. Some degree of standardization of ordering and cataloging procedures is necessary to make such a system operate most efficiently. In some cases the money and personnel saved in technical services operations have been transferred to public services to improve the ability to meet patron needs.

One final method of cooperation commonly used is interlibrary loan. Interlibrary loan is simply one library lending its materials to another library. Depending on their policy, libraries may loan the material itself, send photocopies (i.e., Xerox), or send copies using telefacsimile transmission equipment. Interlibrary loan is one of the earliest forms of library cooperation in the United States. The first code establishing interlibrary loan procedures was the American Library Association Interlibrary Loan Code of 1917. The code has been modified several times over the years; we will later discuss the most recent code, which is the National Interlibrary Loan Code, 1968. Besides the national code, there are numerous other special and local codes in operation, many being less formal and more *ad hoc* arrangements. The library technician should be aware of his library's interlibrary loan policy, the national code, and any special or local codes which may be in use. The decision to make a request for interlibrary loan or to lend material requested by other libraries will usually be made by a librarian. Not all requests are honored, nor is all material available for loan. The experienced library technician may be allowed to make some of these decisions independently, but even then a librarian would always be consulted in special cases. Most of the bibliographic verification and the filling out of interlibrary loan forms, however, can be done by a library technician or even by a supervised clerk.

Because the library technician can be most directly involved in interlibrary loan work, the section below goes into greater detail concerning the forms and procedures used for this method of library cooperation.

INTERLIBRARY LOAN PROCEDURES

Interlibrary loans are transactions between libraries, not between a patron and a library. A library will honor a request for interlibrary loan only if that request comes on a special form (or telephone, TWX, etc.) directly from the library. The library technician must understand this concept in order to avoid misleading the patron into thinking that he can make the request himself.

Before studying some of the special forms and procedures below, it will be helpful to read the National Interlibrary Loan Code, 1968, and any local codes used by libraries in the area.[2]

When a patron requests material to be borrowed from another library, he will usually fill out a special request form stating exactly what is wanted (Figures 1 and 2). After the request is made, a librarian will check to see if it is the type of material which can be requested on interlibrary loan.[3] If it is not acceptable material for interlibrary loan, it can be located nonetheless, and the patron can be sent to the other library, where he can use it. If the request is acceptable, then the library's holdings should be checked to be certain that the material is not already in the library. Because of the complexity of some main entries, even the most experienced patron may not find the correct entry in the catalog. For this reason the request should be checked by trained library personnel.

When accepting the patron's request, the library technician should inform

Figure 1
Patron Interlibrary Loan Request–Book

INTERLIBRARY LOAN REQUEST–BOOK	DO NOT WRITE IN THIS SPACE
Please print as much of the information requested below as you can provide.	
Author _____	Source _____
Title _____	
_____	
_____	Req _____
_____ Edition _____	Rec _____
Place _____ Publisher _____	Due _____
Pub. date _____ Suggested location _____	Ren _____
Source of reference _____	Due _____
_____	Ret _____
_____	Chgs _____
Name _____ Status ____ Dept. _____	Insur _____

Figure 2
Patron Interlibrary Loan Request–Periodical

INTERLIBRARY LOAN REQUEST–PERIODICAL	DO NOT WRITE IN THIS SPACE
Please print as much of the information requested below as you can provide.	
Periodical _____	Source _____
_____	
Volume _____ Date _____ Pages _____	Req _____
Author of article _____	Rec _____
Title of article _____	Due _____
_____	Ren _____
_____	Due _____
Source of reference _____	Ret _____
_____	Chgs _____
Name _____ Status ____ Dept. _____	Insur _____

201

him of the library's interlibrary loan policy. Many libraries, particularly academic libraries, provide handouts—given to all patrons—which explain their policy (Figures 3 and 4). In this way the patron will know what kinds of materials can be requested and whether he will have to pay any of the costs involved, such as photocopy fees and postage. Some libraries absorb this expense, while others pass the cost on to the patron.

Once it has been verified that the library does not have the material a patron has requested, the information is transferred to a special interlibrary loan request form (Figures 5-7). The Interlibrary Loan Request form is used for book and periodical requests for which there is an option of receiving either microfilm or photocopies rather than the material itself (Figure 5). The Library Photoduplication Order Form is used when photocopies are desired or when it is known that the lending library's policy is to send only copies rather than the material itself (Figure 6). An example of a special request form is that used by the California State Library (Figure 7). Many such special forms are in use and the library technician should be aware of the ones used in his library.

Before the request is sent to another library, two more steps are necessary: 1) the existence of the material requested must be verified and the correctness of the bibliographical citation must be checked; and 2) a library which has the material in its collection must be located.

To verify the existence of a book and the correct author, title, date, edition, editor, etc., it will be necessary to consult such reference works as the *National Union Catalog (NUC), Cumulative Book Index (CBI),* and book catalogs of individual libraries. To verify the existence of a periodical, the correct author, title of the article, and paging, it will be necessary to consult reference works such as *National Union Catalog (NUC), New Serials Titles (NST), Union List of Serials in the Libraries of the United States and Canada (ULS),* periodical holdings lists of individual libraries, and periodical indexes and abstracts such as *Readers' Guide, Chemical Abstracts, Education Index,* and *Sociological Abstracts.* Many libraries have a search procedure established, and the library technician should study this procedure and try to get some on-the-job experience.

To find a library which has the material is the second step before sending the request. Requests can be sent "blindly," but verifying the holdings of a library in advance can save much time and expense. Sometimes, however, it may not be possible to verify a location. Some sources used to identify which libraries have certain books are *National Union Catalog (NUC), Register of Additional Locations* (part of the *NUC*), and catalogs of individual libraries. To locate periodicals, the basic tools used are the *Union List of Serials in the Libraries of the United States and Canada (ULS), New Serials Titles (NST),* and the periodicals holdings lists of individual libraries. If a location cannot be verified the library can request that a regional library, the state library, or other bibliographic center locate the material. Below is an example of a form used to request the Library of Congress to help locate a title (Figure 8).

After the verification of bibliographic information and location, the request will be sent to another library. When the request is received by the lending library, it will be examined in light of its own lending policy, and a decision will be made as to whether or not to lend the material. If the material is to be lent, it will be carefully packaged for shipping, along with at least one part of

202

Figure 3
Interlibrary Loan Service Policy: Patron Handout

College Library
California State College, San Bernardino

INTERLIBRARY LOAN SERVICE

Interlibrary loan services are handled by the Reference Department located on the first floor of the library.

Under the terms of the National Interlibrary Loan Code, subscribed to by most academic libraries, loans are restricted to research materials needed by faculty members and graduate students. Copies of the code are available for consultation at the Reference Desk. The Library of Congress and some other research libraries lend to faculty members only.

Recently published books, still in print, should, if possible, be purchased for the library by faculty request rather than requested on interlibrary loan. *Books in Print* should be consulted to determine whether a book is available for purchase. A copy is available for your use in the Technical Services Department.

Request forms for interlibrary loans are available and should be used when submitting a request. Please check CSCSB Library's card catalog and periodical holdings list carefully before making a request. Please provide as much of the information requested on the form as you can *and include the source of your reference.*

Requests for periodical articles present a special problem as most libraries will not lend bound periodicals on interlibrary loan. As a courtesy to us, UCR (main library only) does lend bound periodicals. Other California State College libraries and the Bio-Medical Library at UCLA supply photoprints of periodical articles without charge. The periodical holdings lists of these institutions may be consulted at the Reference Desk. Libraries of other institutions require purchase of photoprints of articles. As this library has no funds for purchases of this type, arrangements for payment must be made between the borrower and the lending library.

In order to continue offering interlibrary loan service, it is necessary to maintain good relations with cooperating libraries. Please return materials promptly and limit requests for renewals. Borrowers should understand that lending libraries often stipulate restrictions, such as use within the library. This library, in fairness, must insist on compliance with such restrictions.

The reference librarians are available to give information and assistance with any problems concerning interlibrary borrowing and use of other libraries.

Figure 4
Interlibrary Loan Service Policy: For Library Use

Interlibrary Loan Policy
Name and address of library _____
_____
_____
_____

NUC Code _____   _____

BOOKS   **MASTERS THESES**
Will lend _____   Will lend _____
Will not lend _____   Will not lend _____
Length of loan _____   Length of loan _____
Renewable _____   Renewable _____
                                    Microfilms available
PERIODICALS   _____
Will lend_____   Photocopying permitted _____
Will not lend _____
Will lend current   _____
   issues _____   **BILLING POLICY**
Will lend bound   Invoiced with
   volumes _____   material _____
Renewable _____   Invoiced monthly _____
Lends if article exceeds   Invoiced on ILL form _____
   ____ pages _____   Charge for formal
                                       billing _____
PHOTOCOPY SERVICE
Free to CSC   **POSTAGE**
   libraries _____   Do charge_____
No charge up to ____ pages   Do not charge _____
Automatic copy of
   articles less than   USUAL LENGTH OF LOAN _____
   ____ pages _____
Charge per page _____   PHOTOCOPY ADDRESS
Minimum charge _____   _____
Handling charge _____   _____
                                    _____
MICROFILMS   _____
Will lend _____
Will not lend _____

MICROFILM SERVICE
Service available _____
Charge per frame
   or per inch _____
Minimum charge _____
Handling charge _____

Interlibrary Loan service is _____ , is not_____ suspended during the
Christmas holidays.

SPECIAL CONDITIONS OR RESTRICTIONS
_____

Figure 5
Interlibrary Loan Request Form: According to the
A.L.A. Interlibrary Loan Code

A INTERLIBRARY LOAN REQUEST
According to the A.L.A. Interlibrary Loan Code

REQUEST

Date of request:

Call-No.

Library
California State College, San Bernardino
5500 State College Parkway
San Bernardino, CA 92407

For use of _____ Status _____ Dept.

Author (or periodical title, vol. and year)

Title (with author & pages for periodical articles) (Incl. edition, place & date)

☐ This edition only

Verified in (or source of reference)

If non-circulating, please supply ☐ Microfilm ☐ Hard copy if cost does not exceed $ _____

AUTHORIZED BY:
(FULL NAME) _____ Title _____

Note: The receiving library
assumes responsibility for
notification of non-receipt.

REPORTS: Checked by _____

SENT BY: ☐ Library rate _____
Charges $ _____ Insured for $ _____
Date sent _____
DUE _____

RESTRICTIONS: ☐ For use in library only _____
☐ Copying not permitted _____

NOT SENT BECAUSE: ☐ In use
☐ Non circulating ☐ Not owned

Estimated Cost of: Microfilm _____
Hard copy _____

BORROWING LIBRARY RECORD:

Date received _____
Date returned _____
By ☐ Library rate _____
Postage
enclosed $ _____ Insured for $ _____

RENEWALS: (Request and report on sheet C)

Requested on _____
Renewed to _____
(or period of renewal)

205

Figure 6
Library Photoduplication Order Form

LIBRARY PHOTODUPLICATION ORDER FORM

Requester's
Order No. ....

Supplier's
Order No. ....

A

Date of request:

Call-No.

Author (or Periodical title, vol. and year)

Fold →

Title (with Author and pages for periodical articles) (incl. edition, place and date)

Verified in (or Source of reference)

☐ Any edition

Request ☐ microfilm ☐ photoprint ☐ Other   Remarks:

REPORTS:

NOT SENT BECAUSE:
☐ Not owned by Library
☐ File is incomplete
☐ In use   ☐ Hold Placed
         ☐ **Request again**
☐ Publication not yet received
☐ Please verify your reference
☐ Other:
☐ Suggest you request of:

← Fold

Estimated Cost of Microfilm ....
               Photoprint ....

☐ Please pay in advance
☐ Please do not pay in advance

Please send cost estimate for
☐ microfilm   ☐ photoprint

Go ahead with the order if it does not
exceed: $ ....

Special instructions:

NOTE: This material is requested in accordance with the A. L. A. recommendations concerning the photocopying of copyrighted materials.

ORDER AUTHORIZED BY:

206

Figure 7
Special Interlibrary Loan Request Form:
California State Library

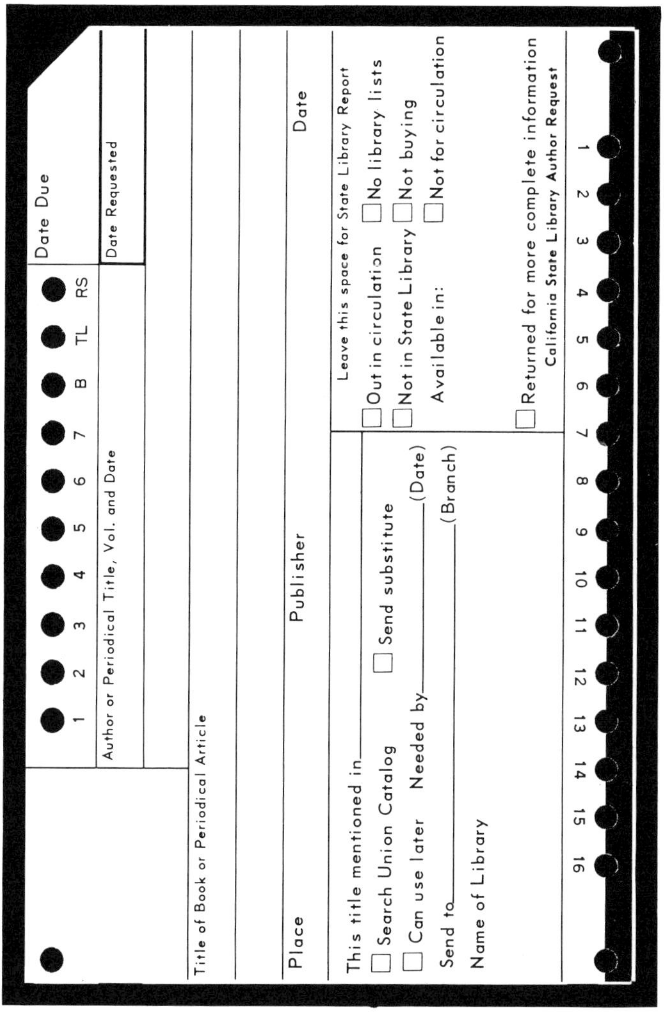

Date Due

Date Requested

1 2 3 4 5 6 7 B TL RS

Author or Periodical Title, Vol. and Date

Title of Book or Periodical Article

Publisher

Place

Date

This title mentioned in

☐ Search Union Catalog   ☐ Send substitute

☐ Can use later   Needed by _____ (Date)

Send to _____ (Branch)

Name of Library

Leave this space for State Library Report

☐ Out in circulation   ☐ No library lists
☐ Not in State Library   ☐ Not buying
Available in: ☐ Not for circulation

☐ Returned for more complete information

California State Library Author Request

1 2 3 4 5 6 7 8 9 10 11 12 13 14 15 16

Figure 8
Request for Locations of Title

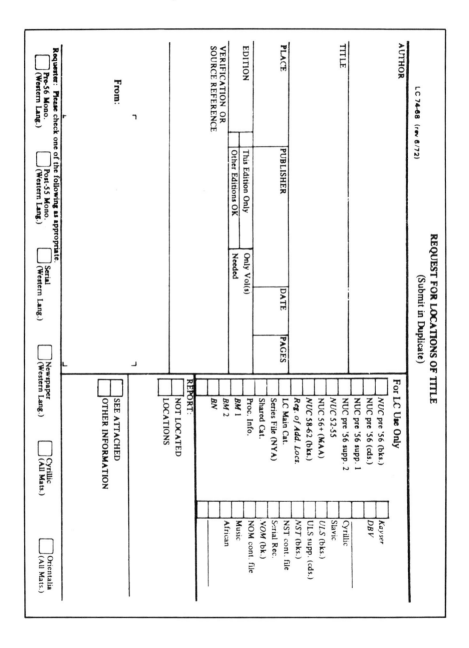

the original request form and a shipping label. The shipping label is to be used when the material is returned so that it will be clearly identified as returned interlibrary loan material (Figure 9). Since special files are used to keep track of materials lent to other libraries, it is necessary that returned materials be clearly labeled as interlibrary loan material, in order to keep these files up to date.

Figure 9
Return Shipping Label: Interlibrary Loan

FROM:	INTERLIBRARY LOAN LIBRARY RATE:
	TO: CALIFORNIA STATE COLLEGE AT SAN BERNARDINO LIBRARY 5500 State College Parkway San Bernardino, Calif. 92407
	Return requested ....Parcel post ....Express collect ....Preinsured ....Express prepaid $...................Value

The borrowing library is responsible for receiving and checking the condition of the borrowed material and for notifying the patron of its availability as quickly as possible. When the borrower picks up the material, he should be told how long he can keep it and whether any restrictions have been placed on its use. Furthermore, the borrowing library is responsible for returning the material to the lending library by the due date. This means that the borrowing library must have packing materials for the safe shipment of material and must follow the mailing instructions of the lending library about such things as insurance.

The preceding is only a general outline of interlibrary loan procedures. The library technician who has responsibilities in this area should read the detailed interpretation of the National Interlibrary Loan Code, 1968, and standard procedures in Thomson's *Interlibrary Loan Procedure Manual*[4] as well as making a careful study of interlibrary loan policies and procedures in his own library.

Figure 10
Interlibrary Loan: Borrowing Procedure

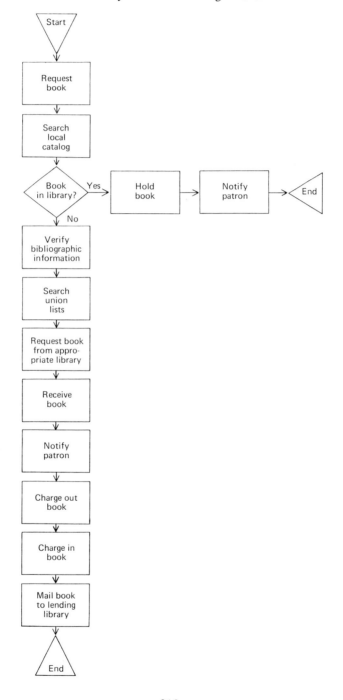

Figure 11
Interlibrary Loan: Lending Procedure

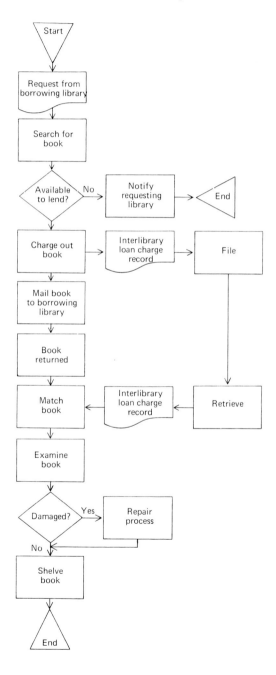

FOOTNOTES

1. You will recall that the Government Printing Office distributes over 12,000 items a year, *Ulrich's International Periodicals Directory* lists over 50,000 periodicals currently available, the *Bowker Annual of Library & Book Trade Information* shows that over 37,000 new books and new editions were published in 1971, and the audiovisual bibliographies we have covered cite over 100,000 separate items currently available.

2. The National Interlibrary Loan Code, 1968, is given in full in Appendix D, page 237.

3. See Section V, "Scope," in the National Interlibrary Loan Code, 1968, for a listing of types of materials which should not be requested. If there are local codes, check them for loan restrictions.

4. Sarah Katharine Thomson, *Interlibrary Loan Procedure Manual* (Chicago, American Library Association, 1970).

BIBLIOGRAPHY

Altman, E. "Independent Study and Interlibrary Loan in Secondary School Libraries," *School Libraries* 21:36-42 (Fall 1971).

Avedon, Don M. "Transmission of Information: New Networks," *Special Libraries* 61:115-18 (March 1970).

Becker, Joseph, ed. *Interlibrary Communications and Information Networks.* Chicago, American Library Association, 1971.

Bird, Warren, and David Skene Melvin, comps. *Library Telecommunications Directory: Canada-United States.* 4th ed. Durham, N.C., Duke University Medical Center Library, 1971.

Boaz, Martha. *Strength Through Cooperation in Southern California Libraries: A Survey.* Los Angeles, 1965.

Brinkley, Cosby, comp. *Directory of Institutional Photocopying Services (Including Selected Interlibrary Loan Policies).* Chicago, 1969.

Budington, William S. "Administrative Aspects of Interlibrary Loans," *Special Libraries* 55:211-15 (April 1964).

Clapp, Verner. "Copyright Dilemma: A Librarian's View," *Library Quarterly* 38:352-87 (October 1968).

Dubester, Henry J., ed. "Issues and Problems in Designing a National Program of Library Automation," *Library Trends* 18:427-568 (April 1970).

Freehafer, Edward G. "Summary Statement of Policy of the Joint Libraries Committee on Fair Use in Photocopying," *Special Libraries* 55:104-106 (February 1964).

Hattery, Lowell H., and George P. Bush, eds. *Reprography and Copyright Law.* Washington, American Institute of Biological Sciences, 1964.

Humphry, John A. "The Place of Urban Main Libraries in Larger Library Networks," *Library Trends* 20:673-92 (April 1972).

Jordan, Robert T. *Tomorrow's Library: Direct Access and Delivery.* New York, R. R. Bowker, 1970.

Kinney, Mary R. *The Abbreviated Citation—A Bibliographical Problem.* Chicago, American Library Association, 1967.

Kruzas, Anthony T., ed. *Encyclopedia of Information Systems and Services.* Ann Arbor, Mich., Edwards Brothers, 1971.

Leigh, Robert D. *The Public Library in the United States: The General Report of the Public Library Inquiry.* New York, Columbia University Press, 1950.

"Librarian, What of the Undergrad? Interlibrary Loan Debate," *RQ* 6:158-63 (Summer 1967).

Lowy, George. *A Searcher's Manual.* Hamden, Conn., Shoe String Press, 1965.

Meise, Norman R. *Conceptual Design of an Automated National Library System.* Metuchen, N.J., Scarecrow Press, 1969.

Morehouse, Harold G. "The Future of Telefacsimile in Libraries: Problems and Prospects," *Library Resources & Technical Services* 13:42-46 (Winter 1969).

Palmour, Vernon E., and others. *A Study of the Characteristics, Costs, and Magnitude of Interlibrary Loans in Academic Libraries.* Westport, Conn., Greenwood Press, 1972.

Schenk, Gretchen Knief. *County and Regional Library Development.* Chicago, American Library Association, 1954.

Stenstrom, Ralph H. *Cooperation Between Types of Libraries, 1940-1968: An Annotated Bibliography.* Chicago, American Library Association, 1970.

Thomson, Sarah Katharine. *Interlibrary Loan Procedure Manual.* Chicago, American Library Association, 1970.

Wall, C. Edward. *Periodical Title Abbreviations.* Detroit, Gale Research, 1969.

CHAPTER 24

REFERENCE SERVICES:
SPECIAL MATERIALS AND SERVICES

INTRODUCTION

This final chapter will present a brief introduction to the functions of several specialized reference materials and services. The topics to be discussed are the vertical file, special reference files, periodicals, public relations, computers, and supervision of personnel. As with other areas of public services, the library technician's role in these specialized services will vary greatly among libraries. Regardless of his role, however, the library technician should have a general knowledge of how his library approaches these special areas. Even if he never sees or uses a vertical file, for example, the library technician should know that such files exist, whether his library has one or not, and if so, where it is located and whom the patron should consult to use it. The same is true for periodicals. If the library has periodical subscriptions, and most do, the library technician should know where the periodicals are located, whether or not they are cataloged or shelved alphabetically, and whether there are special holdings records. Questions like these must be asked about all special areas in a library.

THE VERTICAL FILE AND SPECIAL COLLECTIONS

The vertical file is a useful tool for providing easy access to uncataloged materials which are not shelved with the permanent collection.[1] Types of materials placed in a vertical file collection may include pamphlets, clippings, maps, brochures, photographes, postcards, and other ephemeral items. Generally the vertical file materials have a limited useful life and are on currently popular topics or topics on which questions are continually asked. An example of currently popular material would be pamphlets or brochures on the draft or narcotics. Examples of materials constantly in demand are items on jobs or occupations. The latter must constantly be replaced by updated material.

What a library places in its vertical file depends on patron needs and the philosophy of the librarians. Some libraries maintain a small vertical file and catalog as much as possible with the book collection. Other libraries develop extensive vertical file collections while, at the other extreme, some libraries have no vertical file and reason that anything worth keeping is worth cataloging. Libraries should—and usually do—have a policy on vertical files stating what material is included and how it is arranged.

Two of the most popular ways to arrange materials in a vertical file are alphabetically by subject or by classification number.[2] For example, if the materials are arranged by subjects, items on the same subject are placed in a folder or large envelope and a subject heading is assigned and placed on the folder or envelope. The user can then look in a particular folder to see what material is available. Each item in the folder will have the subject heading placed on it so it can be returned to the correct folder. If the file is arranged by classification number, the same system might be employed using classification numbers in place of subject headings. Some libraries prefer classification numbers so that all the materials on a subject will have the same classification whether in the permanent collection, vertical file, or other special collection. The Decimal Classification is usually used, since the Library of Congress Classification is somewhat cumbersome for this type of material. If subject headings are assigned, some standard guide may be used along with "homemade" subject headings. In order to have some consistency in subject headings, those used by *Readers' Guide to Periodical Literature, Vertical File Index, Public Affairs Information Service Bulletin,* or one of the standard subject heading lists (*Sears List of Subject Headings* or *Subject Headings Used in the Dictionary Catalogs of the Library of Congress*) may be used. Regardless of the source or sources used to obtain subject headings, there will probably be an authority file of the headings used in a library's vertical file in order to maintain consistency in the use of subject headings.

Libraries often have subject references in the catalog directing the user to materials located in the vertical file. These references are filed at the end of the entries for a subject and are often typed on a colored card (Figure 1). The exact wording will vary, of course, depending on the physical layout of the library.

Figure 1
Subject Reference to Vertical File Materials

HEARING AIDS

For more material on this subject, consult the Vertical File located on the first floor. For more information, go to the first floor reference desk.

Some libraries have several vertical files. For example, there may be one for general materials, one for illustrations and pictures, and one for local history. These are only a few of the endless varieties possible.

Another special collection with which the library technician should be familiar is that of college catalogs. College catalogs are not usually kept in a vertical file, but rather are shelved in a special area. The number of catalogs in a collection can range from only a few, limited to local institutions and important universities, to several thousand catalogs of institutions in the United States and foreign countries. Because this collection is frequently used in many libraries, the library technician should know both its physical location and how the catalogs are arranged. The two most popular arrangements are alphabetical by name of the institution or alphabetical by the state where it is located.

Archival collections are the last of the special collections we will discuss. Archives may contain materials on the history of the library, public records, historical documents, personal letters or diaries of persons of distinction.

Archival collections may include books, pamphlets, clippings, pictures and photographs, posters, handbills, non-book materials, etc. The library technician should be aware of the library's policy on such a collection, where the collection is located, whether there are special indexes to the collection, and, if necessary, to whom the patron should be referred.

The library technician should also be aware that many libraries maintain special information files, usually at the reference or information desk on many types of information. Some of these files might be: a file of answers to questions that were particularly difficult to find; a file of answers to questions frequently asked; a file of local speakers and information on how to contact them; and a file listing popular local organizations of all kinds and how to establish contact with them. There may, of course, by many other special files depending on a library's needs. The library technician should be aware of any special files in the library, where they are located, and how to use them.

PERIODICALS[3]

In earlier chapters we discussed some of the special indexes to periodicals, the various lists of periodical holdings of a library, and the union lists with the holdings of many libraries. Now we are concerned with some problems involved in the arrangement of periodicals.[4]

There are several popular methods for arranging periodicals in the library collection. Both bound and unbound periodicals can be classified, using either the Decimal Classification or the Library of Congress Classification, and shelved with the book collection. The current unbound issues of periodicals can be stored in special containers and placed in the proper place on the shelves; however, it is more common to shelve the current issues in a separate area either by classification number, or alphabetically by title or other form of entry. Regardless of the placement of the current periodicals, this method has the advantage of placing bound, and occasionally unbound, periodicals on a subject with the books on the subject. It has the disadvantage of scattering the periodical collection, and it creates an extra cataloging load for technical services.

A second popular arrangement is alphabetically by title or other form of main entry. In this arrangement the periodicals are physically separate from the book collection. The current issues of periodicals may be placed in special containers and placed next to the bound volumes; however, in this arrangement it is more common to shelve the current issues in a separate area. This arrangement has the advantage of bringing all the periodicals together in one place. The disadvantage is that the periodicals are not arranged by subject.

The library technician should know how periodicals are arranged in his library, since there are many variations of these two basic types of arrangement.

Newspapers are often placed near the periodicals, and are usually arranged alphabetically by city on special newspaper racks. Newspapers are among the most popular materials in libraries and the library technician should know their location in order to direct patrons to them.

The library technician should also familiarize himself with the holdings list for periodicals. The holdings may be listed on special cards in a Kardex or Linedex, on a printed list, or possibly on special cards filed in the card catalog.

No matter what system is used, the library technician must know how to interpret the lists to patrons. In addition to recording the periodical holdings, such a list also indicates the location of periodicals if they are stored in more than one place. For example, the list may show that the current issues of a periodical are in the "current section," the bound volumes in a "retrospective section," and microfilm holdings in special cabinets in a third section.

It is obvious by now that familiarity with the physical layout of a library and the location of material is essential if the library technician is to give good service to patrons. Directional questions such as "where are the periodicals?" are not necessarily so easy to answer. To answer such a simple question the library technician must know how periodicals are handled in the library, whether the request is for a current issue or a retrospective bound volume, and whether the library has bound holdings or microfilm holdings.

It is a good idea for the library technician to spend some time looking through the periodical collection. He should also become aware of the library's binding policy and how often materials are sent to the bindery. By looking over the collection he can see the kinds of material included in a particular title, the length of the articles, and the level of scholarship.

PUBLIC RELATIONS

Everything done in a library is either a direct or an indirect act of public relations. Anything that affects the patron's attitude toward the library—negatively or positively—is part of public relations. How long it takes to catalog books, how the telephone is answered, the accuracy of reshelving materials, the inflection in one's voice in answering a question, and the "warmth" or "atmosphere" of a library are only a few examples of things that represent public relations. It is not just reference service that gives a library its image, but a combination of all library activities. In an early chapter we discussed the general techniques of handling patron inquiries.[5] What we will discuss below are some of the activities through which a library can help the patron and improve the services and image of the library. Two of the main goals of the types of public relations presented here are to sell the library and its services and to make patrons aware of the materials available to them. In many libraries a full-time librarian (or even more than one) is assigned to carry out the public relations activities. A professional designer or commercial artist may be on the staff to handle all of the design associated with displays, posters, etc.

One of the most popular ways to sell the library and its materials is through exhibits and displays. The subject possibilities for exhibits and displays are almost endless. There are many traveling exhibits from the Library of Congress, the Smithsonian Institution, other libraries, associations, clubs, etc., that go from library to library. The subjects of these exhibits range from rare books to photographs of famous people to sculpture. Along with these exhibits the library might display its own materials on the topic to let patrons know what is available in their library.

The informational signs in a library are good image-creating devices. Signs that are interestingly designed, well placed, and worded in a friendly way can be a real asset in creating a good library "atmosphere." Hopefully the day is gone when the first sign seen in a library reads "No Talking, No Smoking, No Eating, No Nothing"! The image of the librarian going around maintaining "law and order" was not, unfortunately, conceived without cause.

The bulletin board is another useful and popular public relations tool. Announcements of local cultural events, book talks, library events, etc., can be displayed in an attractive format. This sort of centralized information center can be of real value to patrons.

Other things libraries might do to increase their services and improve their image include sponsoring book reviews, presenting film series, running regular newspaper articles, arranging for lectures on topics of current or community interest, presenting programs on radio and television, offering library facilities to discussion groups or to various other community clubs, and getting librarians into school classrooms—at all levels—to discuss library services.

In the area of publications, topical or subject bibliographies, library service information sheets, bookmarks and reports on research can be made available to the patrons. These projects—especially topical bibliographies—require a lot of hard work by the library staff; they are not projects that can be successful without great effort.

Perhaps the most important library publication is one that is seldom if ever seen by the library's users, yet it has a potentially significant effect on library service. The annual report, a combination of statistical information and a description of library accomplishments, is written to achieve certain political goals. Usually the main goal is to show a governing body—board of trustees, college president, school superintendent, etc.—that the budget should be maintained at present levels or increased to provide better service. If the library does not have personal representation at crucial budgetary meetings, a well-prepared annual report can be of help. The library technician, as a high-ranking non-professional, must be aware that even libraries, full as they are of "culture and virtue," do not exist in an ivory tower but in a real political world.

COMPUTERS AND MECHANIZATION

In public services, and indeed all library services, the computer can be a great labor-saving device. Computers have shown their value in circulation systems, production of bibliographies, cataloging, acquisitions, and financial record-keeping operations. As of now, however, it is safe to assume that the computer will not replace the reference staff in the foreseeable future. There are several projects which are experimenting with a direct patron-computer dialogue to answer reference questions but, even if it is successful, it is not likely to be widely used for many years.

Two of the most useful computer-produced products for public services are periodicals or serials holdings lists and computerized cataloging. By entering into the computer the basic periodical holdings of a library, then entering the latest acquisitions in order to keep the list current, it is possible to produce up-to-date holdings lists. Some of the by-products of computerized cataloging are computer-produced acquisitions lists and bibliographies. The production of bibliographies is of particular importance to public services. Through proper coding of cataloged materials it is possible to extract a list of the library's holdings in any subject area. In some libraries, particularly scientifically oriented special libraries, patrons can tell the library their research interests, and bibliographies can be produced from information previously entered into the computer. This is called selective dissemination of information (SDI).

In the near future more library networks will be communicating by computer; holdings and acquisitions lists will be capable of production by computer; some circulation control systems and computer-produced bibliographies will be the main visible products of the computer in public services. It is probable, however, that even these capabilities will be available only at a minority of libraries. In spite of all the literature about computers, there has not yet been a "computer revolution" in libraries, although some aspects of technical services do seem to be approaching this stage.

In many libraries other aspects of mechanization have had a greater impact than computerization. The Xerox machine for catalog card production and copying, automatic book charging machines, and binding systems have all had profound effects on internal library operations. These may sound like prosaic advances, unless one considers the difference between typing sets of six or seven or even ten cards rather than placing one master card on a Xerox or multilith and producing the card mechanically. These examples of library technology may not be as glamorous as the computer, but at this point in time they are more useful for most libraries.

SUPERVISION OF PERSONNEL

The library technician will be one of the higher level non-professionals on the library staff. Consequently, there is every likelihood that he will be supervising other lower level clerical staff. Below we will introduce the general concepts of supervision that seem most important for the library technician.[6]

The supervisor, first of all, should know what goals are to be accomplished and make certain that his staff is equally aware of the goals. Unless the supervisor knows where he is going and what is required of the staff, the operation will not be effectively carried out.

The goals of a particular operation can be conveyed to the staff through another supervisorial function—training. It is the responsibility of the supervisor to see that every employee receives the training required to carry out his job. The library technician as supervisor need not necessarily do the training himself, but must see that it is done by another competent staff member.

The supervisor must always try to treat all subordinates equally and fairly. If there are "favorites," then the ones who are not favored will soon decide that they will not have a fair break, and communication will be cut off.

The supervisor should communicate with his subordinates. Few, if any, library operations need to be carried out in secrecy. The supervisor has a responsibility to tell the staff any relevant information that may affect their jobs. It is usually a poor policy to spring surprises on the staff when it takes only a few minutes beforehand to forewarn them of possible changes. Communication is a two-way street and the supervisor also has an obligation to listen. The value of open two-way communication between supervisor and subordinate cannot be overstated.

The supervisor should keep subordinates aware of their progress. This involves both praise (publicly if possible) and criticism (always in private), both of which are important. A person doing a good job should be told so. And a person who is doing poorly should be told so that he can make improvements. In fact, if an employee first learns of criticism only after a three- or six-month period has passed, the supervisor has failed in a basic responsibility. Constructive criticism should be given as soon as the supervisor becomes aware of a problem.

The supervisor should be able to make decisions. This sounds simple, but unfortunately many supervisors "muddle through" operations and avoid making decisions. A simple example might be an employee request for a vacation. Here the library technician should evaluate the effect on library service of the employee's absence, make a decision to approve or not to approve the request, and pass the decision on to the librarian, who will probably make final determination in this area. The library technician should try never to leave any request for an operating decision in limbo, but should make the decision as quickly as possible or promptly refer the matter to the supervising librarian.

Finally, the supervisor should supervise subordinates' work, not do it for them. "I'll do it myself so it will get done" is not a good supervisory technique. If a job is not performed correctly or not performed at all, the supervisor should find out the reason and take corrective action. The supervisor who starts "doing" too much is being unfair to subordinates and soon has no time to supervise.

There are, of course, many other aspects of supervision. The six aspects presented above are a good starting point for the library technician. Some libraries or institutions offer management training courses, and it will be to the advantage of the library technician to take them. One must never underestimate the importance of capable supervision. The most skilled and dedicated employees may have their talents wasted unless they are given effective guidance and supervision.

FOOTNOTES

1. "Relatively permanent" may be a better term because a good part of a library's collection is eventually discarded over the years as new editions are published and as material becomes outdated or worn out.

2. Many problems exist in using either of these approaches. For a complete discussion of these problems, see Shirley Miller's *The Vertical File and Its Satellites: A Handbook of Acquisition, Processing and Organization* (Littleton, Colo., Libraries Unlimited, 1971).

3. The term "serial" is used in some libraries rather than "periodical." See the glossary for definitions of both terms.

4. The ordering, cataloging, business record-keeping, binding, and check-in routines for periodicals are often considered technical services functions and are so treated in this text. For a discussion of these functions, see Marty Bloomberg and G. Edward Evans, *Introduction to Technical Services for Library Technicians* (Littleton, Colo., Libraries Unlimited, 1971), pp. 146-59. As the library

technician works with periodicals, it will be apparent that in many areas there is no easy separation between technical service and public service functions.

5. See Chapter 5, pages 80-81.

6. A good, easy-to-read book on supervision is Raymond O. Loen, *Manage More by Doing Less* (New York, McGraw-Hill, 1971). The book was meant for management in business, but many of the basic ideas and suggestions can be modified to suit the management of a library's operations.

BIBLIOGRAPHY

Balmforth, C. K., and N. S. M. Cox, editors. *Interface: Library Automation with Special Reference to Computing Activity.* Cambridge, Mass., M.I.T. Press, 1971.

Bonn, George. *Training Laymen in Use of the Library.* New Brunswick, N.J., Graduate School of Library Science, Rutgers–The State University, 1960.

Coplan, Kate. *Effective Library Exhibits: How to Prepare and Promote Good Displays.* Dobbs Ferry, N.Y., Oceana, 1958.

Coplan, Kate, and Constance Rosenthal. *Guide to Better Bulletin Boards: Time and Labor-Saving Ideas for Teachers and Librarians.* Dobbs Ferry, N.Y., Oceana, 1970.

Coplan, Kate, and Edwin Castagna, editors. *The Library Reaches Out: Reports on Library Service and Community Relations by Some Leading American Librarians.* Dobbs Ferry, N.Y., Oceana, 1965.

Cox, N. S. M., J. D. Dews, and J. L. Dolby. *The Computer and the Library: The Role of the Computer in the Organization and Handling of Information in Libraries.* Hamden, Conn., Archon Books, 1967.

Davinson, D. E. *The Periodicals Collection: Its Purposes and Uses in Libraries.* London, Andre Deutsch, 1969.

Garvey, Mona. *Library Displays: Their Purpose, Construction and Use.* New York, H. W. Wilson, 1969.

Hayes, Robert M., and Joseph Becker. *Handbook of Data Processing for Libraries.* New York, Becker & Hayes, 1970.

Katz, William A. *Introduction to Reference Work.* New York, McGraw-Hill, 1969. 2v. (see especially Volume 2).

Katz, William A. *Magazine Selection: How to Build a Community-Oriented Collection.* New York, R. R. Bowker, 1971.

Katz, William A. *Magazines for Libraries.* New York: R. R. Bowker, 1969.

Kimber, Richard T. *Automation in Libraries.* Oxford, Pergamon Press, 1968.

Loen, Raymond O. *Manage More by Doing Less.* New York, McGraw-Hill, 1971.

Loizeaux, Marie D. *Publicity Primer: An ABC of "Telling All" About the Public Library.* 4th ed. New York, H. W. Wilson, 1959.

Miller, Shirley. *The Vertical File and Its Satellites: A Handbook of Acquisition, Processing and Organization.* Littleton, Colo., Libraries Unlimited, 1971.

Raburn, Josephine. "Public Relations for a Special Public," *Special Libraries* 60:647-50 (December 1969).

Shera, Jesse. *Documentation and the Organization of Knowledge.* Hamden, Conn., Archon Books, 1966.

Wallace, Sara Leslie. *Patrons Are People: How to be a Model Librarian.* Rev. and enl. ed. Chicago, American Library Association, 1956.

Wallick, Clair H. *Looking for Ideas? A Display Manual for Libraries and Bookstores.* Metuchen, N.J., Scarecrow Press, 1970.

GLOSSARY

Accession number. A number assigned, in chronological order, to each book or item as it is received by the library. These numbers are sometimes required to operate a circulation control system.

Added entry. A secondary entry; any entry other than the main entry.

Application card. The form one fills out to apply for library privileges. Usually includes name, address, phone number, and employer or occupation.

Application file. A file of all application cards (filed alphabetically or, if patrons are assigned a number, in numerical order).

Author entry. The name of the author of a book used as an entry in the catalog. This is usually the main entry.

Author number. A combination of letters and numbers assigned to a book to identify the author. The author number and the classification number together make the call number. Also called **book number** or **cutter number.**

Borrower. A person who charges out material from a library.

Call number. The notation used to identify and locate a particular book on the shelves. It consists of the classification number, author number, and may include other identifying symbols.

Catalog. A list of the holdings of a particular library or group of libraries.

Central reference. An organization of the reference department in which all reference material is placed in one physical location in the library.

Central registration. A master file of all registered borrowers in a library system— a main library and its branches—or in several systems.

Charge. A record of the loan of material.

Charging system. See **Circulation control system.** The terms are used interchangeably.

Circulation control system. The method used to lend materials to borrowers and maintain the necessary records.

Circulation statistics. A record of the number of items charged out of a library.

Classification number. The number assigned to a book to show the major subject area of the material.

Classification schedule. The printed scheme of a classification system.

Cutter number. A number from the Cutter-Sanborn Tables used as an author number. Used to maintain an alphabetical author arrangement on the shelves.

Date due. The day material is to be returned to a library. A fine is usually charged for material returned after this date.

Date slip. The strip of paper pasted in the book or on the book pocket, on which the date due is stamped.

Dictionary catalog. A catalog in which all entries are filed in alphabetical order.

Directional question. A question that can be answered by directing the patron to a specific location or to a specific reference tool.

Discharging. The act of cancelling the library's record of a loan.

Divided catalog. A catalog usually divided into two parts. One part has all author, title, and added entries in alphabetical order, and a second part has all subject entries in alphabetical order.

Divisional reference. An organization of the reference department in which the reference materials for a group of related subjects are placed in one physical location.

Fine. The penalty charge for material returned after the date due.

General reference. See **Central reference.**

General reference question. A question that may require several sources to give an answer. The search for an answer may or may not be limited to the reference collection.

Government document. A publication issued by or authorized for issue by a governmental body and paid for with public funds.

Interlibrary loan. The lending of material or copies of material by one library to another library.

Inventory. The process of checking the shelf list with the material on the shelves to discover missing material.

Kardex. A metal file containing a number of shallow drawers in which serial check-in cards are kept.

Librarian. A person who has a B.A. degree and at least one year of academic training in library science.

Library clerk. A person who has the equivalent of at least a high school education and has office skills such as typing, filing, shorthand, etc. Probably has on-the-job training experience in library service.

Library technician. A person who has at least two years of college and some training in library science.

Linedex. A metal file containing a number of flat metal leaves which hold single cardboard strips (lines) listing titles and holdings.

Microfilm. Film on which materials have been photographed in greatly reduced size.

Microfilm reader. A special piece of equipment which magnifies the image on microfilm and projects the enlargement onto a screen.

Overdue material. Material returned to the library after the date due.

Overdue notice. A notice sent to the borrower to remind him to return overdue material.

Pamphlet. An independent publication of 49 pages or less, bound in paper covers.

Periodical. A publication issued in successive parts, each part having the same title but a different number. Most periodicals are issued at regular intervals and in paper covers. Libraries usually secure periodicals on a subscription basis.

Public services. Library work which deals with patrons and the use of the library collection.

Reader's advisory service. The aspect of reference work concerned with recommending reading materials to patrons to meet their needs.

Ready reference question. A question whose answer is short (and usually factual), which can be answered quickly using standard sources.

Reference collection. A special non-circulating collection of selected materials useful in supplying information, kept together for easier access.

Reference services. Library work directly concerned with assistance to readers in securing information and in using other library resources.

Reference work. A work kept in the reference collection. Usually a work consulted for specific facts and statistical information rather than one to be read at length.

Registration. The act of filling out required forms to become an eligible library borrower.

Registration department. The department in a library responsible for registering prospective borrowers.

Research question. A question that may require extensive use of reference and non-reference materials and sources of information from other libraries. There may be no definitive answer to a research question, but only references to information on the subject.

Reserved material. Material held for a borrower for a limited time. The borrower must request this service.

Reserved material collection. A collection of materials with restricted circulation. Usually found in college and university libraries.

Serial. A publication issued in successive parts at regular or irregular intervals, usually to be continued indefinitely. Included are periodicals, newspapers, proceedings, reports, annuals, and numbered monographic series.

Shelf list. A record of books in a library, with the entries arranged in the order of the books on the shelves.

Shelving. Placing materials on shelves in proper order.

Subject entry. The entry for a work in the catalog under the subject heading.

Subject heading. A word or group of words indicating a subject.

Subject subdivision. A restrictive word or group of words added to a subject heading to limit it to a more specific area.

Technical services. Work performed in or for a library to insure that materials are made available for patron use. This work does not normally require direct contact with library patrons. Includes acquisitions, cataloging, and materials preparation.

Title entry. The entry of a work in the catalog under the title.

Vertical file. A collection of materials such as pamphlets, clippings, or illustrations kept in special containers and usually stored in a vertical position.

APPENDIX A

U.S. CIVIL SERVICE COMMISSION
GS-1411 Series, June 1966

A SUMMARY OF POSITION CLASSIFICATION STANDARDS

LIBRARY AID SERIES

POSITION	NATURE OF POSITION	TYPICAL TASKS (Illustrative, but not all-inclusive)	REQUIREMENTS
Library Aid GS-1	Under close supervision, simple routine tasks requiring repetitive application of a few specific instructions. Full performance expected after a few days training and on-the-job practice.	Shelving, loading, counting, assembling, stapling, stamping ownership, applying book pockets and other one-step operations connected with receiving materials.	No previous experience required.
Library Aid GS-2	Under close supervision, follows instructions for performing accurately a variety of library duties of limited complexity. Such duties are simple and repetitive.	Routines in paging, shelving, preparing materials, charging and discharging books. Alphabetical and numerical filing. Limited contact with users—may give directional information. Lettering, etc.	No previous experience required, but limited training in or acquaintance with library services and procedures is required.
Library Aid GS-3	Under supervision, performs tasks, clerical or manual, of limited complexity involving use of a working knowledge and understanding of the library's services, practices and procedures related to the specific function or activity involved. Works according to established procedures. Some discretion or choice in application of guidelines to a situation at hand may be exercised.	Giving and receiving information which is routine and recurrent, simple and clearcut. Searching, shelving, shifting, shelf-reading library publications. Locates according to shelving scheme. Performs circulation or registration duties or both where knowledge of library rules is applied; explains rules to users; registers borrowers, files applications; enters and clears records of overdues; inspects books for damage, maintains	Previous library experience desirable, but not required. Working knowledge and understanding of library's services, practices and procedures related to specific functions or activities which may be gained through instruction on the job. Tact, courtesy, poise, alertness and good judgment required for contact work.

POSITION	NATURE OF POSITION	TYPICAL TASKS	REQUIREMENTS
Library Aid GS-3 (cont'd)		inter-library loan records; prepares and sends notices; prepares materials, pamphlets, music, etc. Makes preliminary separation of books to be bound and discarded.	
Library Technician GS-4	Under supervision of a librarian or supervisory library technician, performs a variety of detailed, non-routine, or more complex or nonprofessional duties following prescribed or standardized methods or instructions, including a variety of steps or operations, with various alternative courses of action where choices must be made and judgment exercised. Applies library policies, rules, and instructions.	Coding, searching for, recording or filing materials. Processing duplicate non-fiction and adult fiction titles which are being added, reclassified or reinstated; searching catalogs and shelf list. Identifying and maintaining records of foreign language serial publications. Shelf maintenance of special collections. Maintenance of system of circulation controls, such as reserves, renewals, overdues and inter-library loans. Receive calls requiring skill in sensing the meaning and intent of the request.	Working knowledge of library rules and procedures. May include some knowledge of cataloging practices, bibliographic entries, basic reference sources, acquisition sources and familiarity with library terminology. Working knowledge of one or two foreign languages may be required.
Library Technician GS-5	Under supervision of a librarian or supervisory library technician, performs tasks which involve use of a significant specialized knowledge of (a) the particular library's functions, services, practices and procedures, (b) the terminology content and classification scheme of the library's collection or a specialized collection, or (c) both. Performs technical or quasi-	Bibliographic work—preparing entries for acquisition, verifies data, searches trade journals, catalogs, and reference tools. Maintains serial checklist—recording and searching. Performs cataloging, either temporary or preliminary and original cataloging in brief form, adaption of LC cards, cataloging new editions.	In addition to the requirements for GS-4, are considerable knowledge of the library's organization, services facilities, and classification system and procedures.

POSITION	NATURE OF POSITION	TYPICAL TASKS	REQUIREMENTS
Library Technician GS-5 (cont'd)	professional library operations of limited scope or difficulty in one or more library functions. Must apply considerable judgment in application of operating guides.	Aids individuals in use of library resources by locating materials through catalog, on shelves, etc.	
Library Technician GS-6	Under general technical supervision of a librarian or supervisory library technician, performs work in one or more of the functional areas of librarianship (such as acquisition, cataloging and reference) to provide technical support and relieve the professional librarian for higher level and more demanding responsibilities.	Performs bibliographic searching of difficulty requiring extensive searching. Performs descriptive cataloging of specific library materials. On second shift, serves as person in charge; aids individuals, answers ready-reference questions, etc. May supervise one or two lower grade employees.	In addition to requirements for GS-4 and GS-5, are knowledge of a specialized technical or quasi-professional area of library work and skill and understanding of established library techniques and methods and the use of standard library tools within the library in which employed. Ability to speak for the library when serving as the person-in-charge. Intensive knowledge of library's holdings; good understanding of searching techniques.
Library Technician GS-7	Under general technical supervision of a librarian who is located either within the local library or at a higher organizational level, works on the basis of a general assignment or responsibilities and follows through the full continuity of the job. Involves substantial specialized knowledge of the library's functions, services, practices, and procedures.	Responsible for operation of a small branch, bookmobile, or hospital library where the subject area is relatively narrow or non-technical, and where acquisition and cataloging are done centrally. Acquisition services for a library of significant size or group of libraries, responsible for checking order data,	In addition to requirements for lower levels of Librarian-Technician, possesses a store of knowledge related to the functions, services, practices and procedures of *the* library or special type of library *in which* employed. (NOTE: The GS-7 *Librarian*, on the other hand, possesses a pro-

POSITION	NATURE OF POSITION	TYPICAL TASKS	REQUIREMENTS
Library Technician GS-7 (cont'd)		etc. Performs descriptive cataloging, possibly of materials in foreign languages. Performs difficult searching in special subject fields. Gives book talks or other presentation to groups. Establishes working relationships within the library and with library clientele.	fessional knowledge of the fundamentals of library science, and of the principles, theories and techniques which are applicable to *any* type of library.)

APPENDIX B

CODE OF ETHICS FOR LIBRARIANS*

Preamble

1. The library as an institution exists for the benefit of a given constituency, whether it be the citizens of a community, members of an educational institution, or some larger or more specialized group. Those who enter the library profession assume an obligation to maintain ethical standards of behavior in relation to the governing authority under which they work, to the library constituency, to the library as an institution and to fellow workers on the staff, to other members of the library profession, and to society in general.

2. The term librarian in this code applies to any person who is employed by a library to do work that is recognized to be professional in character according to standards established by the ALA.

This code sets forth principles of ethical behavior for the professional librarian. It is not a declaration of prerogatives nor a statement of recommended practices in specific situations.

Relations of the Librarian to the Governing Authority

4. The librarian should perform his duties with realization of the fact that final jurisdiction over the administration of the library rests in the officially constituted governing authority. This authority may be vested in a designated individual, or in a group such as a committee or board.

5. The chief librarian should keep the governing authority informed on professional standards and progressive action. Each librarian should be responsible for carrying out the policies of the governing authorities and its appointed executives with a spirit of loyalty to the library.

6. The chief librarian should interpret decisions of the governing authority to the staff, and should act as liaison officer in maintaining friendly relations between staff members and those in authority.

7. Recommendations to the governing authority for the appointment of a staff member should be made by the chief librarian solely upon the basis of the candidate's professional and personal qualifications for the position. Continuance in service and promotion should depend upon the quality of performance, following a definite and known policy. Whenever the good of the service requires a change in personnel, timely warning should be given. If desirable adjustment cannot be made, unsatisfactory service should be terminated in accordance with the policy of the library and the rules of tenure.

8. Resolutions, petitions and requests of a staff organization or group should be submitted through a duly appointed representative to the chief librarian. If a mutually satisfactory solution cannot be reached, the chief librarian, on request of the staff, should transmit the matter to the governing authority. The staff may further request that they be allowed to send a representative to the governing authority, in order to present their opinions in person.

*Reprinted by permission of the American Library Association. Please note that the Code is in the process of revision.

231

Relation of the Librarian to His Constituency

9. The chief librarian, aided by staff members in touch with the constituency, should study the present and future needs of the library, and should acquire materials on the basis of those needs. Provision should be made for as wide a range of publications and as varied a representation of viewpoints as is consistent with the policies of the library and with the funds available.

10. It is the librarian's responsibility to make the resources and services of the library known to its potential users. Impartial service should be rendered to all who are entitled to use the library.

11. It is the librarian's obligation to treat as confidential any private information obtained through contact with library patrons.

12. The librarian should try to protect library property and to inculcate in users a sense of their responsibility for its preservation.

Relations of the Librarian Within His Library

13. The chief librarian should delegate authority, encourage a sense of responsibility and initiative on the part of staff members, provide for their professional development and appreciate good work. Staff members should be informed of the duties of their positions and the policies and problems of the library.

14. Loyalty to fellow workers and a spirit of courteous cooperation, whether between individuals or between departments, are essential to effective library service.

15. Criticism of library policies, service and personnel should be offered only to the proper authority for the sole purpose of improvement of the library.

16. Acceptance of a position in a library incurs an obligation to remain long enough to repay the library for the expense incident to adjustment. A contract signed or agreement made should be adhered to faithfully until it expires or is dissolved by mutual consent.

17. Resignations should be made long enough before they are to take effect to allow adequate time for the work to be put in shape and a successor appointed.

18. A librarian should never enter into a business dealing on behalf of the library which will result in personal profit.

19. A librarian should never turn the library's resources to personal use, to the detriment of services which the library renders to its patrons.

Relations of the Librarian to His Profession

20. Librarians should recognize librarianship as an educational profession and realize that the growing effectiveness of their service is dependent upon their own development.

21. In view of the importance of ability and personality traits in library work, a librarian should encourage only those persons with suitable aptitudes to enter the library profession and should discourage the continuance in service of the unfit.

22.   Recommendations should be confidential and should be fair to the candidate and the prospective employer by presenting an unbiased statement of strong and weak points.

23.   Librarians should have a sincere belief and a critical interest in the library profession. They should endeavor to achieve and maintain adequate salaries and proper working conditions.

24.   Formal appraisal of the policies or practices of another library should be given only upon the invitation of that library's governing authority or chief librarian.

25.   Librarians, in recognizing the essential unity of their profession, should have membership in library organizations and should be ready to attend and participate in library meetings and conferences.

Relations of the Librarian to Society

26.   Librarians should encourage a general realization of the value of library service and be informed concerning movements, organizations, and institutions whose aims are compatible with those of the library.

27.   Librarians should participate in public and community affairs and so represent the library that it will take its place among educational, social and cultural agencies.

28.   A librarian's conduct should be such as to maintain public esteem for the library and library work.

APPENDIX C

FORMAT OF THE LIBRARY OF CONGRESS AND
SEARS LIST OF SUBJECT HEADINGS

(1) *Subject Headings Used in the Dictionary Catalogs of the Library of Congress* (7th ed.)

The subject headings which are used as subject entries are in bold-face type. Following the subject heading, the suggested references are listed in lighter type.

HOUSE-BOATS

    sa — Shantyboats and shantyboaters

    x — Houseboats

    xx — Boats and boating

            Riverlife

The meanings of the "sa," "x," and "xx" are:

    sa — see also

    x — subject heading that is not used; make a "see" reference from the term to the heading under which it is placed

    xx — make "see also" references from these subject headings which are used back to the subject heading under which it is placed

Applied to the example above, these references mean:

HOUSE-BOATS *see also* SHANTYBOATS AND SHANTYBOATERS

HOUSEBOATS *see* HOUSE-BOATS

BOATS AND BOATING *see also* HOUSE-BOATS

RIVERLIFE *see also* HOUSE-BOATS

and the following reference cards would be placed in the catalog:

HOUSE-BOATS
See also
SHANTYBOATS AND SHANTYBOATERS

HOUSEBOATS
See
HOUSE-BOATS

BOATS AND BOATING
See also
HOUSE-BOATS

RIVERLIFE
See also
HOUSE-BOATS

(2) *Sears List of Subject Headings*

Subject headings which may be used are in bold face type; terms not to
be used are in light face type.

DRILL AND MINOR TACTICS

See also — MILITARY ART AND SCIENCE
x — Military drill; Minor tactics
xx — MILITARY ART AND SCIENCE

The meaning of the "see also," "x" and "xx" are:

See also — see also

x — subject heading that is not used; make a "see"
reference from the term to the heading under
which it is placed (same as LC)

xx — make "see also" references from these subject
headings which are used back to the subject heading
under which it is placed (same as LC)

DRILL AND MINOR TACTICS

See also

MILITARY ART AND SCIENCE

MILITARY DRILL

See

DRILL AND MINOR TACTICS

MINOR TACTICS

See

DRILL AND MINOR TACTICS

MILITARY ART AND SCIENCE

See also

DRILL AND MINOR TACTICS

APPENDIX D

NATIONAL INTERLIBRARY LOAN CODE, 1968*

Introduction

This code, adopted by the Reference Services Division, acting for the American Library Association on June 27, 1968, governs the interlibrary lending relations among libraries on the national level, among research libraries, and among libraries not operating under special or local codes. Libraries of a common geographical area or those specializing in the same field may find it advantageous to develop codes for their own needs. There is appended to this national code a model code (for regional, state, local or other special groups of libraries) which may be considered for adoption by such groups of libraries with common interests.

On the national level interlibrary loan requests should be restricted to materials which cannot be obtained readily and at moderate cost by other means. The costs involved in lending and the conflict in demand for certain kinds of materials necessitate this restriction.

The American Library Association has published a manual explaining in detail the procedures which should be used in implementing the principles of this code. Libraries requesting materials on interlibrary loan are expected to have copies of this manual and to abide by its recommendations.

The present interlibrary loan system may be radically changed by less conventional methods of transmission of materials, such as telefacsimile and computer networks. Until such methods have gained widespread acceptance, their use must be based on special agreements among libraries.

I. Definition

Interlibrary loans are transactions in which library materials are made available by one library to another for the use of an individual; for the purposes of this code they include the provision of copies as substitutes for loans of the original materials.

II. Purpose

The purpose of interlibrary loans is to make available, for *research*, materials not owned by a given library, in the belief that the furtherance of knowledge is in the general interest. Interlibrary loan service supplements a library's resources by making available, for the use of an individual, materials from other libraries not owned by the borrowing library.

III. Responsibility of Borrowing Libraries

1. It is assumed that each library will provide the resources to meet the study, instructional, informational, and normal research needs of its users, and

*Reprinted by permission of the American Library Association.

that requests for materials from another library will be limited to unusual items which the borrowing library does not own and cannot readily obtain at moderate cost. Requests for individuals with academic affiliations should be limited to those materials needed for faculty and staff research, and the thesis and dissertation research of graduate students.

2. Thesis topics should be selected according to the resources on hand and should not require extensive borrowing from other libraries. If an individual needs to use a large number of items located in another library, he should make arrangements to use them at that library.

3. The borrowing library should screen carefully all applications for loans and should reject those which do not conform to this code.

IV. Responsibility of Lending Libraries

1. In the interests of furthering research it is desirable that lending libraries interpret as generously as possible their own lending policies, with due consideration to the interests of their primary clientele.

2. A lending library has the responsibility of informing any borrowing library of its apparent failure to follow the provisions of this code.

V. Scope

1. Any type of library materials needed for the purpose of research may be requested on loan or in photocopy from another library. The lending library has the privilege of deciding in each case whether a particular item should or should not be provided, and whether the original or a copy should be sent.

2. Libraries should not ordinarily ask, however, to borrow the following types of materials: a) U.S. books in print of moderate cost; b) Serials, when the particular item needed can be copied at moderate cost; c) Rare materials, including manuscripts; d) Basic reference materials; e) Genealogical, heraldic, and similar materials; f) Bulky or fragile materials which are difficult and expensive to pack (e.g., newspapers); g) Typescript doctoral dissertations, when fully reproduced in microfilm and readily available.

VI. Expenses

1. The borrowing library assumes the responsibility for all costs charged by the lending library, including transportation, insurance, copying, and any service charges. If the charges are more than nominal, and not authorized beforehand by the borrowing library, the lending library should inform the requesting library and ask for authorization to proceed with the transaction. Borrowing libraries should try to anticipate charges, such as for copies, and authorize them on the original request.

2. It is recommended that in the interests of efficiency the lending library absorb costs which are nominal, such as for postage.

VII. Conditions of Loans

1. The safety of borrowed materials is the responsibility of the borrowing library. In case of loss or damage the borrowing library is obligated to meet all costs of repair or replacement, in accordance with the preferences of the lending library.

2. The borrowing library is bound by any limitations on use imposed by the lending library. It is recommended to lending libraries that any limitations (such as "for use in library only") be based on the physical condition or the bibliographic character of the particular item rather than be imposed on all materials lent.

3. Unless specifically forbidden by the lending library, copying by the borrowing library is permitted provided that it is in accordance with copyright law and American Library Association policy.

VIII. Placement of Requests

1. Libraries should exhaust local resources and make an effort to locate copies through the use of bibliographical tools, union lists, and union catalogs. Requests should be made to one of the nearer institutions known to possess the desired material. Care should be taken, however, to avoid concentrating requests on a few libraries.

2. In the absence of special agreements, requests should normally be placed by mail using the standard ALA forms, or by teletype using a format based on the ALA interlibrary loan form. When an urgent request is made by telephone, this initial request should be immediately followed by the confirming ALA form.

IX. Form of Request

1. Materials requested must be described completely and accurately following accepted bibliographic practice.

2. Items requested should be verified and sources of verification given, and for this purpose borrowing libraries should have access to basic bibliographic tools. When the item requested cannot be verified, the statement "cannot verify" should be included with complete information on the original source of reference. If this provision is disregarded and the bibliographic data appear to be incorrect, the request may be returned unfilled without special effort to identify the reference.

3. The name and status (position or other identifying information) of the individual for whom the material is being requested should be included on the request form.

4. A standard ALA interlibrary loan form should be used for each item requested (or an ALA photoduplication order form, when it is known that copies will be supplied and payment required).

5. All correspondence and shipments should be conspicuously labeled "Interlibrary Loan."

X. Duration of Loan

1. Unless otherwise specified by the lending library, the duration of loan is normally calculated to mean the period of time the item may remain with the borrowing library, disregarding the time spent in transit.

2. The borrowing library should ask for renewal only in unusual circumstances, and a second renewal should never be asked for without a specific explanation. The renewal request should be sent in time to reach the lending library on or before the date due. The lending library should respond to renewal requests promptly; if it does not, it will be assumed that renewal for the same length as the original loan period is granted.

3. Material on loan is subject to recall at any time and the borrowing library should comply promptly.

4. The loan period specified by the lending library should be appropriate to the type of material.

XI. Notification and Acknowledgment

1. The lending library is expected to notify the requesting library promptly whether or not the material is being sent; if the material cannot be supplied, the lending library should state the reason.

2. Except in the case of very valuable shipments, no acknowledgment of receipt is necessary. If there is undue delay in receipt, however, the receiving library has a responsibility to notify the lending library so that a search may be initiated promptly.

XII. Violation of Code

Continued disregard of any of the provisions of this code is sufficient reason for suspension of borrowing privileges.

APPENDIX E

A SELECT LIST OF ABBREVIATIONS
COMMONLY SEEN IN PUBLIC SERVICES

AACR	Anglo-American Cataloging Rules
ALA	American Library Association
BIP	*Books in Print*
CBI	*Cumulative Book Index*
DAB	*Dictionary of American Biography*
DC (or DDC)	Decimal Classification (or Dewey Decimal Classification)
DNB	*Dictionary of National Biography*
GPO	United States Government Printing Office
ILL	Interlibrary loan
LC	Library of Congress
LJ	*Library Journal*
NST	*New Serials Titles*
NUC	*National Union Catalog*
PTLA	*Publisher's Trade List Annual*
PW	*Publisher's Weekly*
SDI	Selective dissemination of information
ULS	*Union List of Serials*

INDEX

245